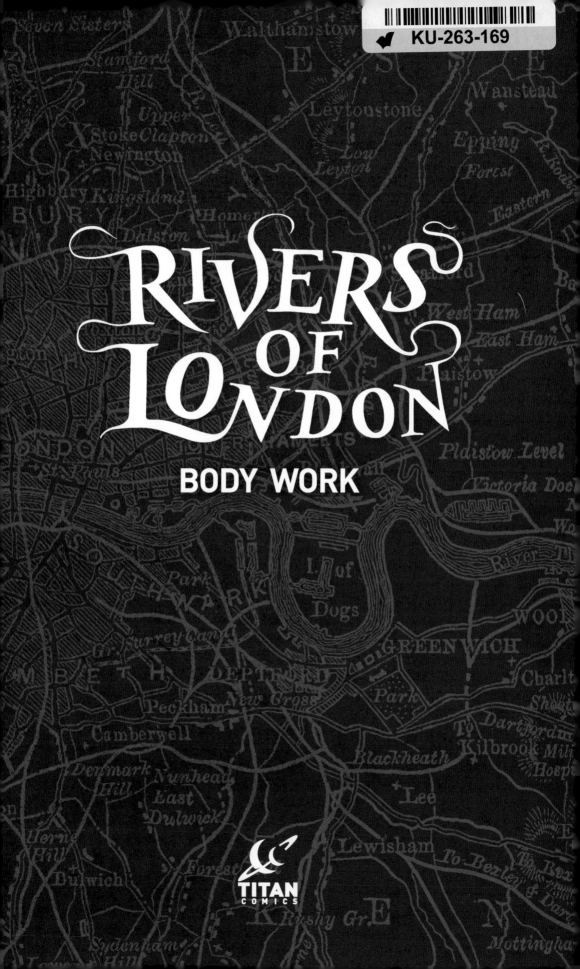

RIVERS OF LONDON

BODY WORK

TITAN
COMICS

RIVERS OF LONDON: BODY WORKS
SC ISBN: 9781782761877
HB ISBN: 9781785853647

TITAN COMICS

EDITOR STEVE WHITE
DEPUTY EDITOR ANDREW JAMES
DESIGNER ROB FARMER

Titan Comics Editorial Jessica Burton, Lizzie Kaye, Tom Williams
Production Supervisors Jackie Flook, Maria Pearson
Production Assistant Peter James
Production Manager Obi Onuora
Art Director Oz Browne
Studio Manager Selina Juneja
Senior Sales Manager Steve Tothill
Press Officer Cara Fielder
Senior Marketing & Press Officer Owen Johnson
Marketing Manager Ricky Claydon
Commercial Manager Michelle Fairlamb
Publishing Manager Darryl Tothill
Publishing Director Chris Teather
Operations Director Leigh Baulch
Executive Director Vivian Cheung
Publisher Nick Landau

Published by Titan Comics
A division of Titan Publishing Group Ltd.
144 Southwark St.
London
SE1 0UP

A CIP catalogue record for this title is available from the British Library.

First edition: March 2016

10 9 8 7 6 5 4 3

Printed in Spain.
Titan Comics. TC0420

WWW.TITAN-COMICS.COM

Become a fan on Facebook.com/comicstitan

Follow us on Twitter @ComicsTitan

RIVERS OF LONDON

BODY WORK

WRITTEN BY
BEN AARONOVITCH & ANDREW CARTMEL

ART BY
LEE SULLIVAN

COLORS BY
LUIS GUERRERO

LETTERING BY
RONA SIMPSON (#1); JANICE CHIANG (#2-5)

Titan
COMICS

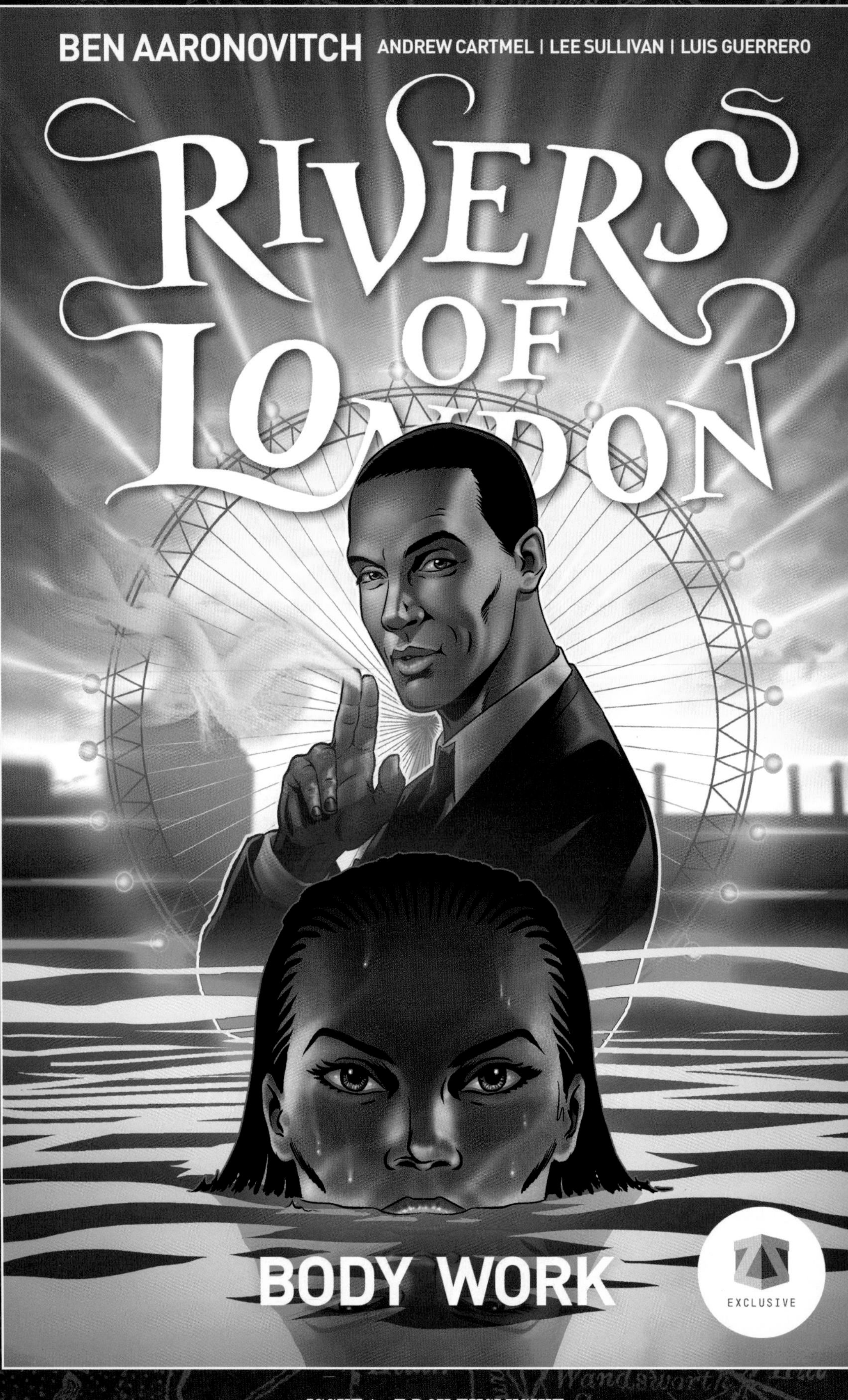
BEN AARONOVITCH
ANDREW CARTMEL | LEE SULLIVAN | LUIS GUERRERO
RIVERS OF LONDON
BODY WORK
EXCLUSIVE

ISSUE 1 - Z BOX EXCLUSIVE

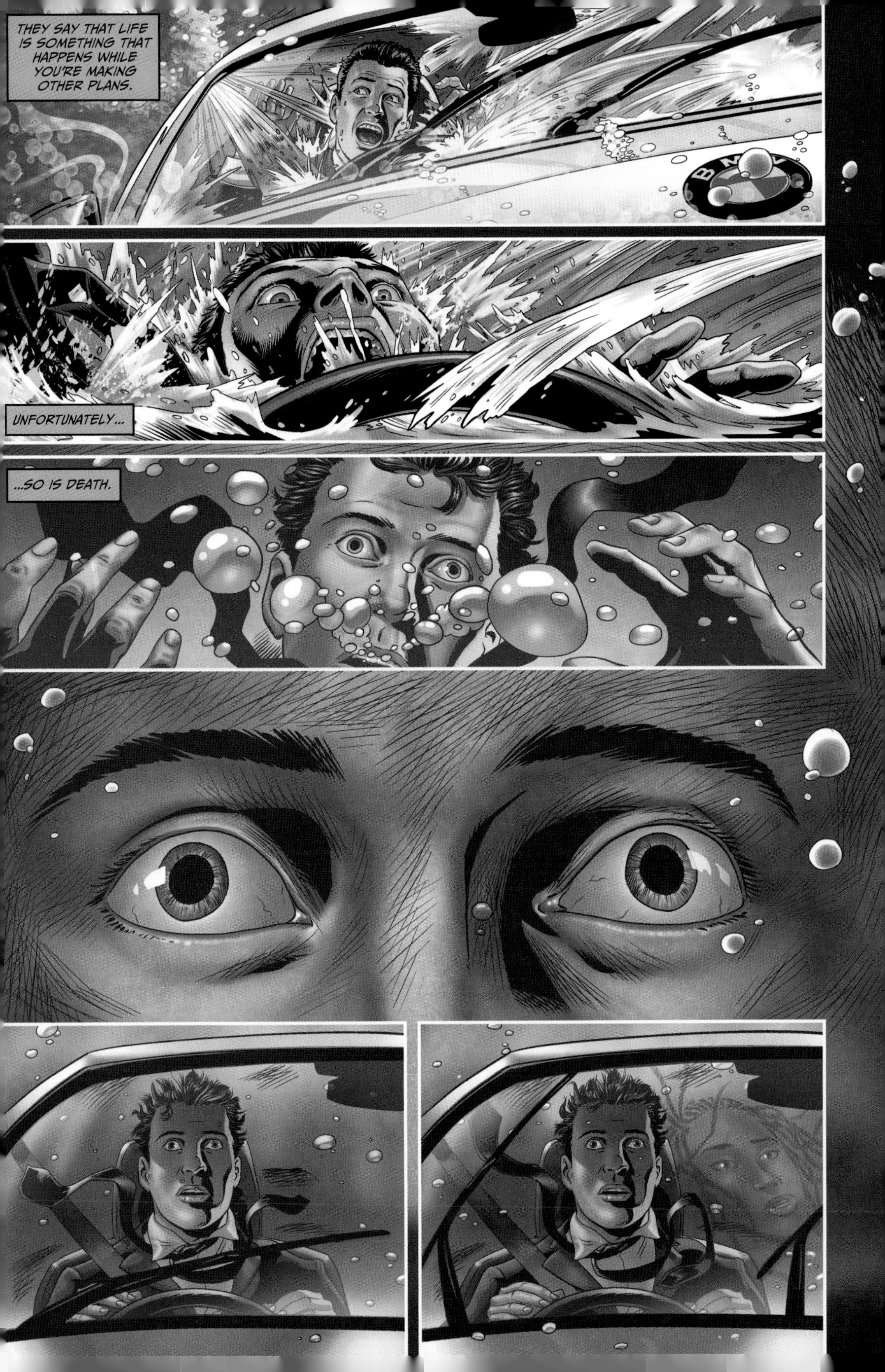
THEY SAY THAT LIFE IS SOMETHING THAT HAPPENS WHILE YOU'RE MAKING OTHER PLANS.
BMW
UNFORTUNATELY...
...SO IS DEATH.

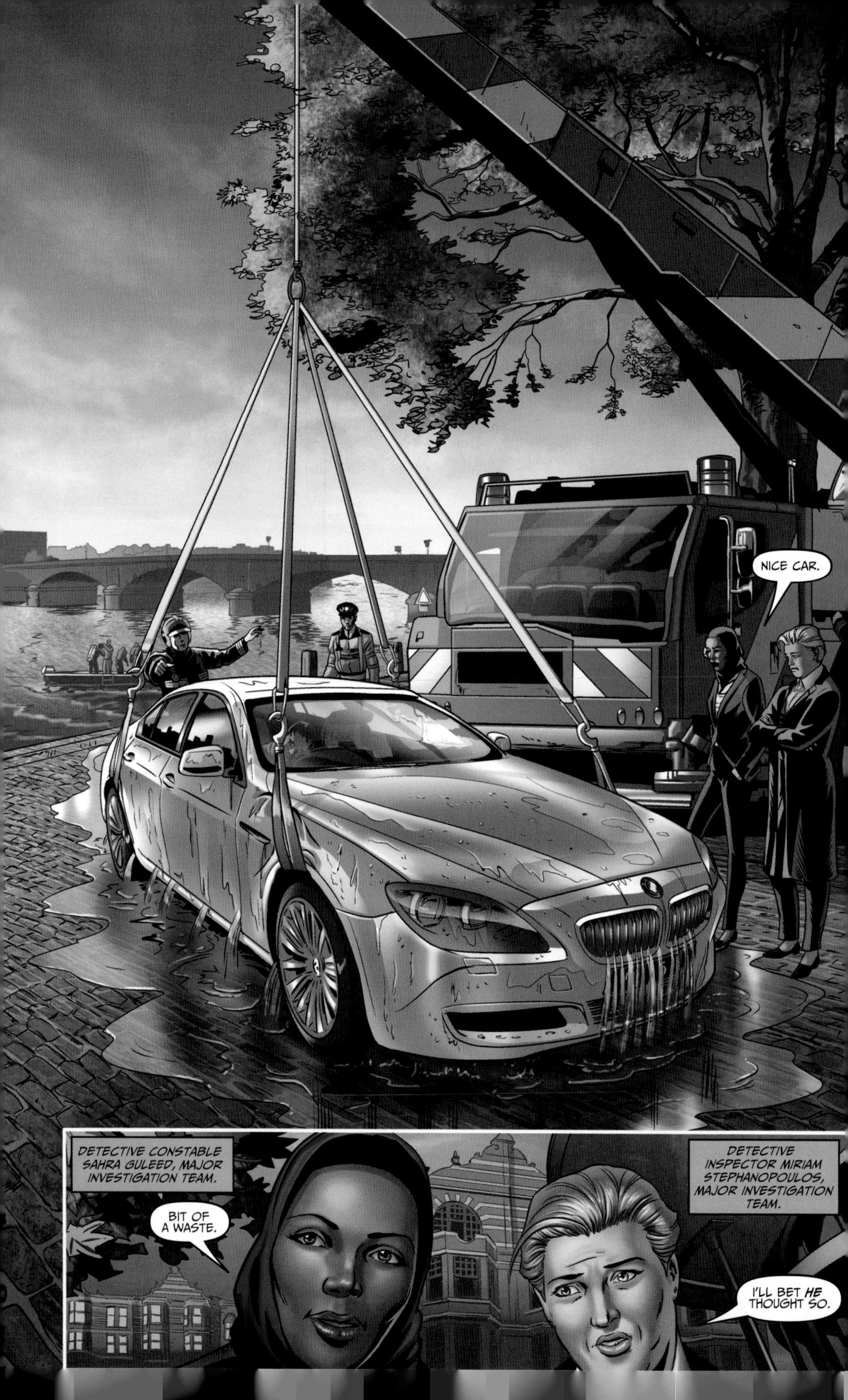
NICE CAR.
DETECTIVE CONSTABLE SAHRA GULEED, MAJOR INVESTIGATION TEAM.
BIT OF A WASTE.
DETECTIVE INSPECTOR MIRIAM STEPHANOPOULOS, MAJOR INVESTIGATION TEAM.
I'LL BET *HE* THOUGHT SO.

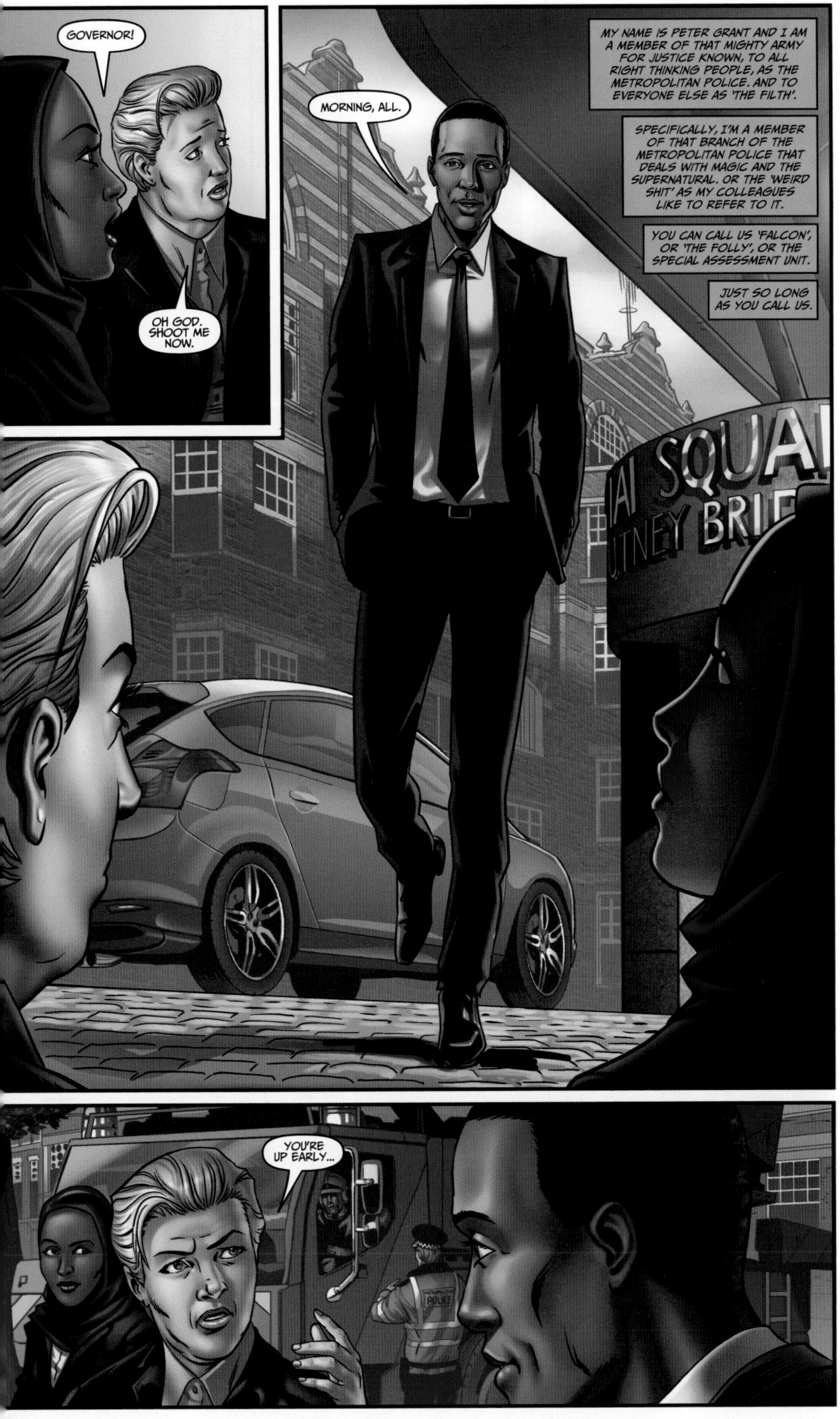
GOVERNOR!
OH GOD. SHOOT ME NOW.
MORNING, ALL.
MY NAME IS PETER GRANT AND I AM A MEMBER OF THAT MIGHTY ARMY FOR JUSTICE KNOWN, TO ALL RIGHT THINKING PEOPLE, AS THE METROPOLITAN POLICE. AND TO EVERYONE ELSE AS 'THE FILTH'.
SPECIFICALLY, I'M A MEMBER OF THAT BRANCH OF THE METROPOLITAN POLICE THAT DEALS WITH MAGIC AND THE SUPERNATURAL. OR THE 'WEIRD SHIT' AS MY COLLEAGUES LIKE TO REFER TO IT.
YOU CAN CALL US 'FALCON', OR 'THE FOLLY', OR THE SPECIAL ASSESSMENT UNIT.
JUST SO LONG AS YOU CALL US.
YOU'RE UP EARLY...
POLICE

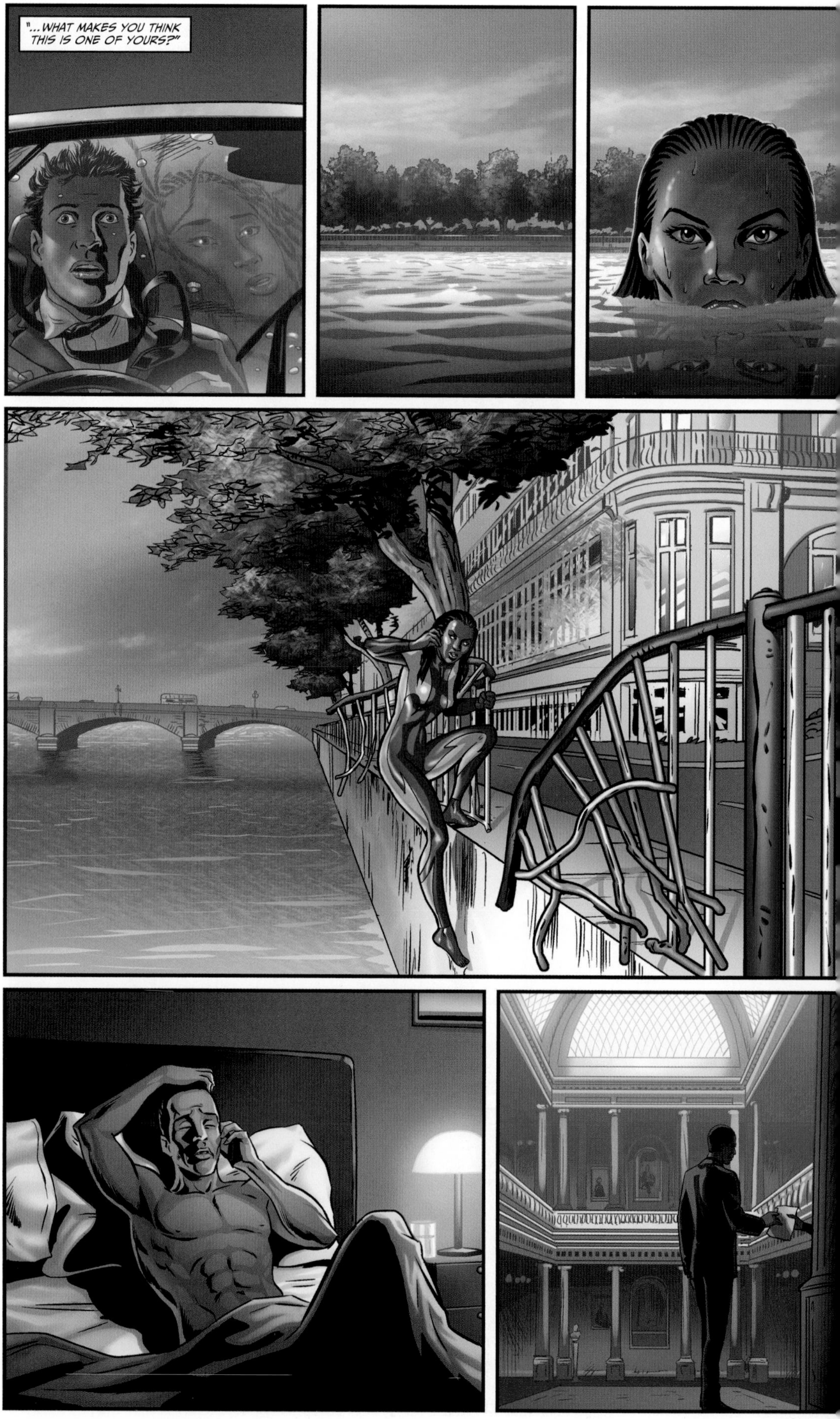
"...WHAT MAKES YOU THINK THIS IS ONE OF YOURS?"

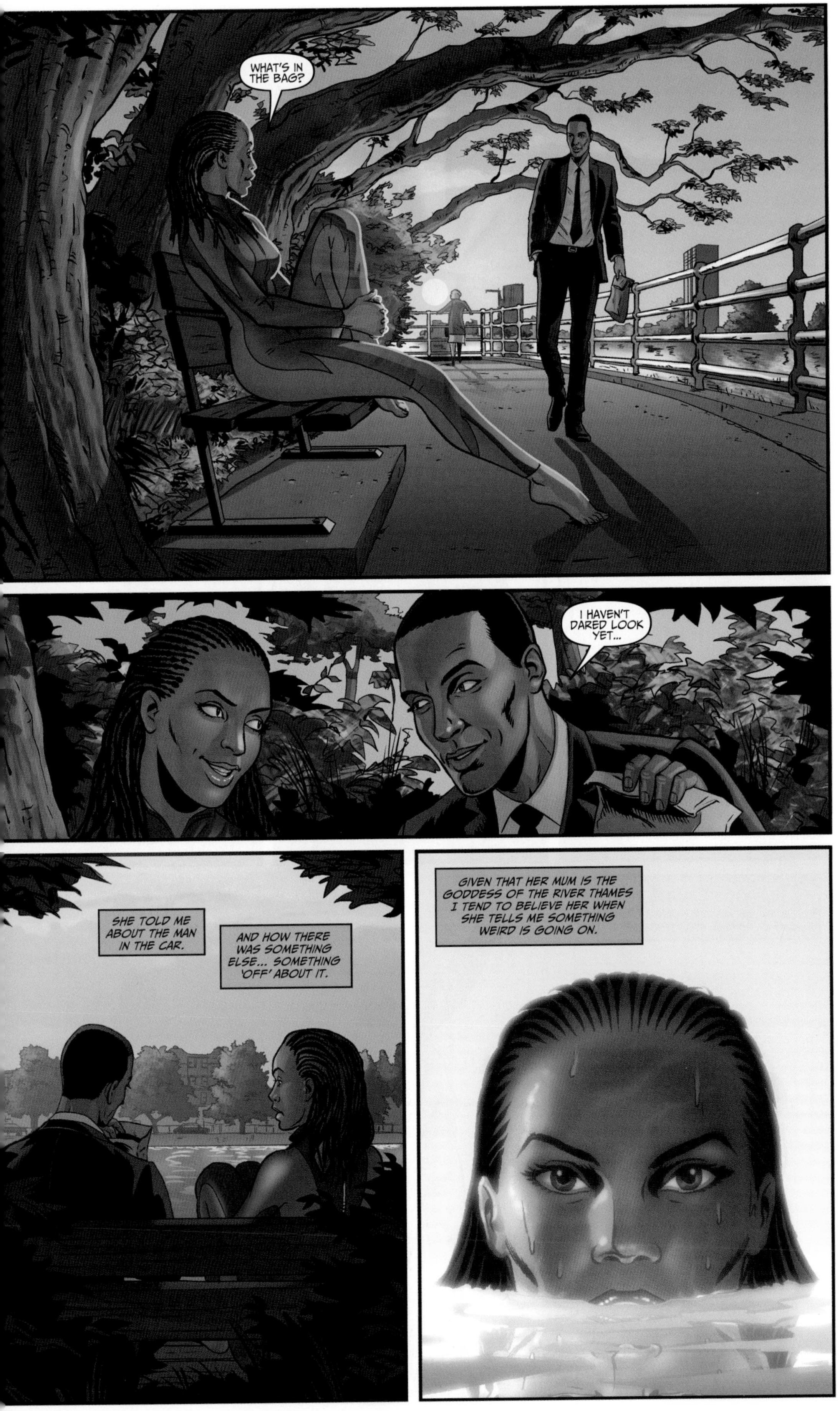
WHAT'S IN THE BAG?
I HAVEN'T DARED LOOK YET...
SHE TOLD ME ABOUT THE MAN IN THE CAR.
AND HOW THERE WAS SOMETHING ELSE... SOMETHING 'OFF' ABOUT IT.
GIVEN THAT HER MUM IS THE GODDESS OF THE RIVER THAMES I TEND TO BELIEVE HER WHEN SHE TELLS ME SOMETHING WEIRD IS GOING ON.

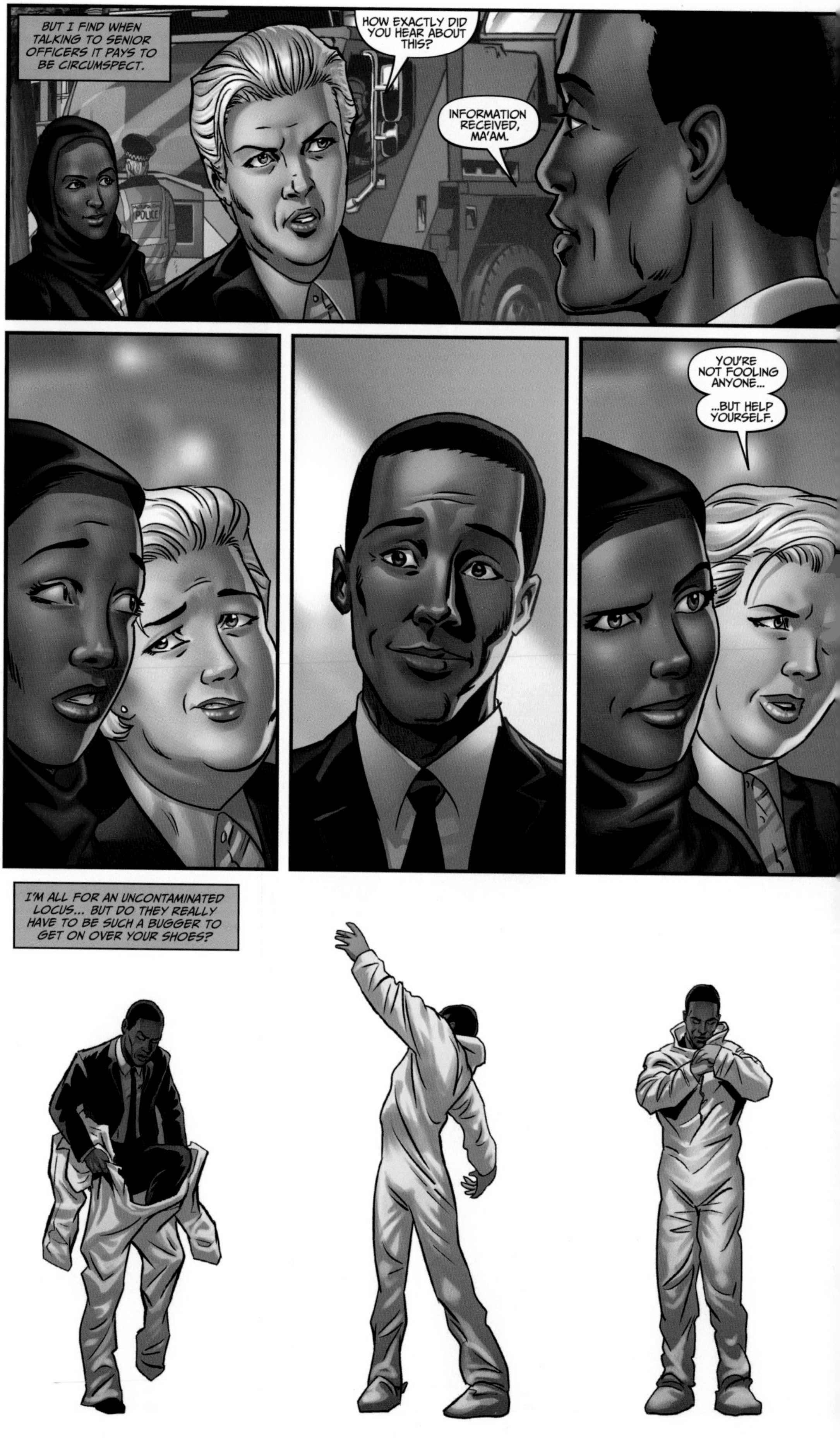
BUT I FIND WHEN TALKING TO SENIOR OFFICERS IT PAYS TO BE CIRCUMSPECT.
HOW EXACTLY DID YOU HEAR ABOUT THIS?
INFORMATION RECEIVED, MA'AM.
POLICE
YOU'RE NOT FOOLING ANYONE...
...BUT HELP YOURSELF.
I'M ALL FOR AN UNCONTAMINATED LOCUS... BUT DO THEY REALLY HAVE TO BE SUCH A BUGGER TO GET ON OVER YOUR SHOES?

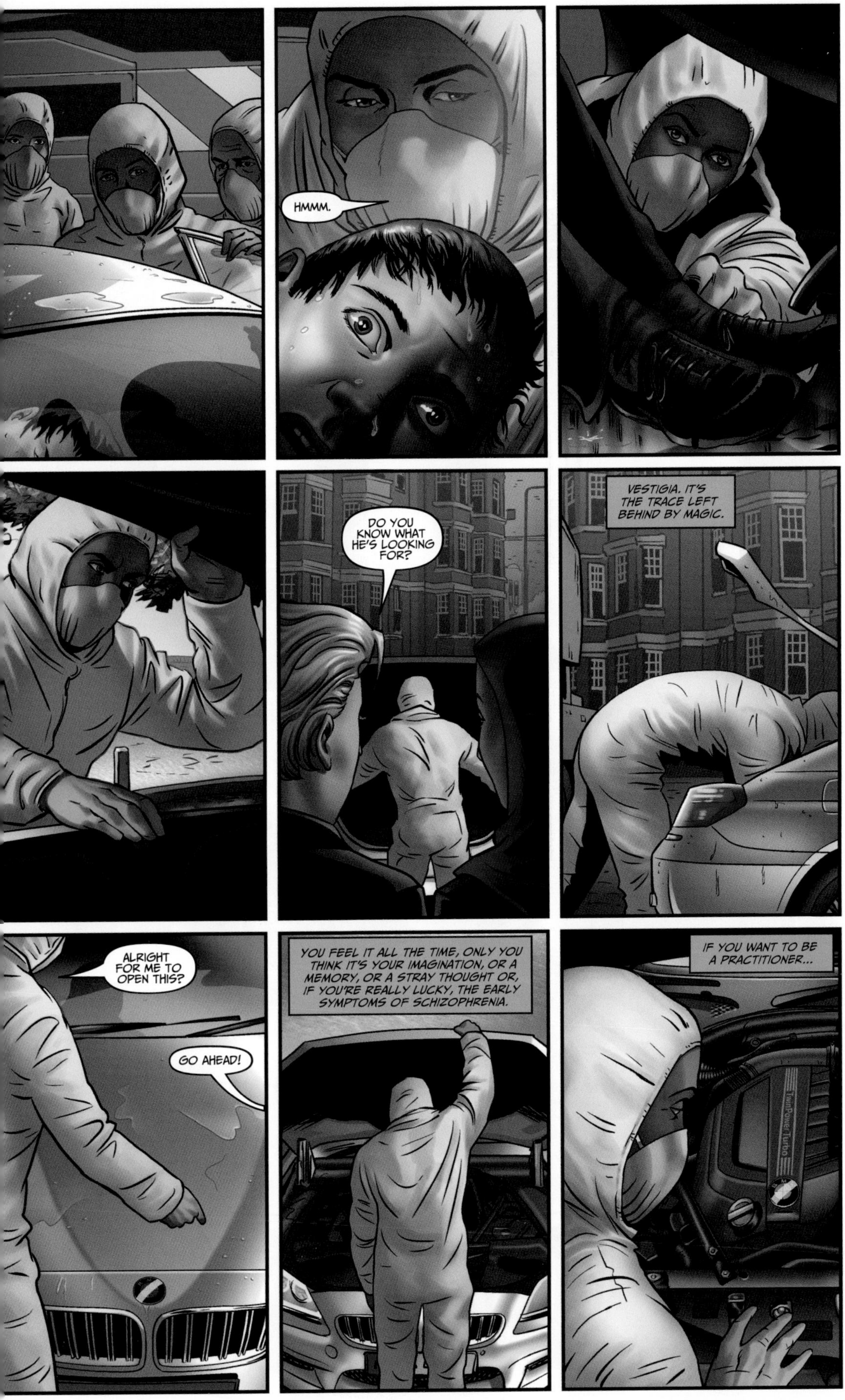
HMMM.
DO YOU KNOW WHAT HE'S LOOKING FOR?
VESTIGIA. IT'S THE TRACE LEFT BEHIND BY MAGIC.
ALRIGHT FOR ME TO OPEN THIS?
GO AHEAD!
YOU FEEL IT ALL THE TIME, ONLY YOU THINK IT'S YOUR IMAGINATION, OR A MEMORY, OR A STRAY THOUGHT OR, IF YOU'RE REALLY LUCKY, THE EARLY SYMPTOMS OF SCHIZOPHRENIA.
IF YOU WANT TO BE A PRACTITIONER...

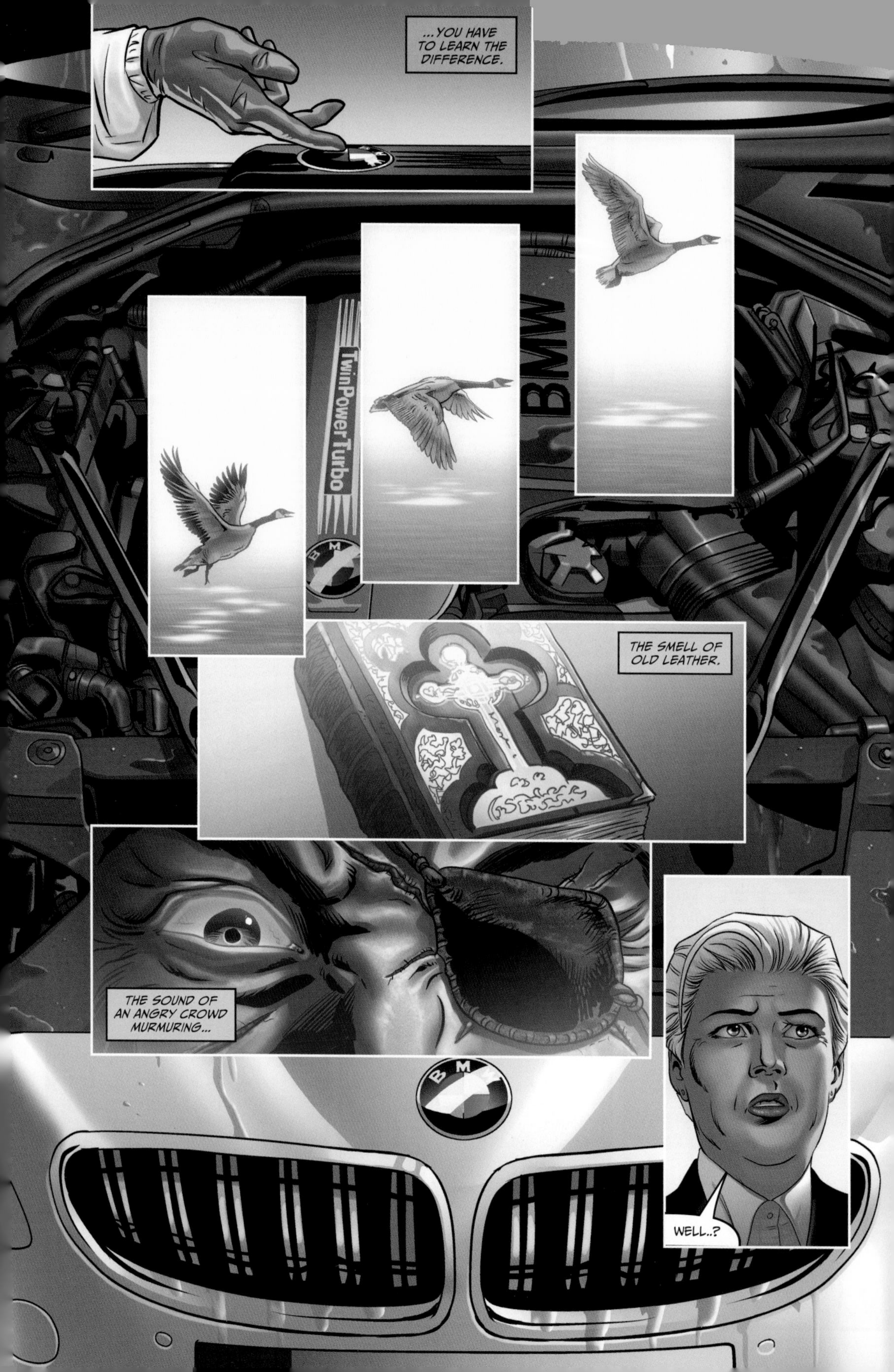
...YOU HAVE TO LEARN THE DIFFERENCE.
TwinPowerTurbo
BMW
THE SMELL OF OLD LEATHER.
THE SOUND OF AN ANGRY CROWD MURMURING...
WELL..?

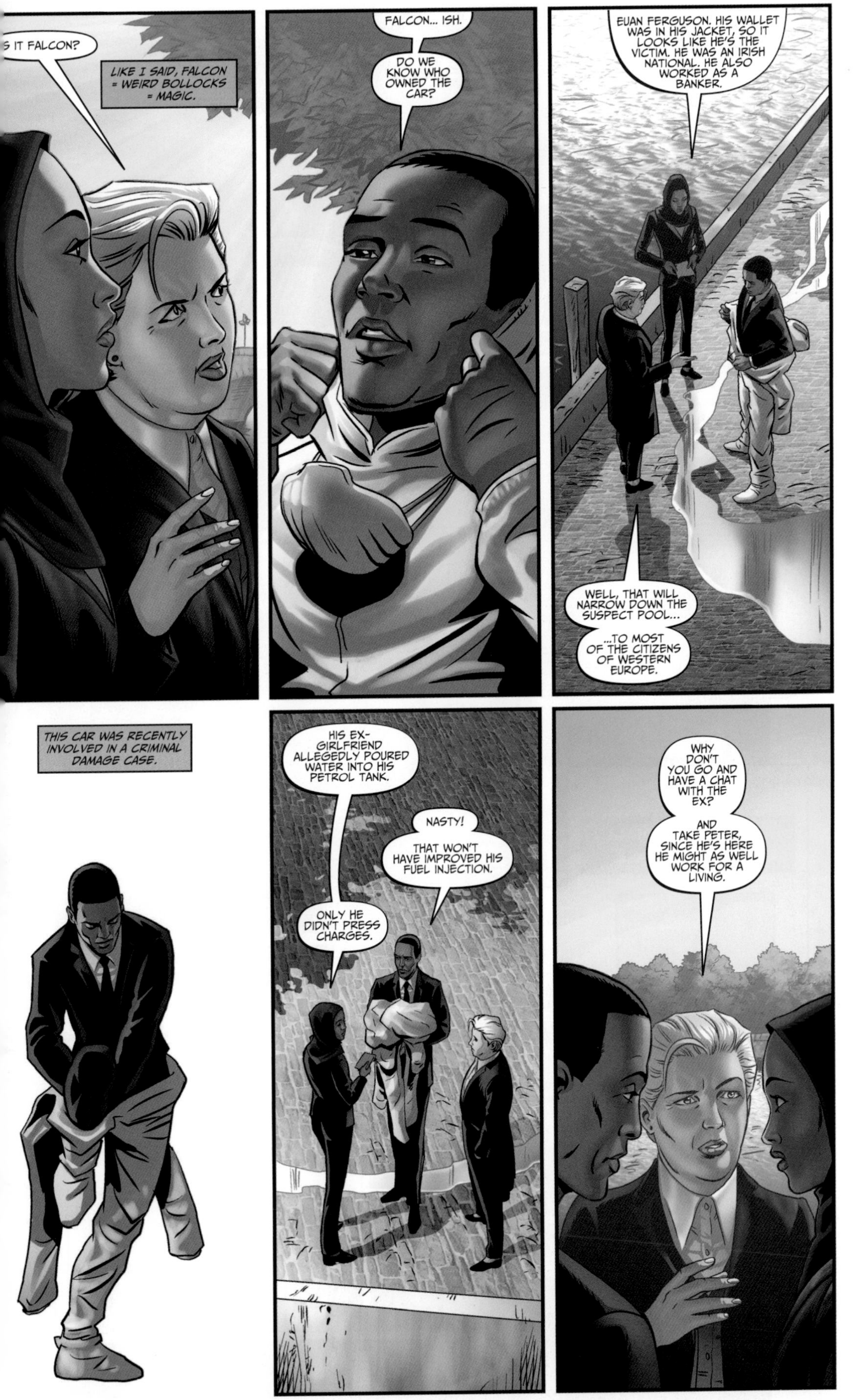

S IT FALCON?
LIKE I SAID, FALCON = WEIRD BOLLOCKS = MAGIC.
FALCON... ISH.
DO WE KNOW WHO OWNED THE CAR?
EUAN FERGUSON. HIS WALLET WAS IN HIS JACKET, SO IT LOOKS LIKE HE'S THE VICTIM. HE WAS AN IRISH NATIONAL. HE ALSO WORKED AS A BANKER.
WELL, THAT WILL NARROW DOWN THE SUSPECT POOL...
...TO MOST OF THE CITIZENS OF WESTERN EUROPE.
THIS CAR WAS RECENTLY INVOLVED IN A CRIMINAL DAMAGE CASE.
HIS EX-GIRLFRIEND ALLEGEDLY POURED WATER INTO HIS PETROL TANK.
NASTY!
THAT WON'T HAVE IMPROVED HIS FUEL INJECTION.
ONLY HE DIDN'T PRESS CHARGES.
WHY DON'T YOU GO AND HAVE A CHAT WITH THE EX?
AND TAKE PETER, SINCE HE'S HERE HE MIGHT AS WELL WORK FOR A LIVING.

YOU DON'T JUST RUSH OVER TO A POTENTIAL SUSPECT'S HOUSE AND TAKE POTLUCK.

FIRST YOU CALL IN FOR AN IIP (INTEGRATED INTELLIGENCE PLATFORM) CHECK, WHICH LOOKS AT EVERYTHING...

...FROM THE DVLA...

DRIVING LICENCE

UK

1. GORING
2. JULIE ANN
3. 11-09-90 LONDON
4a. 30-04-08 4b.
5.
7.
8. 42 DORKING
LONDON

9. B B1 C1 AK

...THE UK BORDER AGENCY...

UNITED KINGDOM OF GREAT BRITAIN AND NORTHERN IRELAND

P   GBR   920575485
GORING
JULIE ANN
BRITISH CITIZEN
11 SEP /SEPT 90
F   CROYDON
16 JUL /JUIL 10 IPS
16 JUL /JUIL 20   J Goring

P<GBRGORING<JULIE<ANN<<<<<<<<<<<<<<<<<<<<<<<<<

...THE POLICE NATIONAL COMPUTER...

METROPOLITAN POLICE

INCIDENT REPORT

CHARGE 0174170144

Mail   Search   Social Media   File Sharin

SEARCH RESULTS
did you mean Julie GOERING?

...AND OF COURSE YOU LOOK THEM UP IN THE SAME PLACE EVERYBODY ELSE LOOKS THINGS UP.

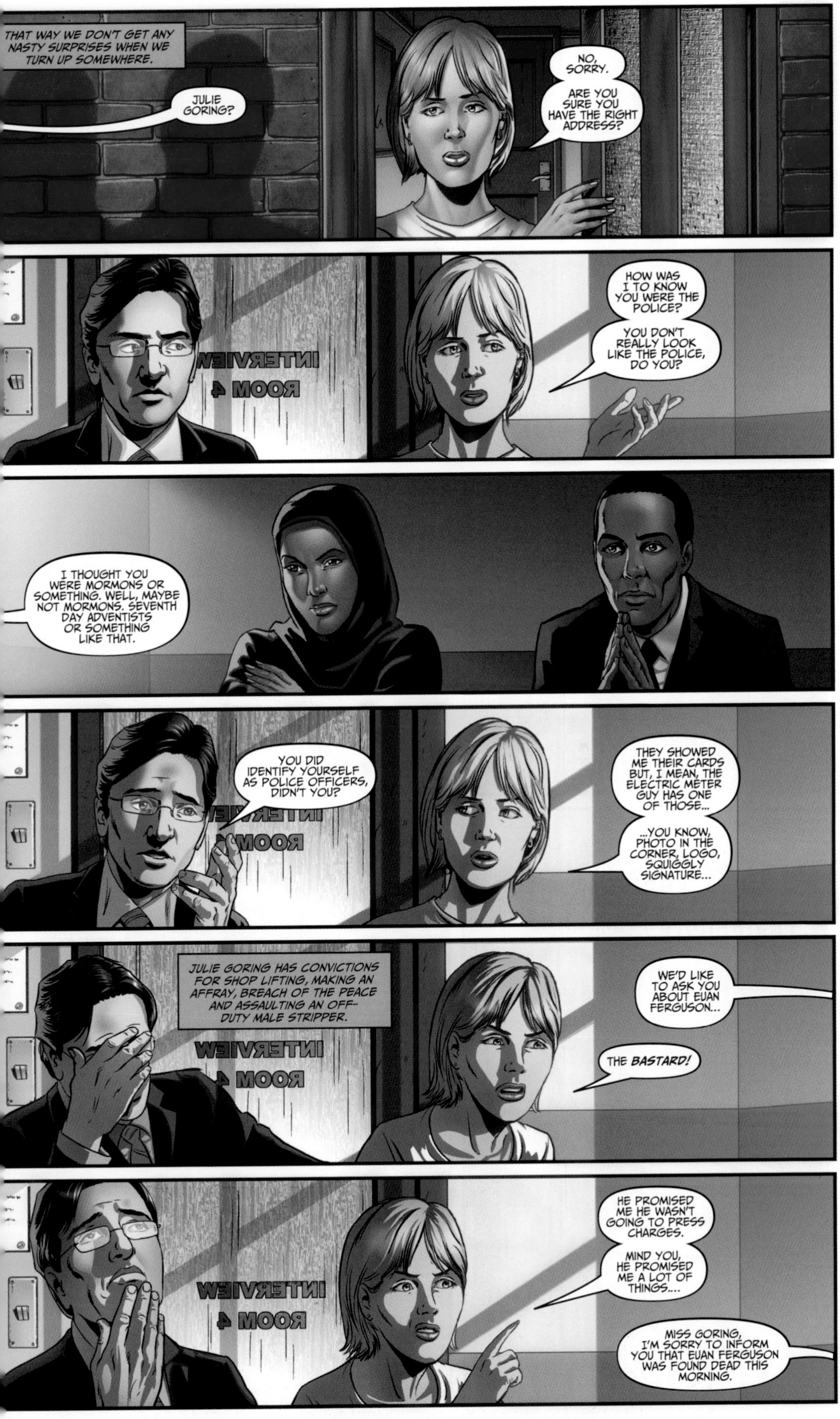
THAT WAY WE DON'T GET ANY NASTY SURPRISES WHEN WE TURN UP SOMEWHERE.
JULIE GORING?
NO, SORRY.
ARE YOU SURE YOU HAVE THE RIGHT ADDRESS?
INTERVIEW ROOM 4
HOW WAS I TO KNOW YOU WERE THE POLICE?
YOU DON'T REALLY LOOK LIKE THE POLICE, DO YOU?
I THOUGHT YOU WERE MORMONS OR SOMETHING. WELL, MAYBE NOT MORMONS. SEVENTH DAY ADVENTISTS OR SOMETHING LIKE THAT.
YOU DID IDENTIFY YOURSELF AS POLICE OFFICERS, DIDN'T YOU?
THEY SHOWED ME THEIR CARDS BUT, I MEAN, THE ELECTRIC METER GUY HAS ONE OF THOSE...
...YOU KNOW, PHOTO IN THE CORNER, LOGO, SQUIGGLY SIGNATURE...
JULIE GORING HAS CONVICTIONS FOR SHOP LIFTING, MAKING AN AFFRAY, BREACH OF THE PEACE AND ASSAULTING AN OFF-DUTY MALE STRIPPER.
WE'D LIKE TO ASK YOU ABOUT EUAN FERGUSON...
THE *BASTARD!*
HE PROMISED ME HE WASN'T GOING TO PRESS CHARGES.
MIND YOU, HE PROMISED ME A LOT OF THINGS....
MISS GORING, I'M SORRY TO INFORM YOU THAT EUAN FERGUSON WAS FOUND DEAD THIS MORNING.

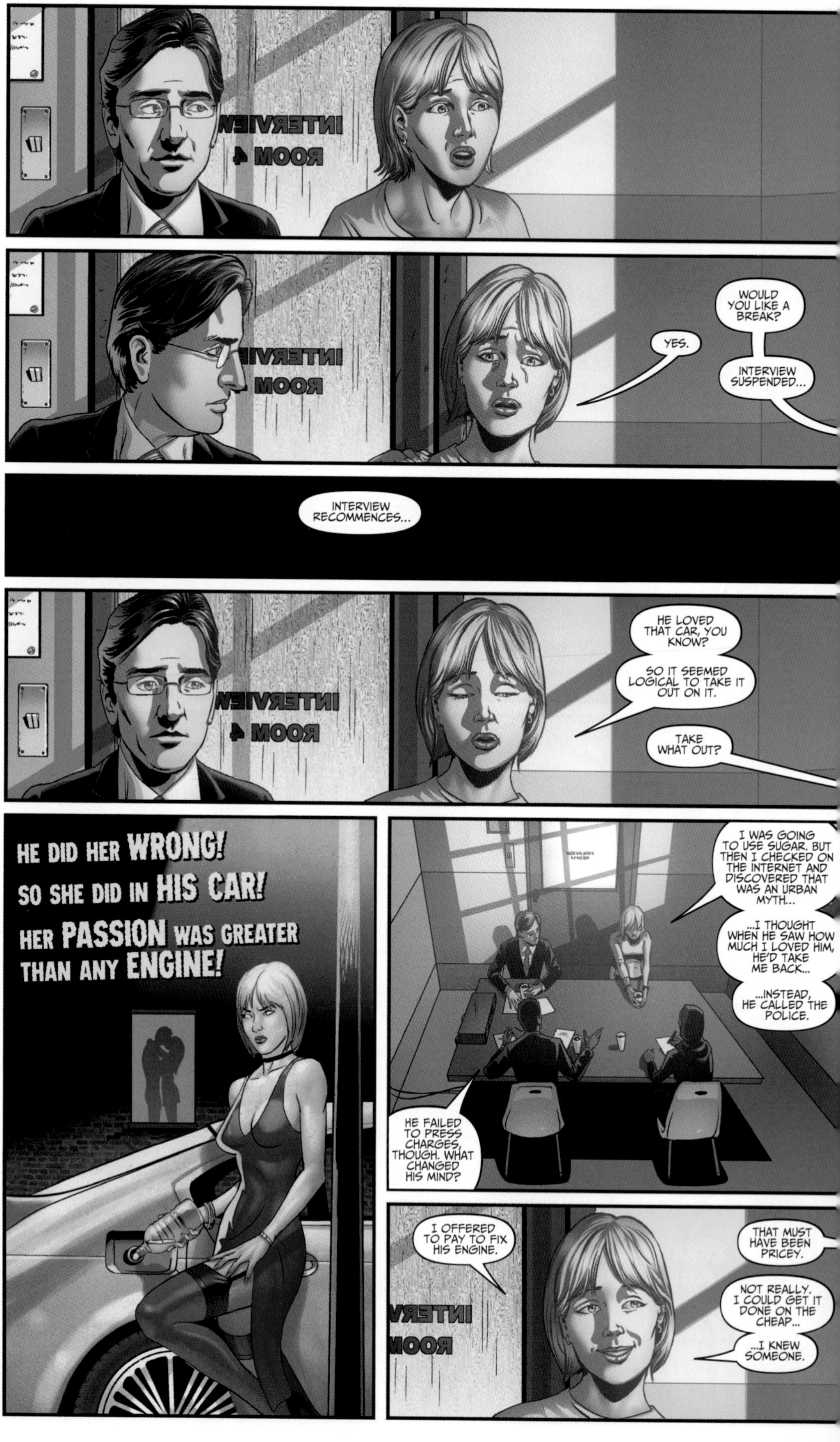

WOULD YOU LIKE A BREAK?
YES.
INTERVIEW SUSPENDED...
INTERVIEW RECOMMENCES...
HE LOVED THAT CAR, YOU KNOW?
SO IT SEEMED LOGICAL TO TAKE IT OUT ON IT.
TAKE WHAT OUT?
HE DID HER WRONG!
SO SHE DID IN HIS CAR!
HER PASSION WAS GREATER THAN ANY ENGINE!
I WAS GOING TO USE SUGAR, BUT THEN I CHECKED ON THE INTERNET AND DISCOVERED THAT WAS AN URBAN MYTH...
...I THOUGHT WHEN HE SAW HOW MUCH I LOVED HIM, HE'D TAKE ME BACK...
...INSTEAD, HE CALLED THE POLICE.
HE FAILED TO PRESS CHARGES, THOUGH. WHAT CHANGED HIS MIND?
I OFFERED TO PAY TO FIX HIS ENGINE.
THAT MUST HAVE BEEN PRICEY.
NOT REALLY. I COULD GET IT DONE ON THE CHEAP...
...I KNEW SOMEONE.

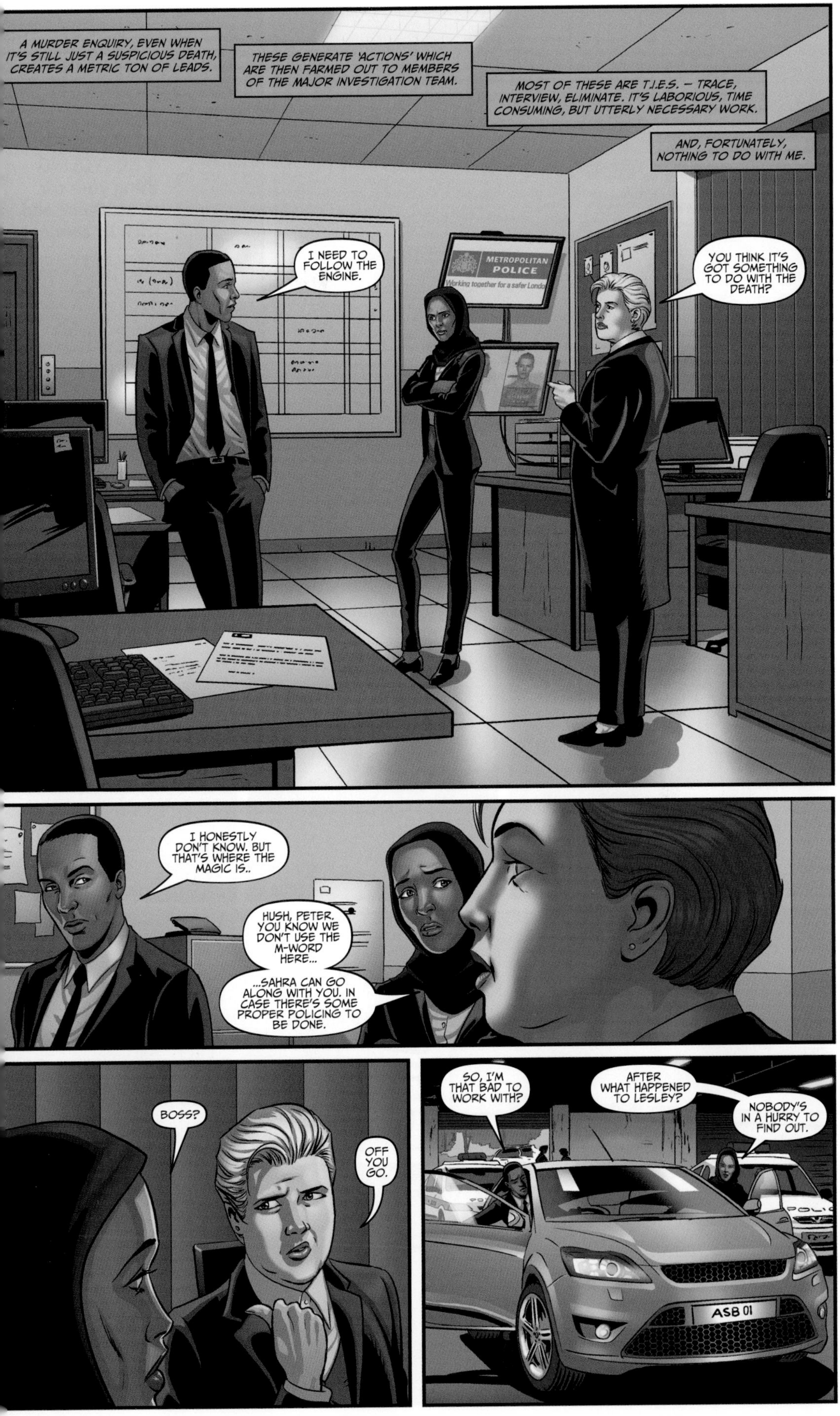
A MURDER ENQUIRY, EVEN WHEN IT'S STILL JUST A SUSPICIOUS DEATH, CREATES A METRIC TON OF LEADS.
THESE GENERATE 'ACTIONS' WHICH ARE THEN FARMED OUT TO MEMBERS OF THE MAJOR INVESTIGATION TEAM.
MOST OF THESE ARE T.I.E.S. — TRACE, INTERVIEW, ELIMINATE. IT'S LABORIOUS, TIME CONSUMING, BUT UTTERLY NECESSARY WORK.
AND, FORTUNATELY, NOTHING TO DO WITH ME.
I NEED TO FOLLOW THE ENGINE.
METROPOLITAN POLICE
Working together for a safer London
YOU THINK IT'S GOT SOMETHING TO DO WITH THE DEATH?
I HONESTLY DON'T KNOW. BUT THAT'S WHERE THE MAGIC IS..
HUSH, PETER. YOU KNOW WE DON'T USE THE M-WORD HERE...
...SAHRA CAN GO ALONG WITH YOU. IN CASE THERE'S SOME PROPER POLICING TO BE DONE.
BOSS?
OFF YOU GO.
SO, I'M THAT BAD TO WORK WITH?
AFTER WHAT HAPPENED TO LESLEY?
NOBODY'S IN A HURRY TO FIND OUT.
ASB 01

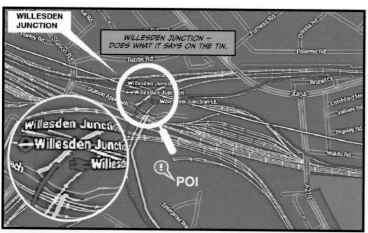

WILLESDEN JUNCTION

WILLESDEN JUNCTION — DOES WHAT IT SAYS ON THE TIN.

POI

A DEBDEN'S SCRAP METAL & RECYCLING Bring your car to us. Quick and friendly service!

THOMAS DEBDEN Esq. CARS BOUGHT

WELL THIS EXPLAINS WHY SHE GOT IT CHEAP!

HELLO?

PRESS TO SPEAK!

WARUMMMMMMMM

PRESS TO SPEAK!

PRESS TO SPEAK!

HELP! SHE'S TRYING TO KILL ME!

THERE ARE STRICT AND RIGOROUS CONDITIONS LAID DOWN TO REGULATE THE CIRCUMSTANCES IN WHICH AN OFFICER OF THE LAW CAN LEGALLY ENTER PRIVATE PREMISES...

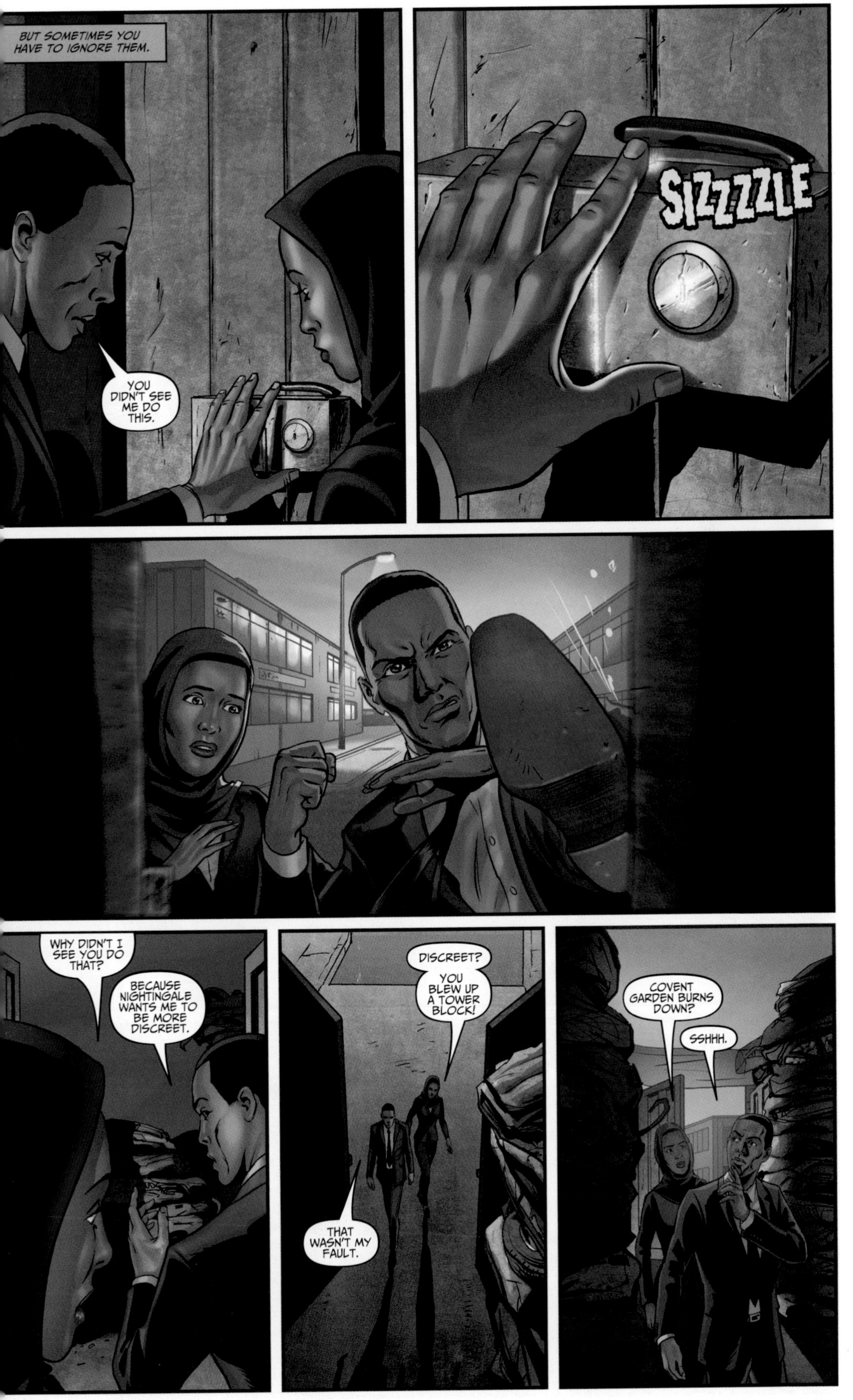
BUT SOMETIMES YOU HAVE TO IGNORE THEM.
YOU DIDN'T SEE ME DO THIS.
SIZZZZLE
WHY DIDN'T I SEE YOU DO THAT?
BECAUSE NIGHTINGALE WANTS ME TO BE MORE DISCREET.
DISCREET?
YOU BLEW UP A TOWER BLOCK!
THAT WASN'T MY FAULT.
COVENT GARDEN BURNS DOWN?
SSHHH.

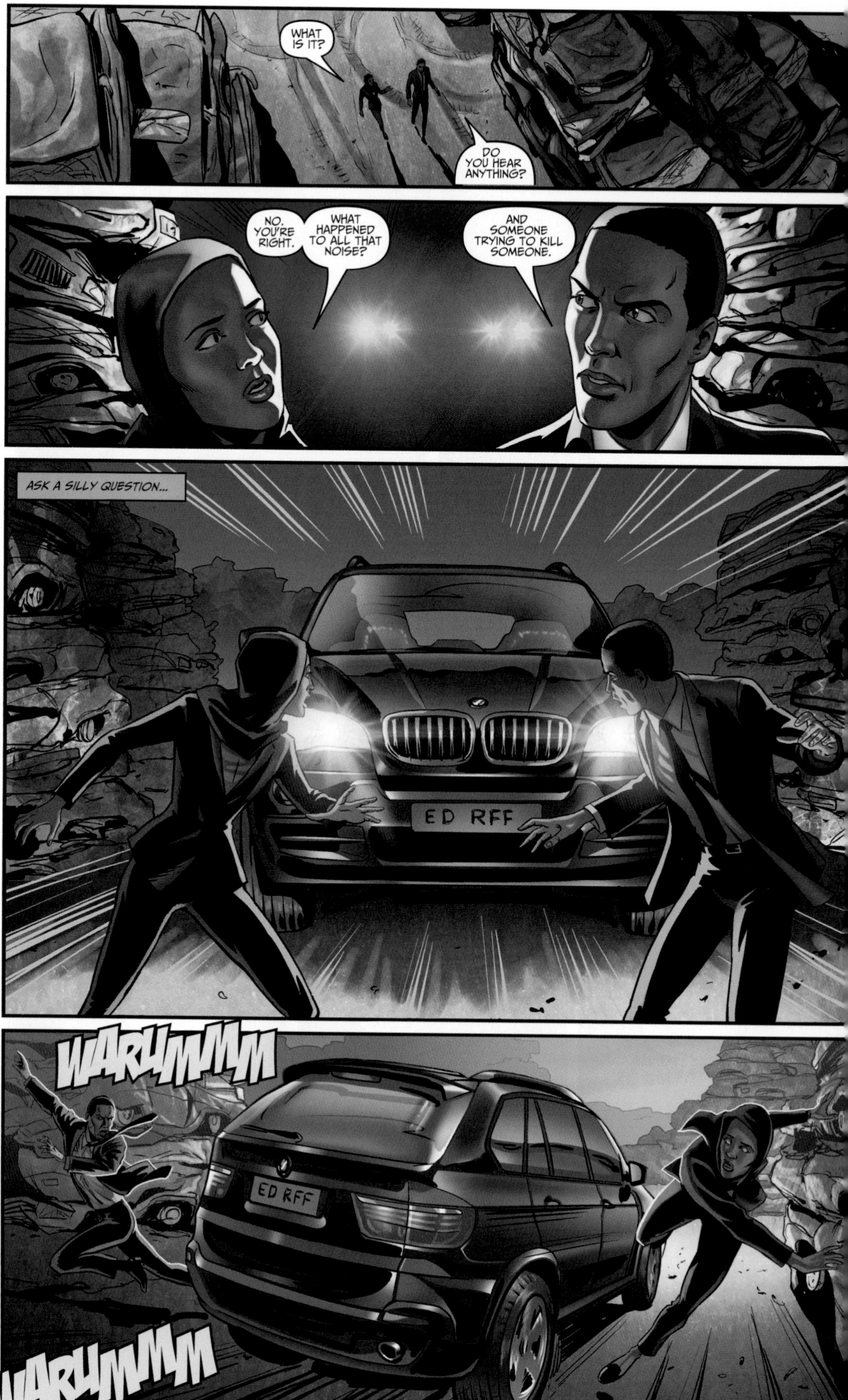
WHAT IS IT?
DO YOU HEAR ANYTHING?
NO. YOU'RE RIGHT.
WHAT HAPPENED TO ALL THAT NOISE?
AND SOMEONE TRYING TO KILL SOMEONE.
ASK A SILLY QUESTION...
ED RFF
WARUMMM
ED RFF
WARUMMM

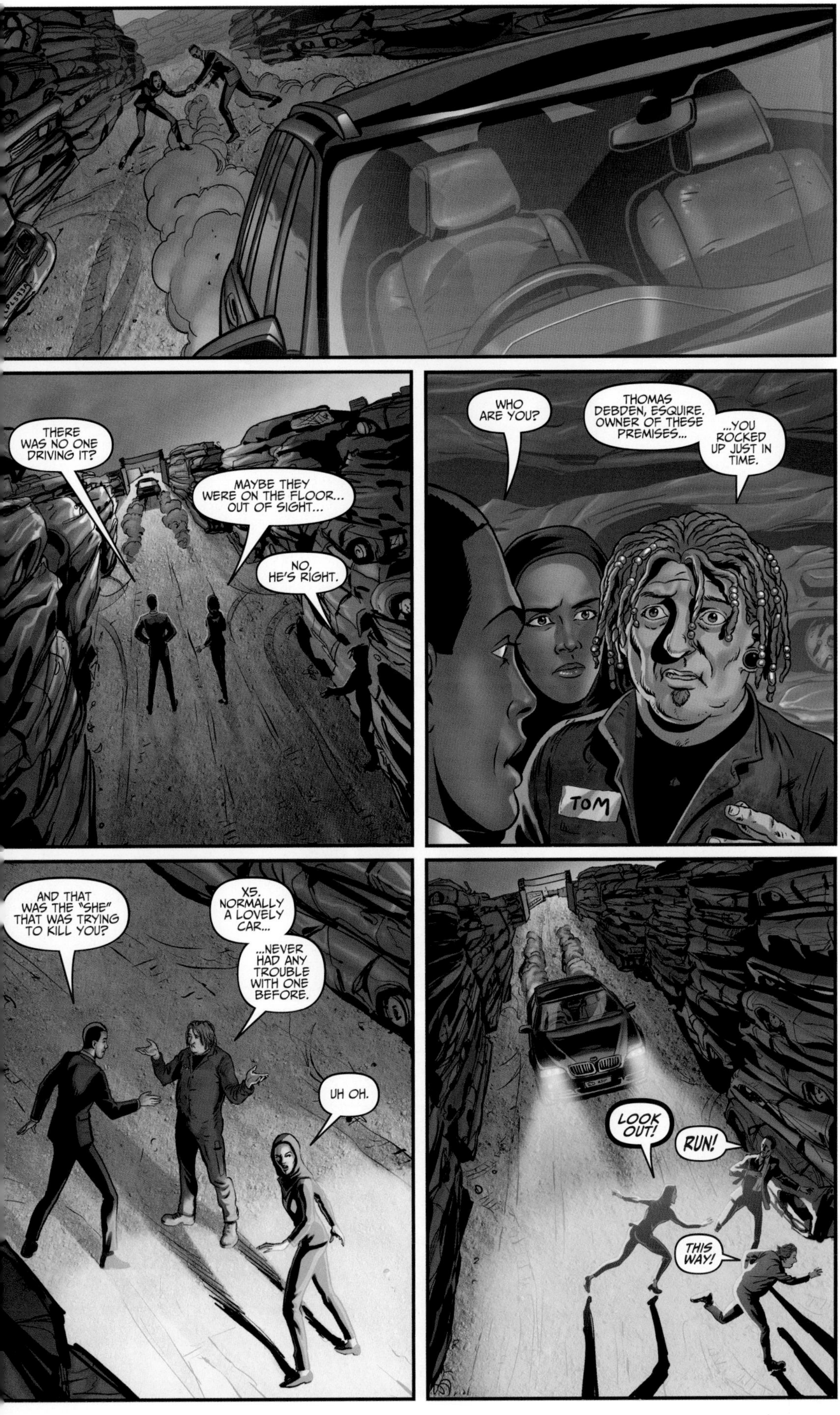
THERE WAS NO ONE DRIVING IT?
MAYBE THEY WERE ON THE FLOOR... OUT OF SIGHT...
NO, HE'S RIGHT.
WHO ARE YOU?
THOMAS DEBDEN, ESQUIRE. OWNER OF THESE PREMISES...
...YOU ROCKED UP JUST IN TIME.
TOM
AND THAT WAS THE "SHE" THAT WAS TRYING TO KILL YOU?
X5. NORMALLY A LOVELY CAR...
...NEVER HAD ANY TROUBLE WITH ONE BEFORE.
UH OH.
LOOK OUT!
RUN!
THIS WAY!

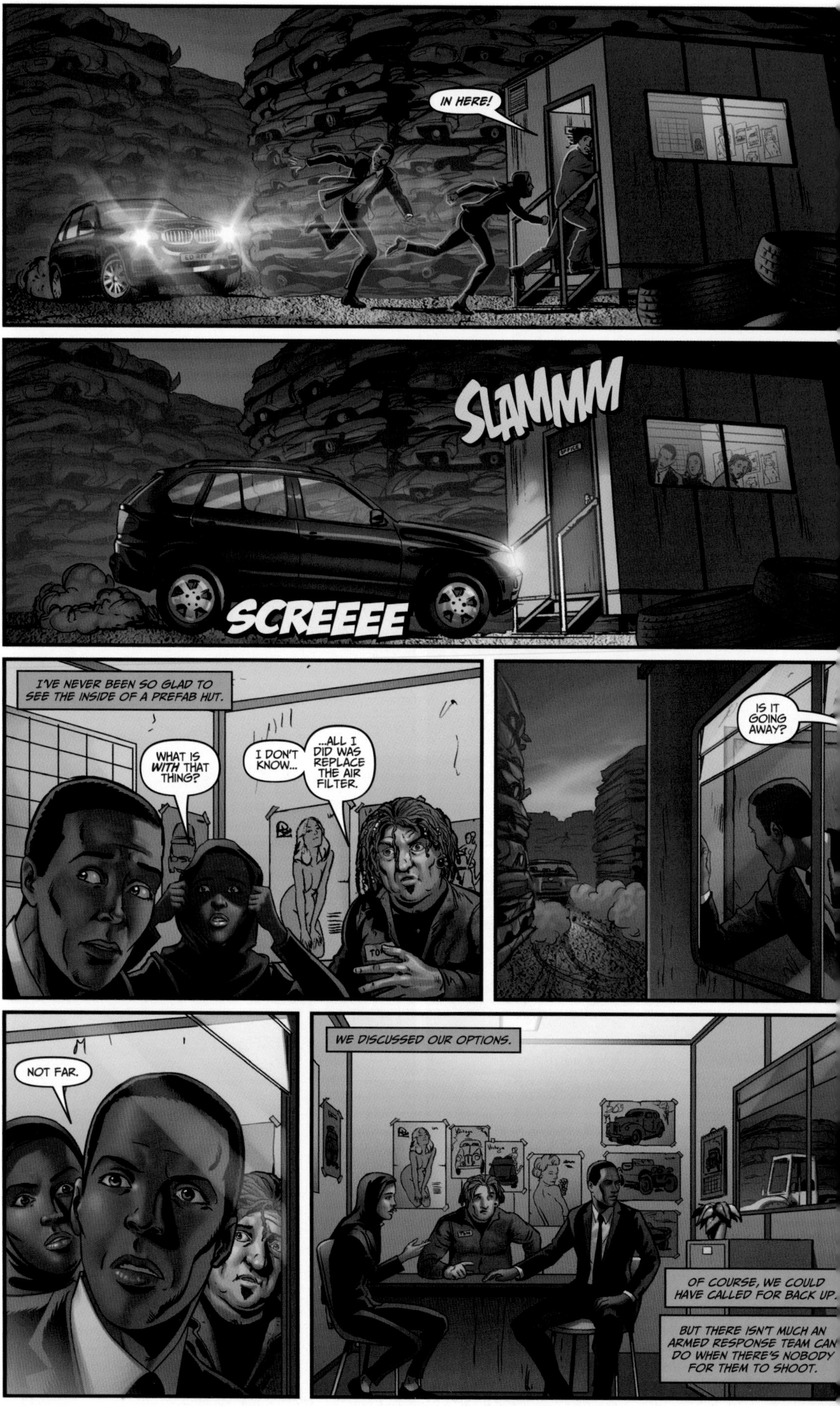
IN HERE!
SLAMMM
SCREEEE
I'VE NEVER BEEN SO GLAD TO SEE THE INSIDE OF A PREFAB HUT.
WHAT IS *WITH* THAT THING?
I DON'T KNOW...
...ALL I DID WAS REPLACE THE AIR FILTER.
IS IT GOING AWAY?
NOT FAR.
WE DISCUSSED OUR OPTIONS.
OF COURSE, WE COULD HAVE CALLED FOR BACK UP.
BUT THERE ISN'T MUCH AN ARMED RESPONSE TEAM CAN DO WHEN THERE'S NOBODY FOR THEM TO SHOOT.

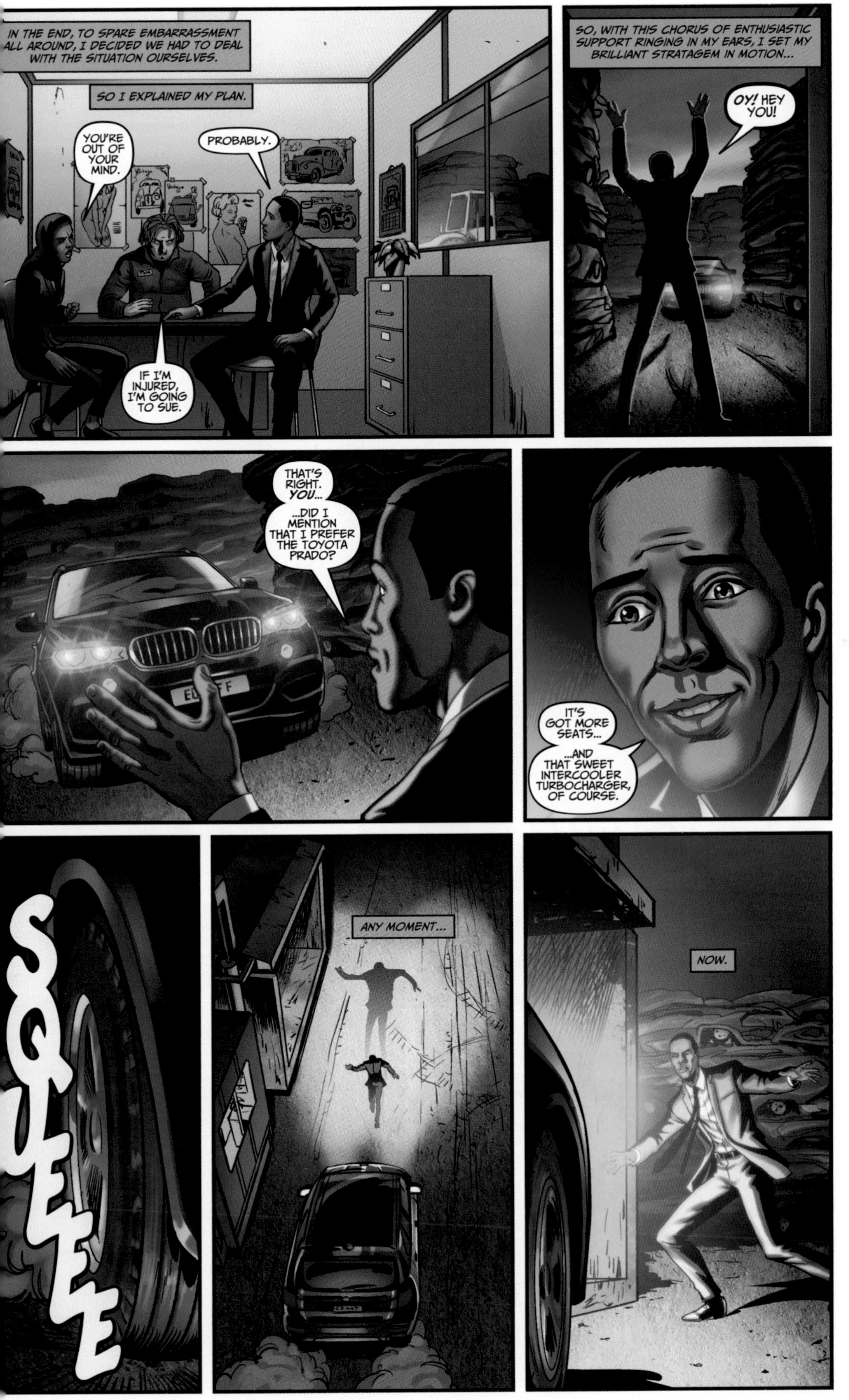

IN THE END, TO SPARE EMBARRASSMENT ALL AROUND, I DECIDED WE HAD TO DEAL WITH THE SITUATION OURSELVES.
SO I EXPLAINED MY PLAN.
YOU'RE OUT OF YOUR MIND.
PROBABLY.
IF I'M INJURED, I'M GOING TO SUE.
SO, WITH THIS CHORUS OF ENTHUSIASTIC SUPPORT RINGING IN MY EARS, I SET MY BRILLIANT STRATAGEM IN MOTION...
OY! HEY YOU!
THAT'S RIGHT. YOU...
...DID I MENTION THAT I PREFER THE TOYOTA PRADO?
IT'S GOT MORE SEATS...
...AND THAT SWEET INTERCOOLER TURBOCHARGER, OF COURSE.
SQUEEE
ANY MOMENT...
NOW.

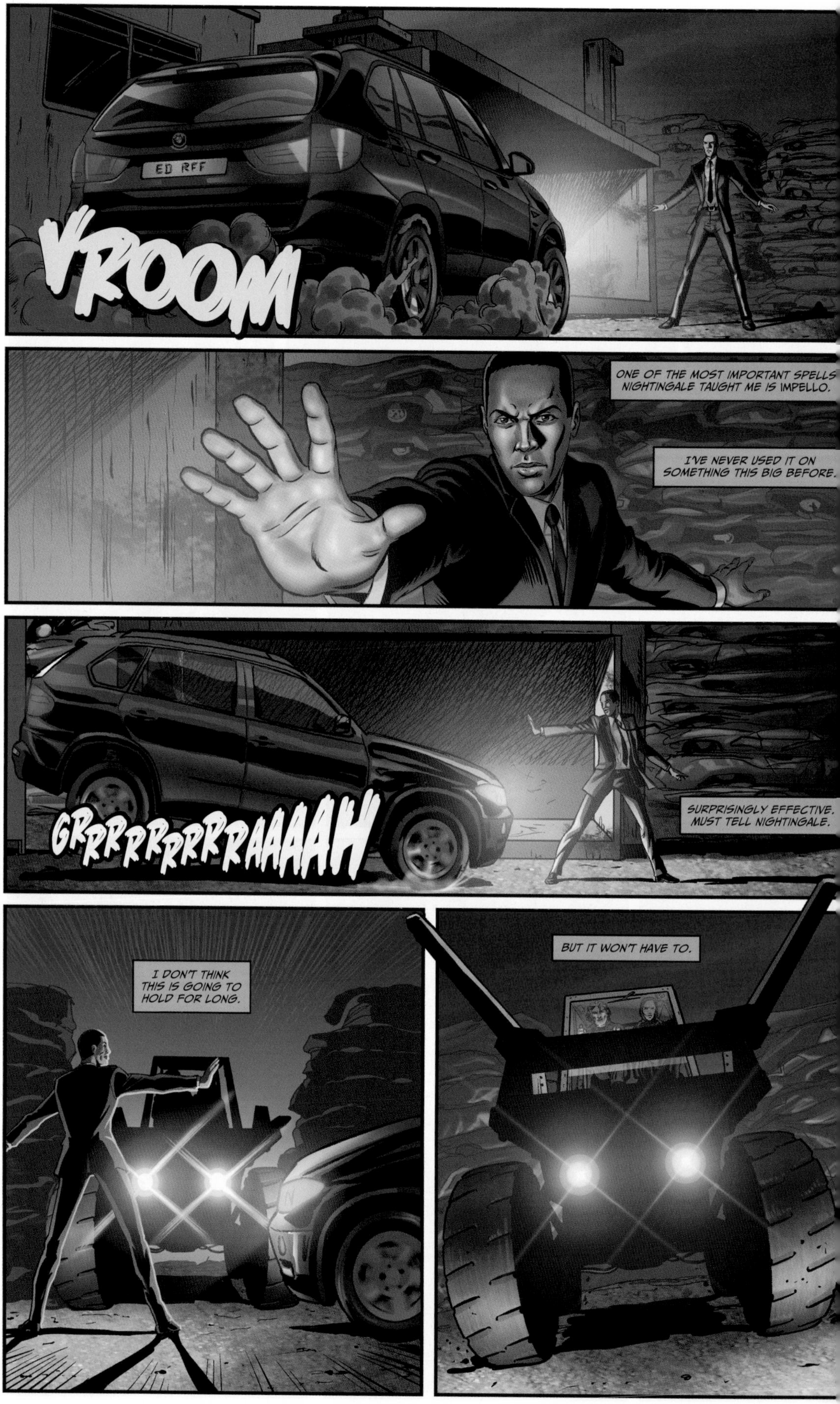
ED RFF
VROOM
ONE OF THE MOST IMPORTANT SPELLS NIGHTINGALE TAUGHT ME IS IMPELLO.
I'VE NEVER USED IT ON SOMETHING THIS BIG BEFORE.
GRRRRRRRRAAAAAH
SURPRISINGLY EFFECTIVE. MUST TELL NIGHTINGALE.
I DON'T THINK THIS IS GOING TO HOLD FOR LONG.
BUT IT WON'T HAVE TO.

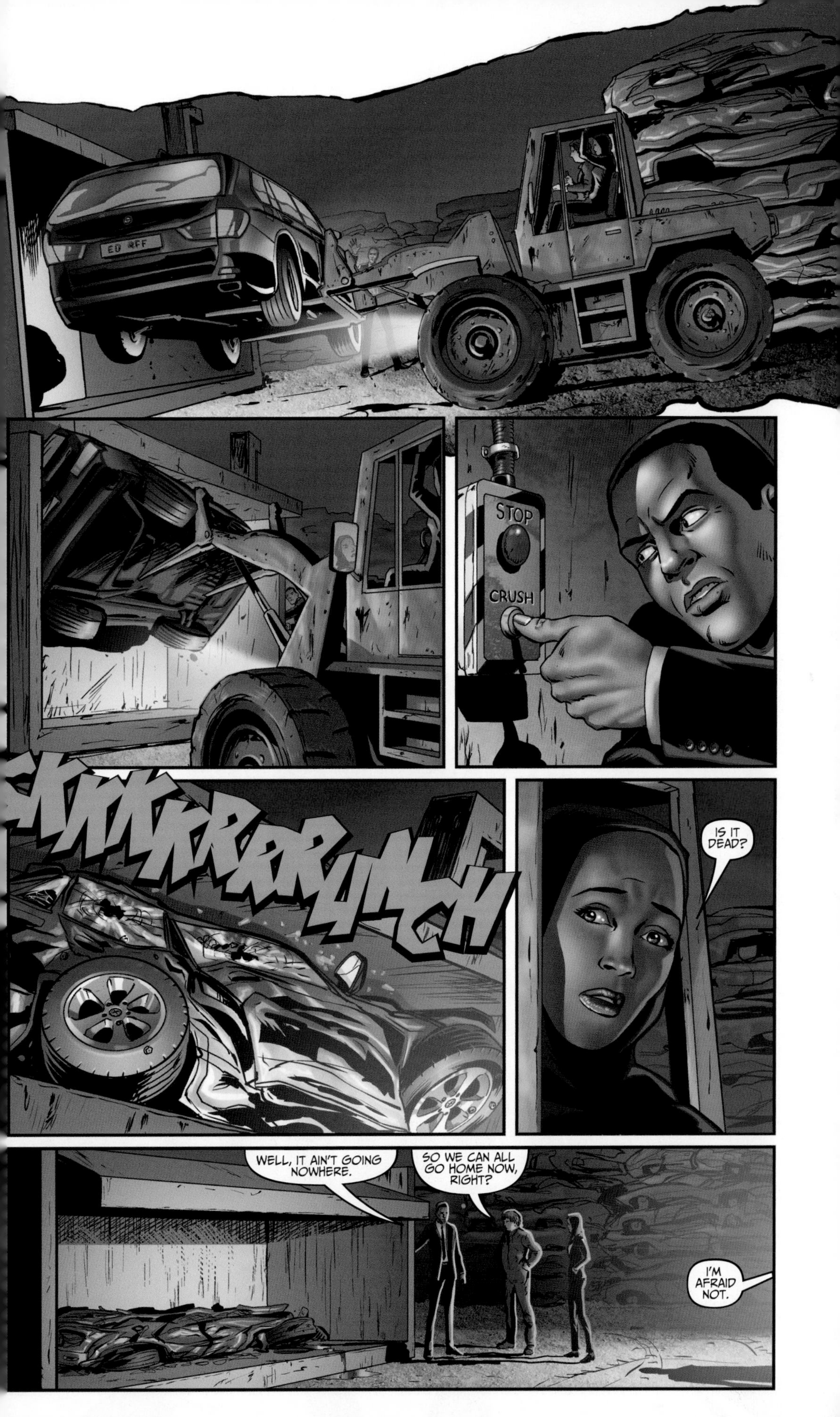

E0 OFF
STOP
CRUSH
SKKKRRRRUNCH
IS IT DEAD?
WELL, IT AIN'T GOING NOWHERE.
SO WE CAN ALL GO HOME NOW, RIGHT?
I'M AFRAID NOT.

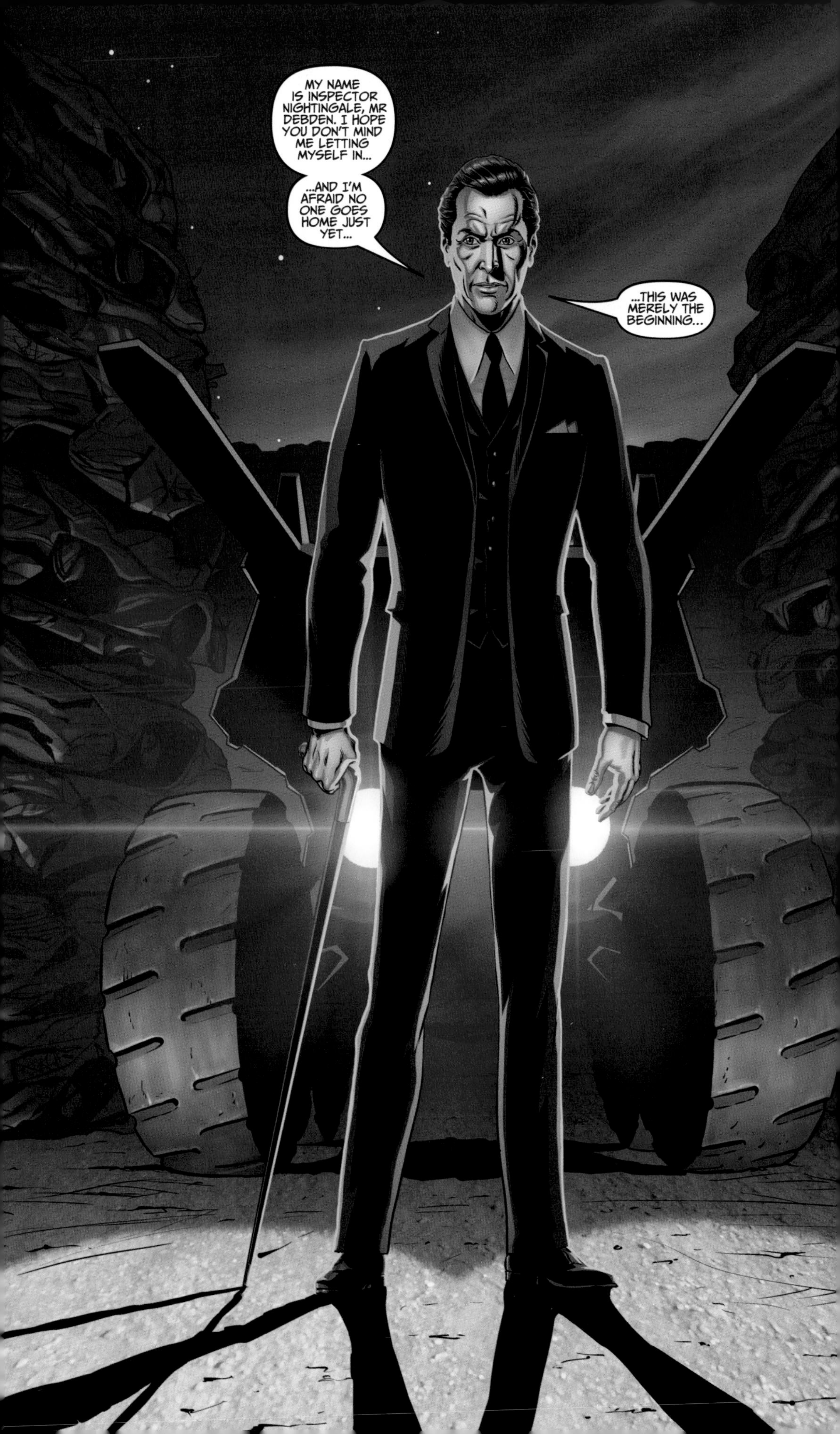
MY NAME IS INSPECTOR NIGHTINGALE, MR DEBDEN. I HOPE YOU DON'T MIND ME LETTING MYSELF IN...
...AND I'M AFRAID NO ONE GOES HOME JUST YET...
...THIS WAS MERELY THE BEGINNING...

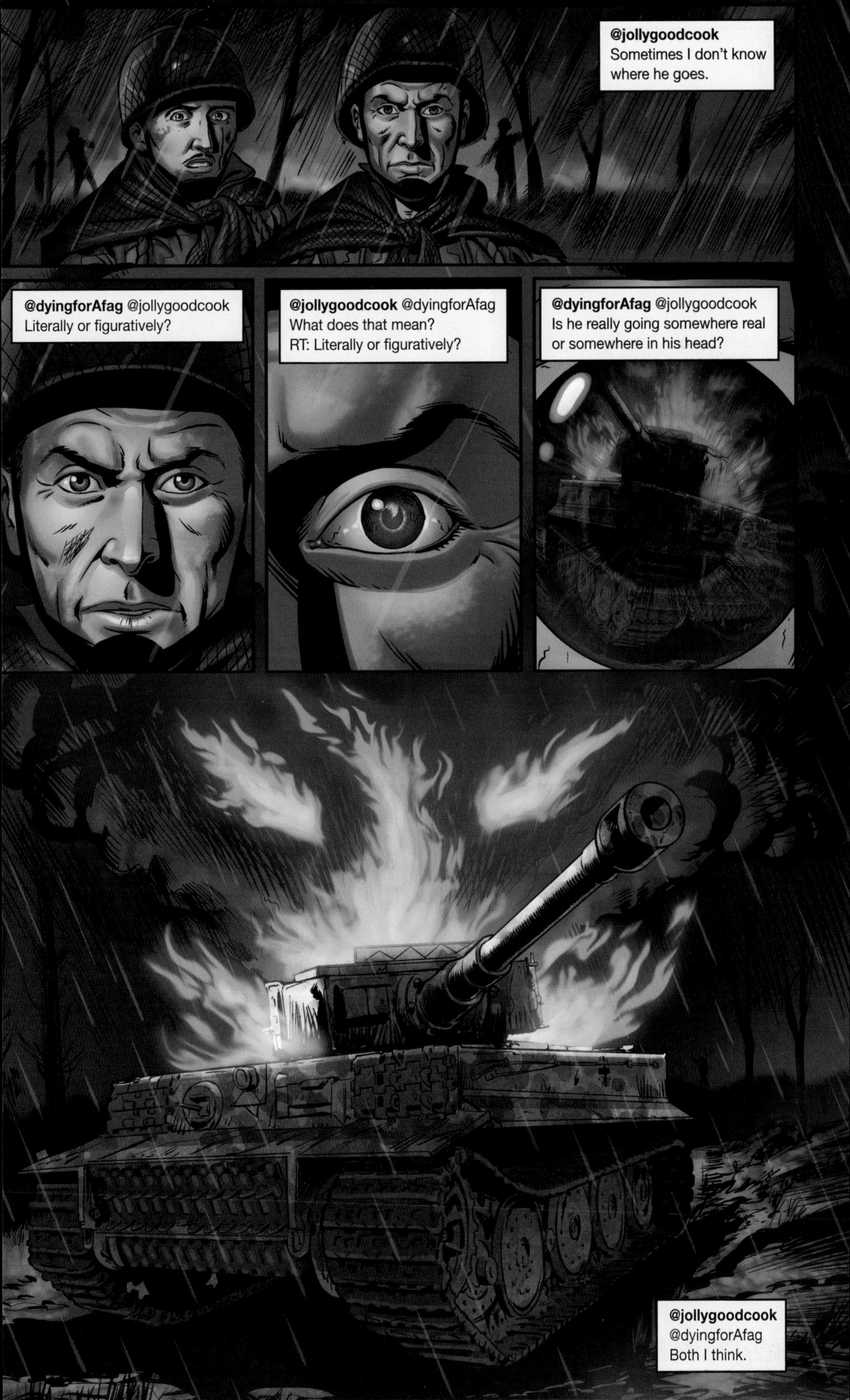
@jollygoodcook
Sometimes I don't know where he goes.
@dyingforAfag @jollygoodcook
Literally or figuratively?
@jollygoodcook @dyingforAfag
What does that mean?
RT: Literally or figuratively?
@dyingforAfag @jollygoodcook
Is he really going somewhere real or somewhere in his head?
@jollygoodcook
@dyingforAfag
Both I think.

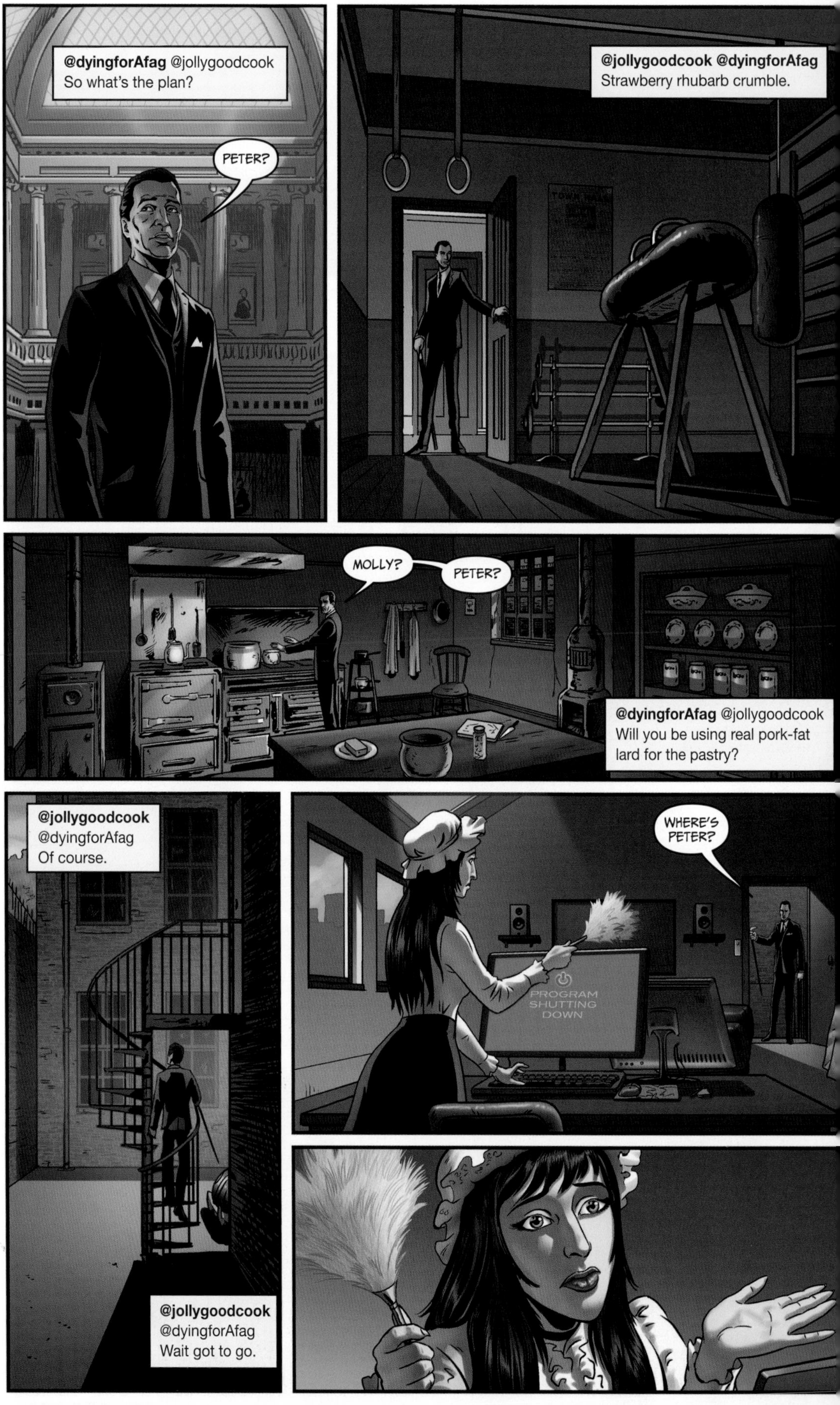
@dyingforAfag @jollygoodcook
So what's the plan?
PETER?
@jollygoodcook @dyingforAfag
Strawberry rhubarb crumble.
MOLLY?
PETER?
@dyingforAfag @jollygoodcook
Will you be using real pork-fat lard for the pastry?
@jollygoodcook
@dyingforAfag
Of course.
@jollygoodcook
@dyingforAfag
Wait got to go.
WHERE'S PETER?
PROGRAM SHUTTING DOWN

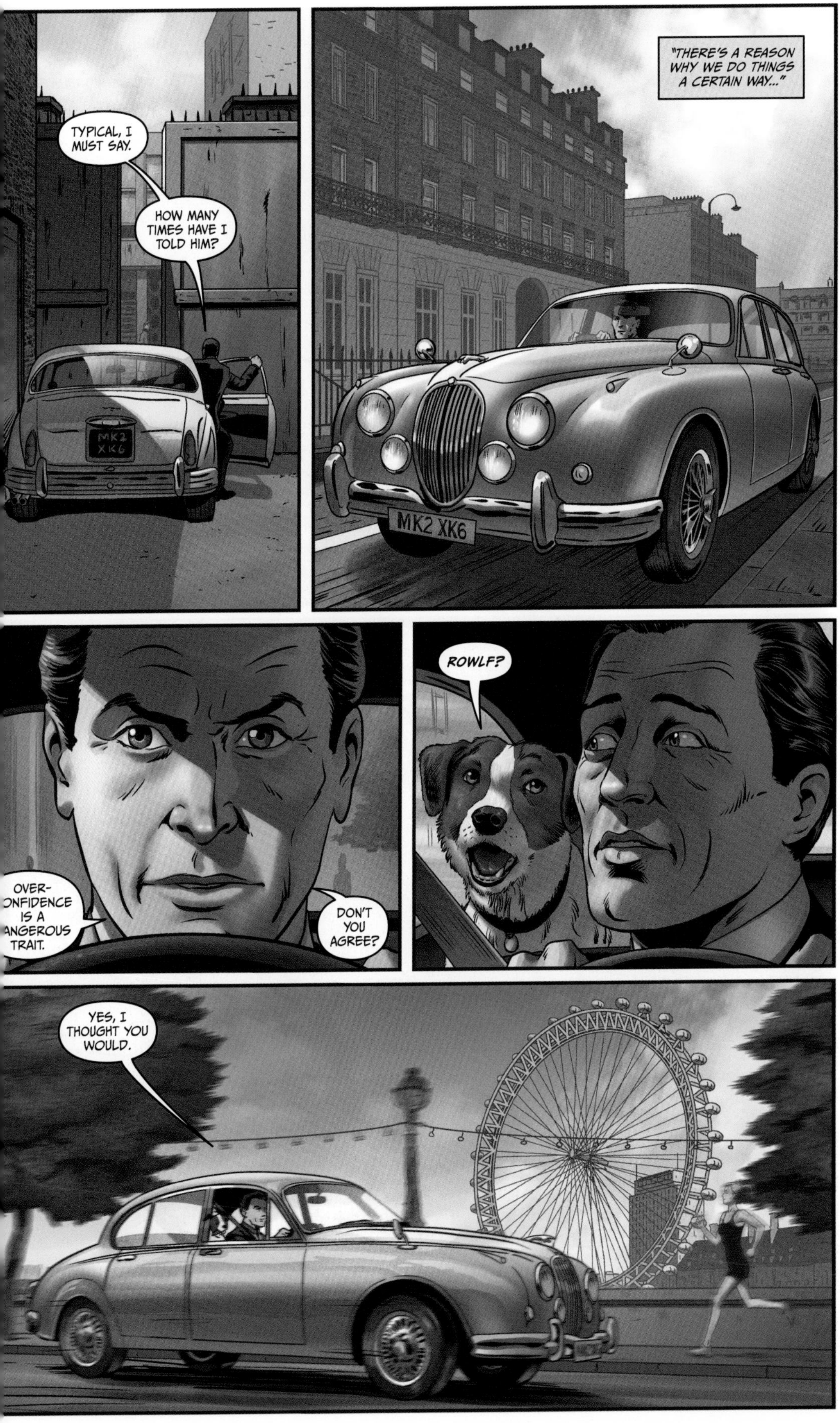

TYPICAL, I MUST SAY.
HOW MANY TIMES HAVE I TOLD HIM?
MK2 XK6
"THERE'S A REASON WHY WE DO THINGS A CERTAIN WAY..."
MK2 XK6
OVER-
ONFIDENCE IS A
ANGEROUS TRAIT.
DON'T YOU AGREE?
ROWLF?
YES, I THOUGHT YOU WOULD.

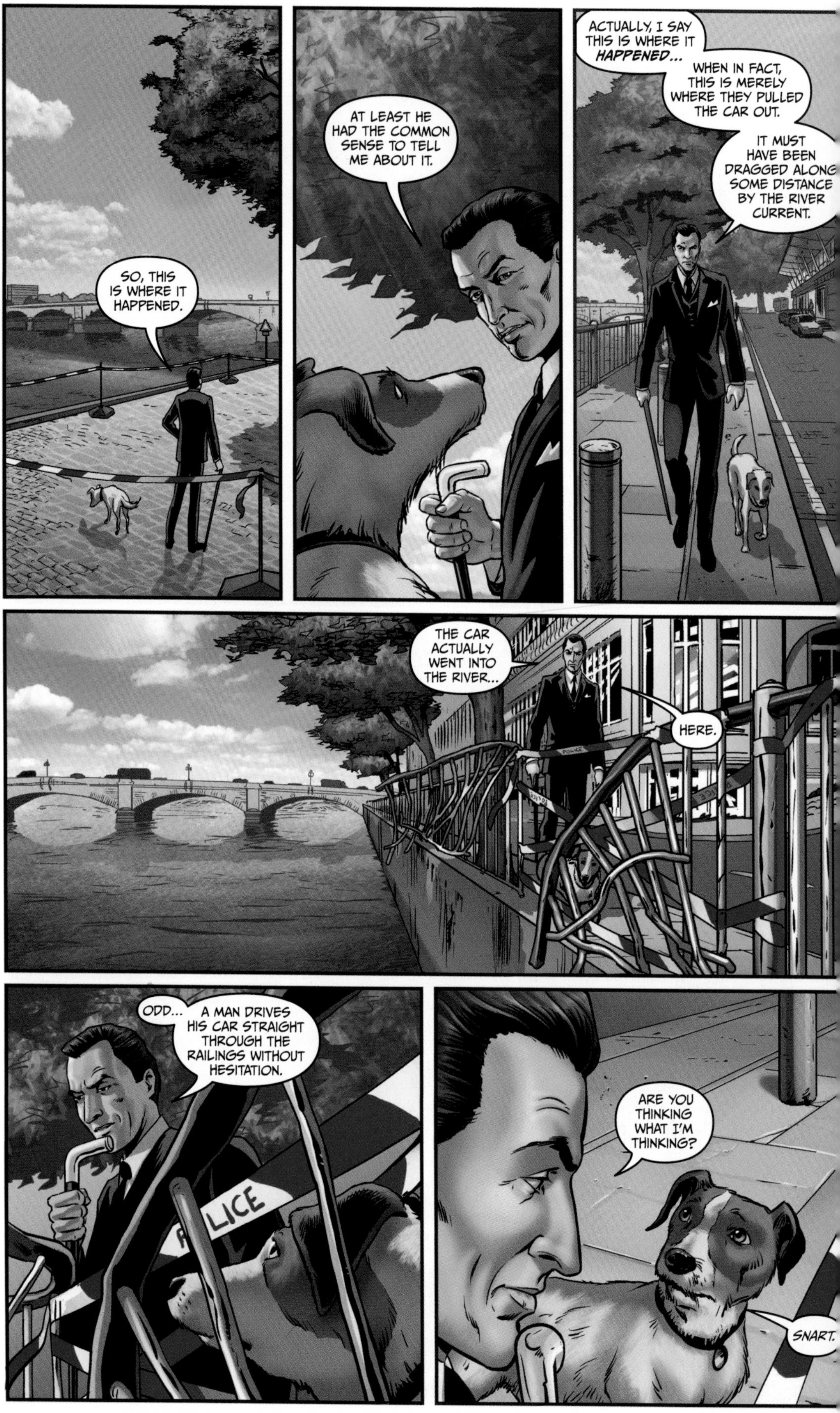
SO, THIS IS WHERE IT HAPPENED.
AT LEAST HE HAD THE COMMON SENSE TO TELL ME ABOUT IT.
ACTUALLY, I SAY THIS IS WHERE IT *HAPPENED...*
WHEN IN FACT, THIS IS MERELY WHERE THEY PULLED THE CAR OUT.
IT MUST HAVE BEEN DRAGGED ALONG SOME DISTANCE BY THE RIVER CURRENT.
THE CAR ACTUALLY WENT INTO THE RIVER...
HERE.
POLICE
ODD...
A MAN DRIVES HIS CAR STRAIGHT THROUGH THE RAILINGS WITHOUT HESITATION.
LICE
ARE YOU THINKING WHAT I'M THINKING?
SNART.

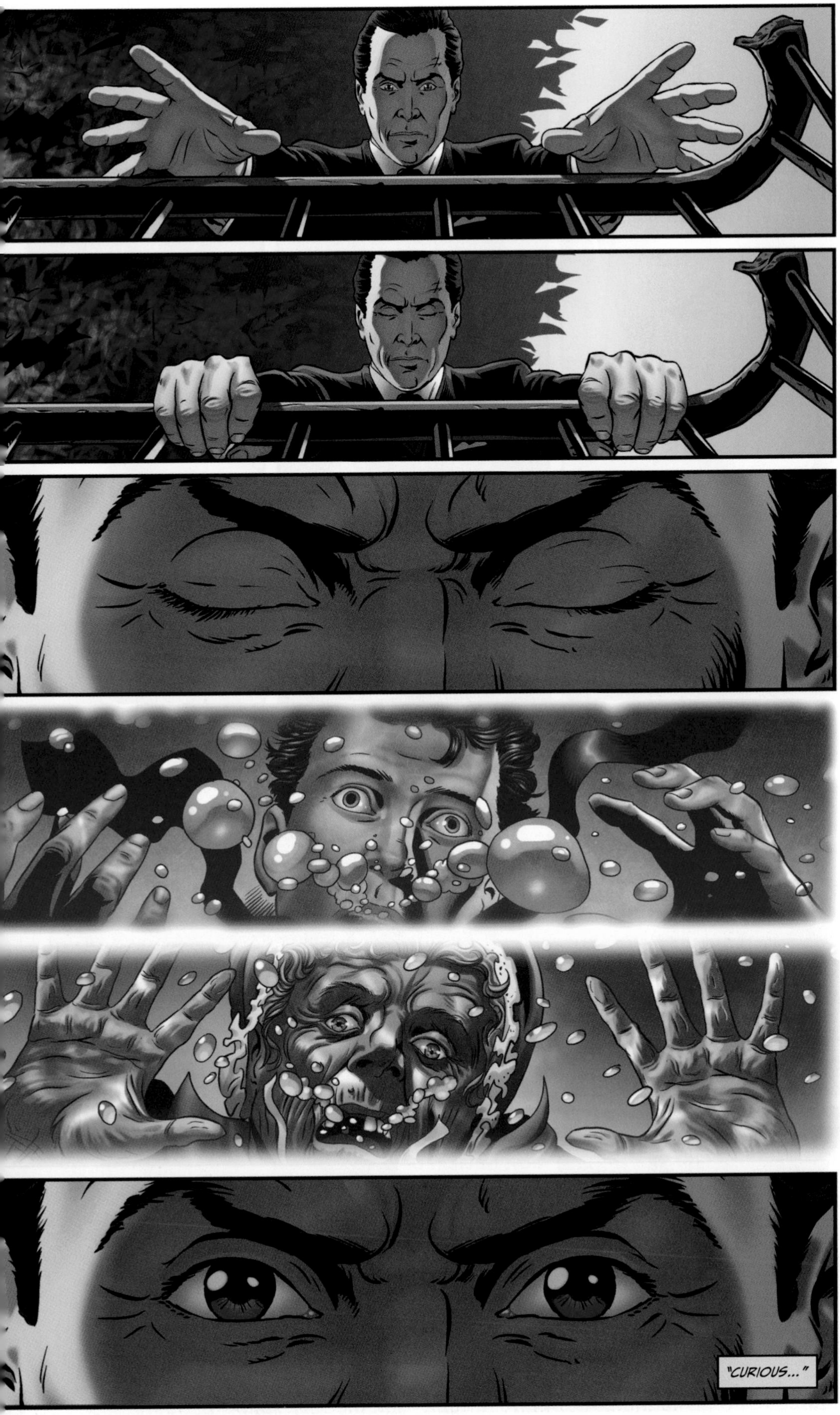
"CURIOUS..."

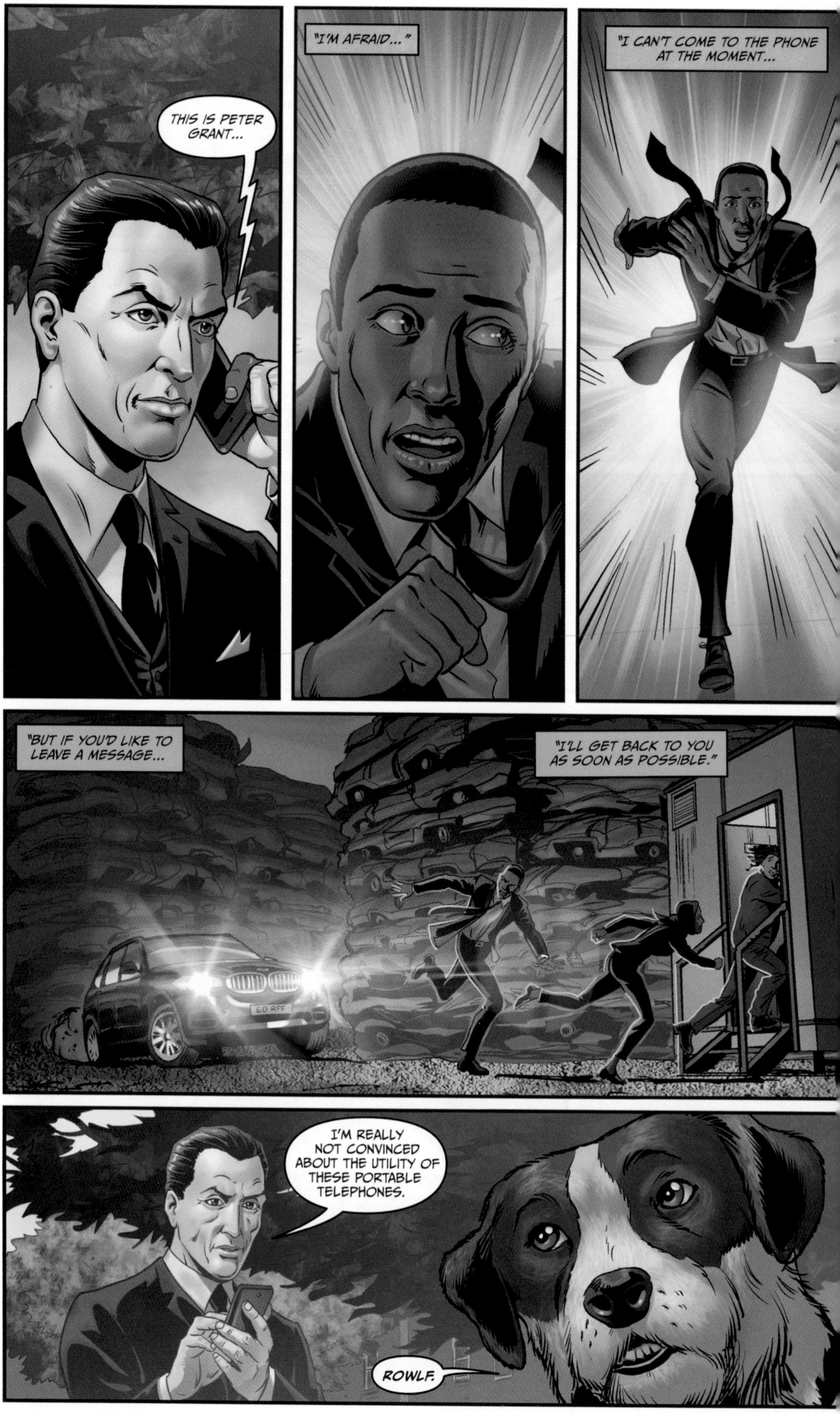
THIS IS PETER GRANT...
"I'M AFRAID..."
"I CAN'T COME TO THE PHONE AT THE MOMENT...
"BUT IF YOU'D LIKE TO LEAVE A MESSAGE...
"I'LL GET BACK TO YOU AS SOON AS POSSIBLE."
I'M REALLY NOT CONVINCED ABOUT THE UTILITY OF THESE PORTABLE TELEPHONES.
ROWLF.

"ON THE OTHER HAND...

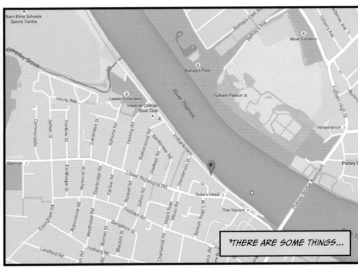

"THERE ARE SOME THINGS...

Beverley Brook

"FOR WHICH THEY ARE VERY USEFUL."

THAT'S ALL I CAN TELL YOU...

THEN I'LL HAVE TO RESORT TO OTHER MEANS TO FIND PETER.

I HAVE A SUSPICION HE MIGHT BE IN TROUBLE.

DON'T YOU THINK HE CAN TAKE CARE OF HIMSELF?

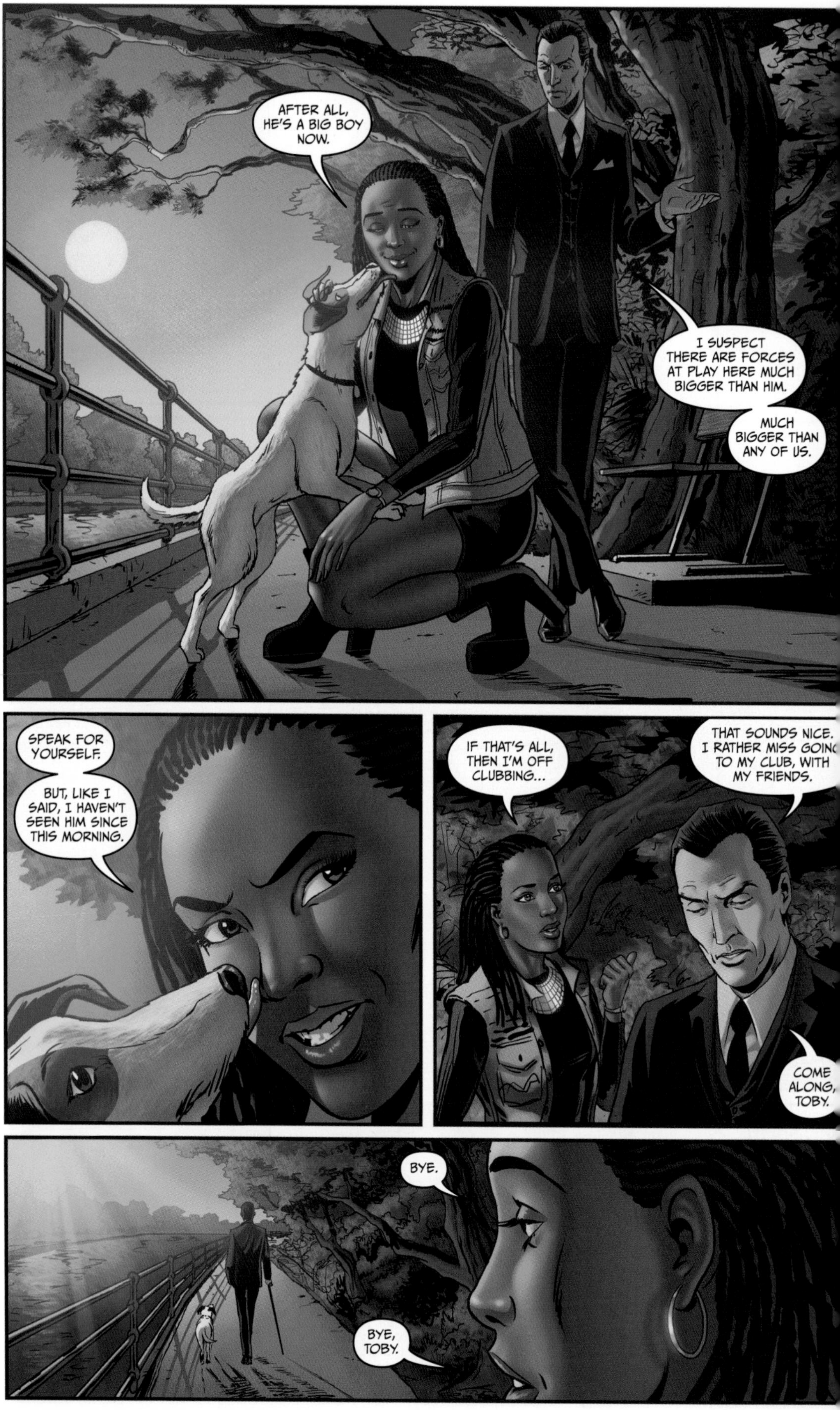
AFTER ALL, HE'S A BIG BOY NOW.
I SUSPECT THERE ARE FORCES AT PLAY HERE MUCH BIGGER THAN HIM.
MUCH BIGGER THAN ANY OF US.
SPEAK FOR YOURSELF.
BUT, LIKE I SAID, I HAVEN'T SEEN HIM SINCE THIS MORNING.
IF THAT'S ALL, THEN I'M OFF CLUBBING...
THAT SOUNDS NICE. I RATHER MISS GOING TO MY CLUB, WITH MY FRIENDS.
COME ALONG, TOBY.
BYE.
BYE, TOBY.

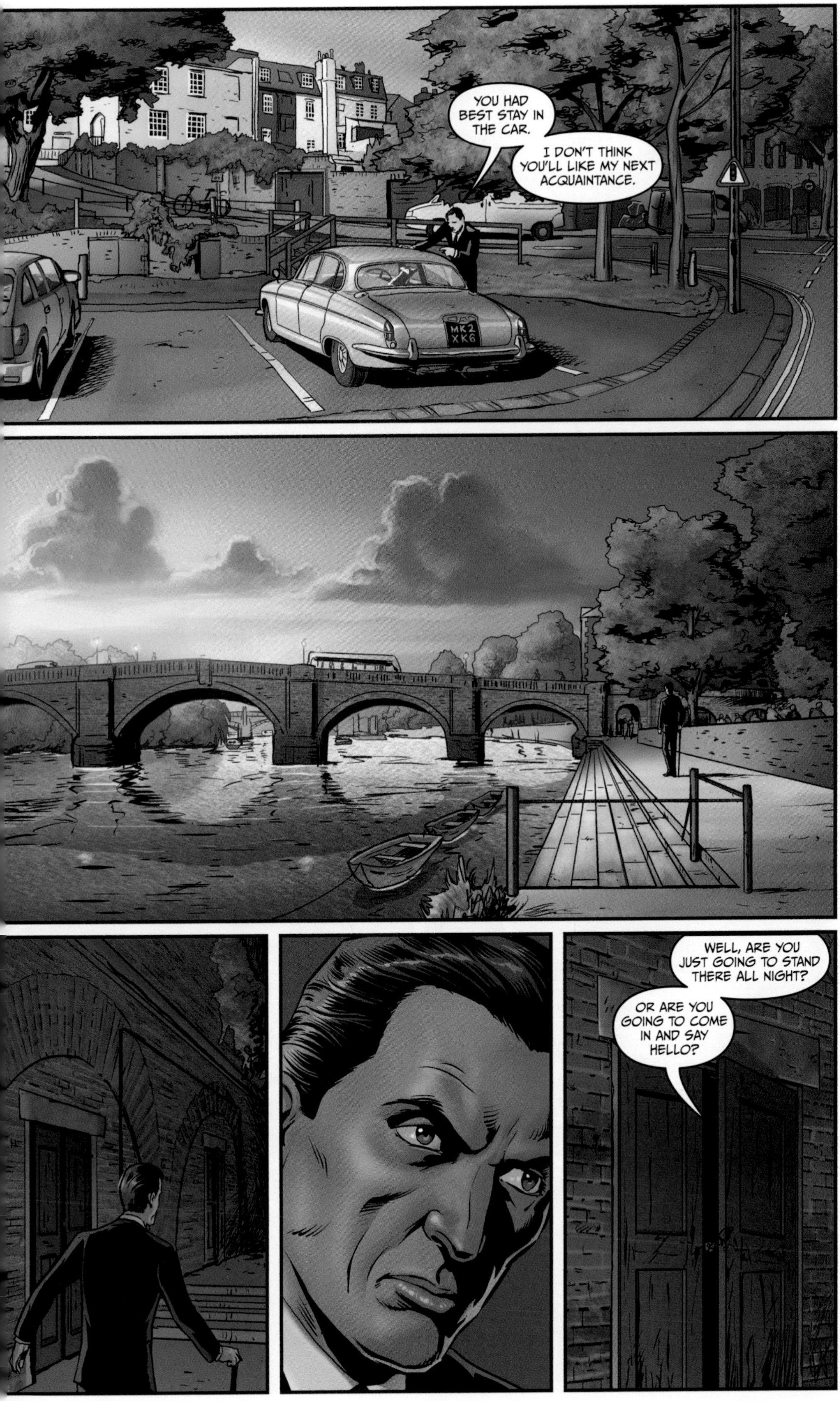

YOU HAD BEST STAY IN THE CAR.
I DON'T THINK YOU'LL LIKE MY NEXT ACQUAINTANCE.
MK2 XK6
WELL, ARE YOU JUST GOING TO STAND THERE ALL NIGHT?
OR ARE YOU GOING TO COME IN AND SAY HELLO?

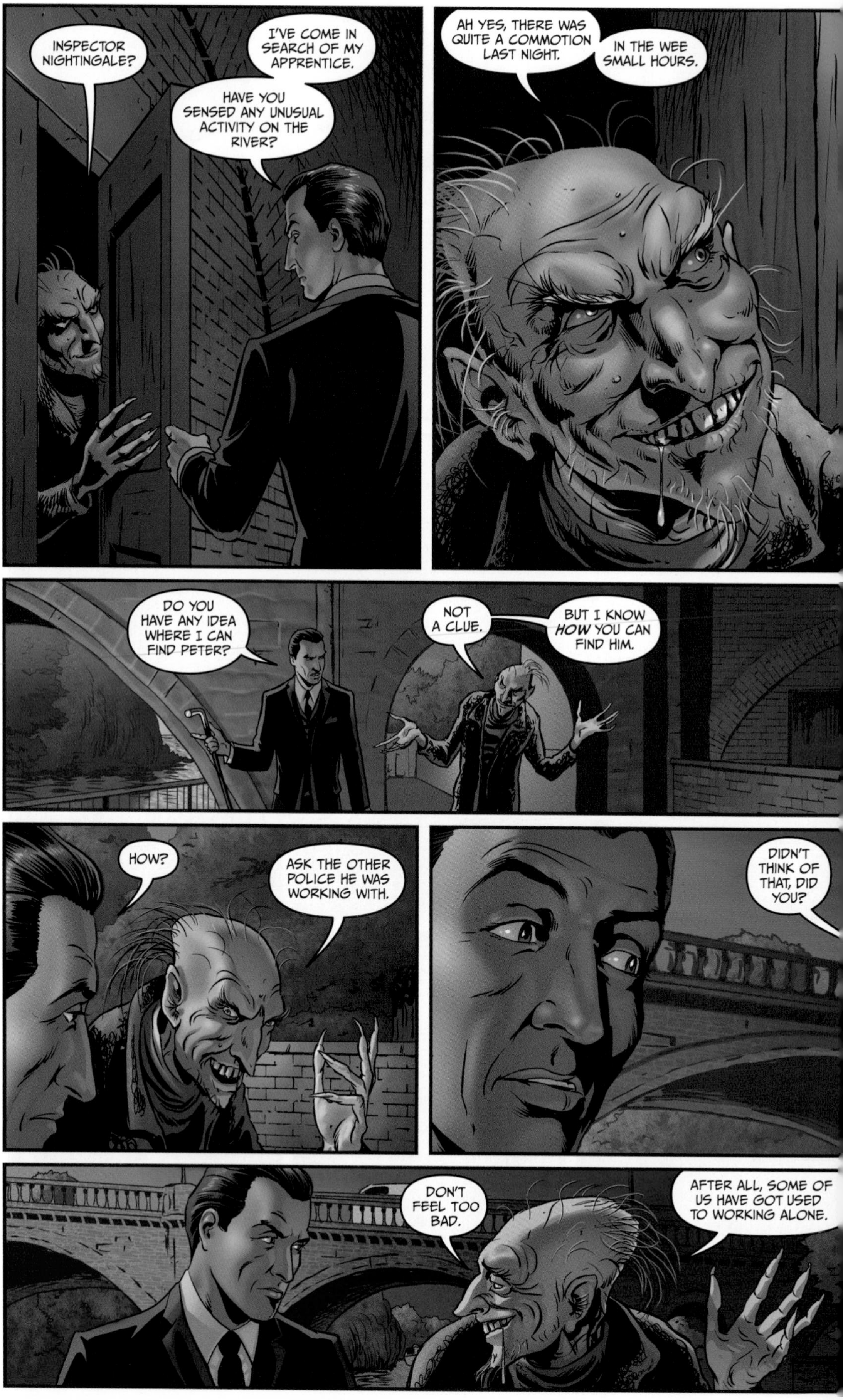
INSPECTOR NIGHTINGALE?
I'VE COME IN SEARCH OF MY APPRENTICE.
HAVE YOU SENSED ANY UNUSUAL ACTIVITY ON THE RIVER?
AH YES, THERE WAS QUITE A COMMOTION LAST NIGHT.
IN THE WEE SMALL HOURS.
DO YOU HAVE ANY IDEA WHERE I CAN FIND PETER?
NOT A CLUE.
BUT I KNOW HOW YOU CAN FIND HIM.
HOW?
ASK THE OTHER POLICE HE WAS WORKING WITH.
DIDN'T THINK OF THAT, DID YOU?
DON'T FEEL TOO BAD.
AFTER ALL, SOME OF US HAVE GOT USED TO WORKING ALONE.

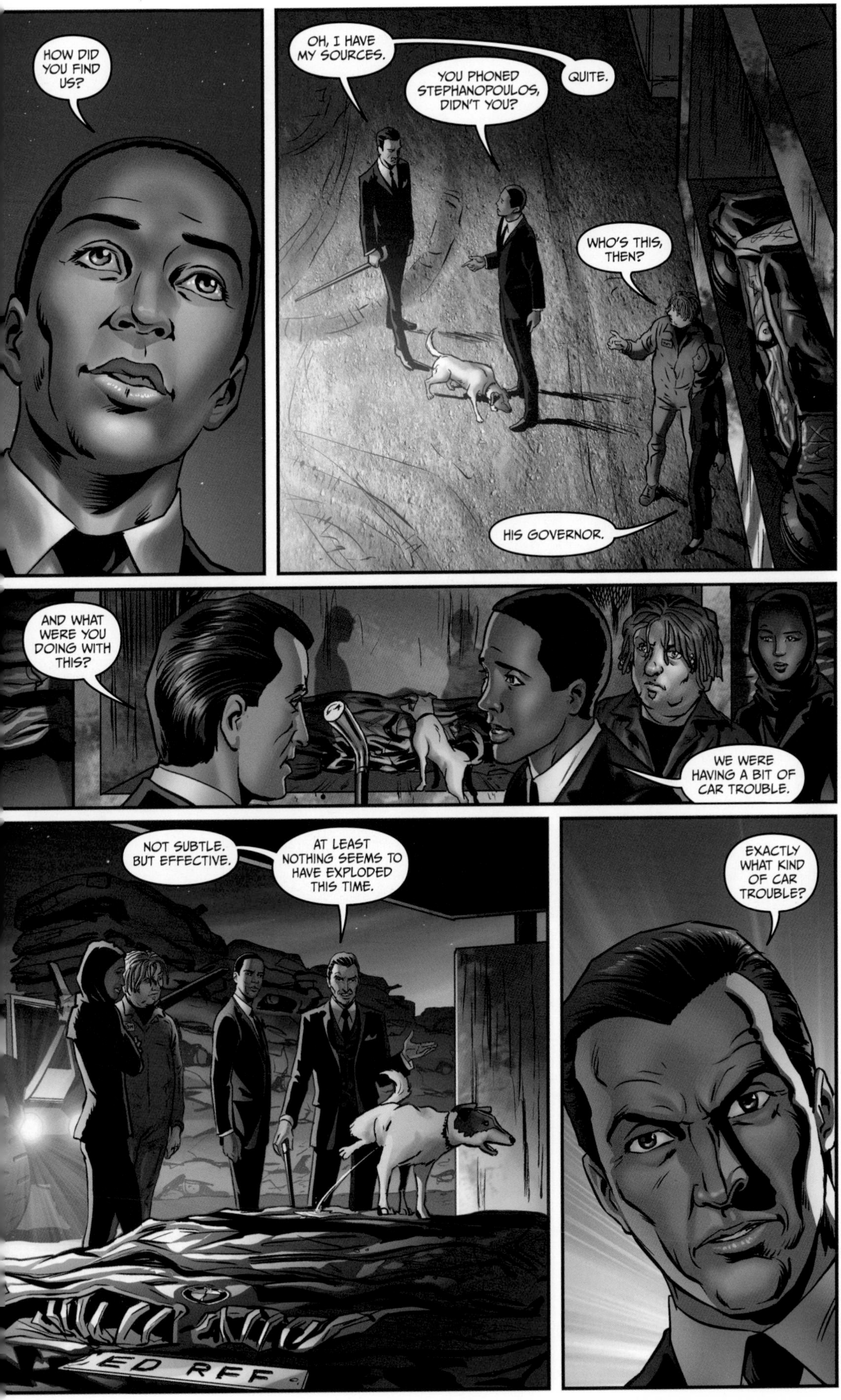
HOW DID YOU FIND US?
OH, I HAVE MY SOURCES.
YOU PHONED STEPHANOPOULOS, DIDN'T YOU?
QUITE.
WHO'S THIS, THEN?
HIS GOVERNOR.
AND WHAT WERE YOU DOING WITH THIS?
WE WERE HAVING A BIT OF CAR TROUBLE.
NOT SUBTLE. BUT EFFECTIVE.
AT LEAST NOTHING SEEMS TO HAVE EXPLODED THIS TIME.
ED RFF
EXACTLY WHAT KIND OF CAR TROUBLE?

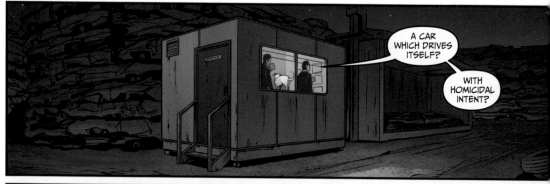

A CAR WHICH DRIVES ITSELF?

WITH HOMICIDAL INTENT?

WHAT COULD CAUSE SOMETHING LIKE THAT?

THAT'S WHAT I WAS HOPING YOU COULD TELL US.

SOMEONE IS GOING TO HAVE TO BRIEF STEPHANOPOULOS.

GOOD OF YOU TO VOLUNTEER.

YOU WALKED INTO THAT ONE.

STORY OF MY LIFE.

MR. DEBDEN, CAN YOU REPAIR CARS LIKE THESE?

I'D GIVE MY LEFT OCTAGONAL CHROMED 42 MILLIMETRE NUT FOR THE CHANCE.

YOU MAY HAVE JUST SUCH AN OPPORTUNITY.

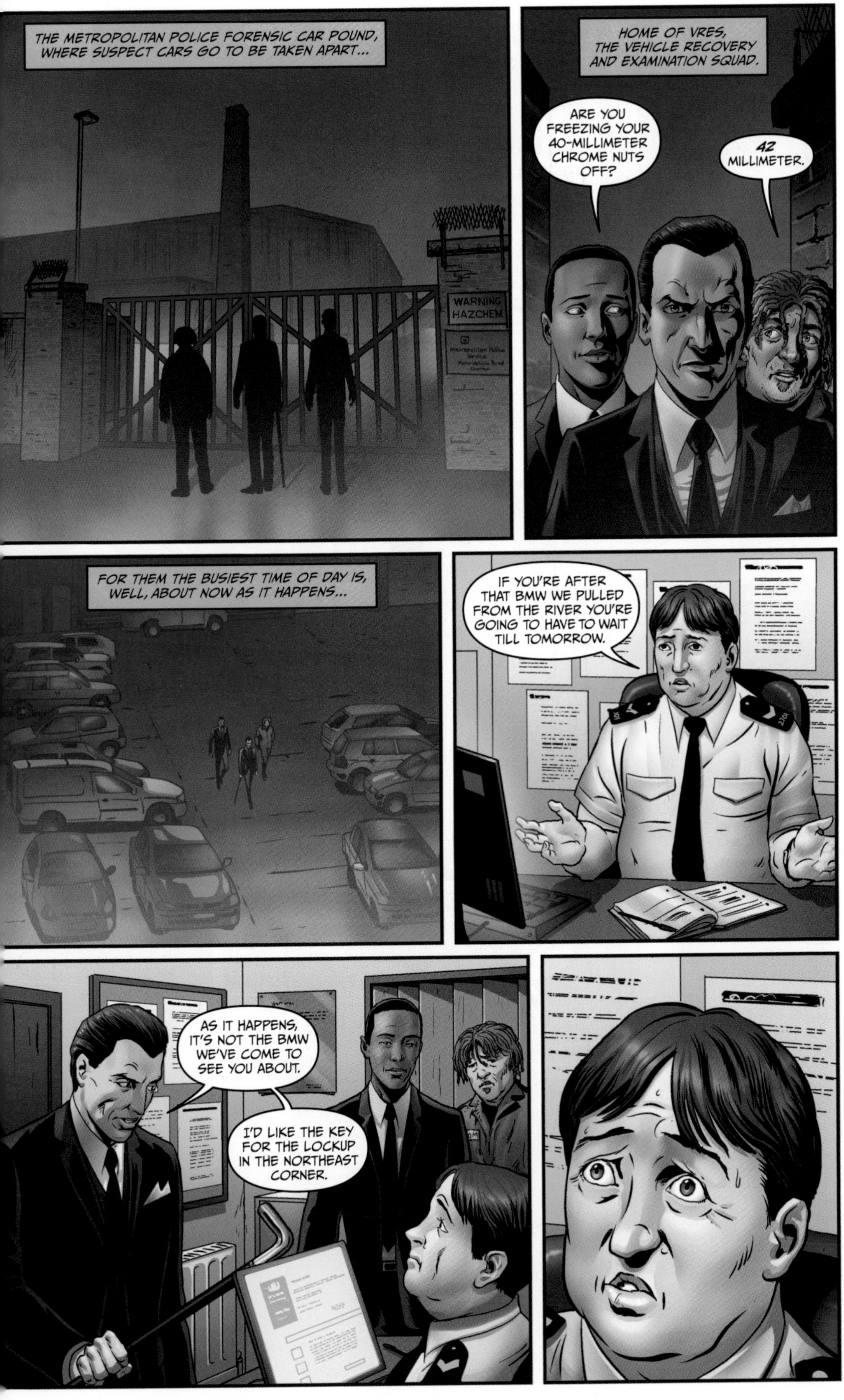
THE METROPOLITAN POLICE FORENSIC CAR POUND, WHERE SUSPECT CARS GO TO BE TAKEN APART...
WARNING HAZCHEM
HOME OF VRES, THE VEHICLE RECOVERY AND EXAMINATION SQUAD.
ARE YOU FREEZING YOUR 40-MILLIMETER CHROME NUTS OFF?
42 MILLIMETER.
FOR THEM THE BUSIEST TIME OF DAY IS, WELL, ABOUT NOW AS IT HAPPENS...
IF YOU'RE AFTER THAT BMW WE PULLED FROM THE RIVER YOU'RE GOING TO HAVE TO WAIT TILL TOMORROW.
AS IT HAPPENS, IT'S NOT THE BMW WE'VE COME TO SEE YOU ABOUT.
I'D LIKE THE KEY FOR THE LOCKUP IN THE NORTHEAST CORNER.

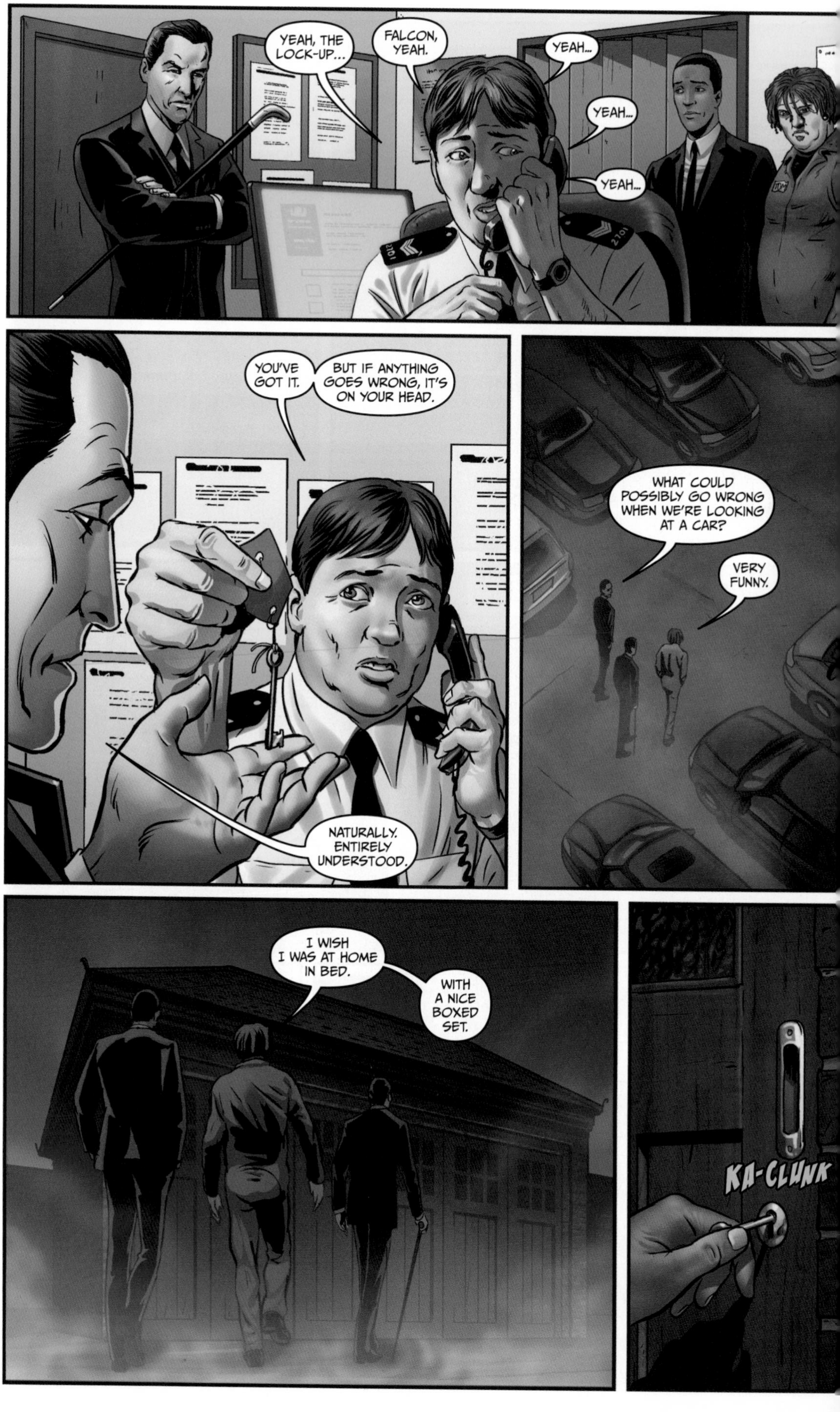
YEAH, THE LOCK-UP...
FALCON, YEAH.
YEAH...
YEAH...
YEAH...
YOU'VE GOT IT.
BUT IF ANYTHING GOES WRONG, IT'S ON YOUR HEAD.
NATURALLY. ENTIRELY UNDERSTOOD.
WHAT COULD POSSIBLY GO WRONG WHEN WE'RE LOOKING AT A CAR?
VERY FUNNY.
I WISH I WAS AT HOME IN BED.
WITH A NICE BOXED SET.
KA-CLUNK

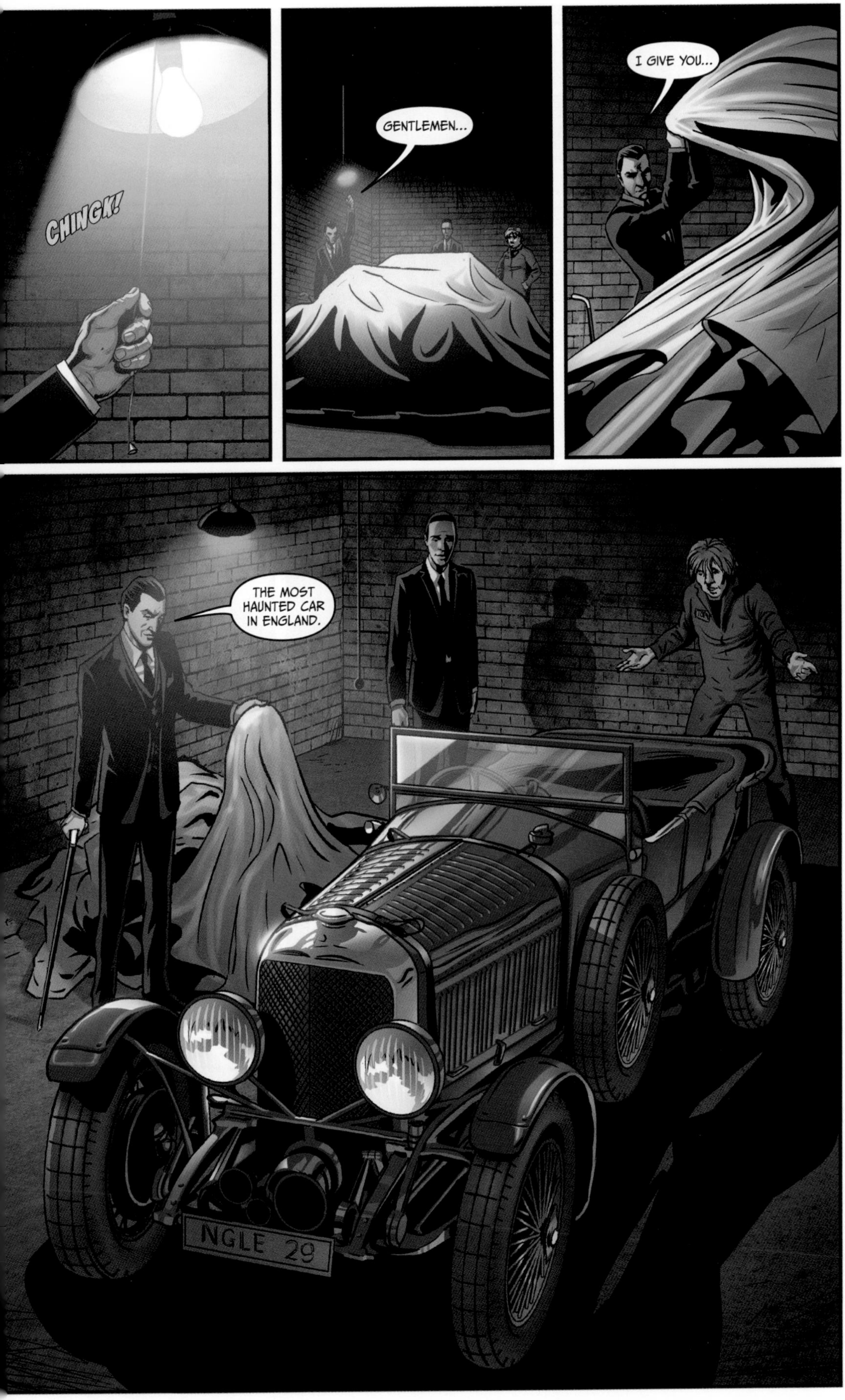
CHINGK!
GENTLEMEN...
I GIVE YOU...
THE MOST HAUNTED CAR IN ENGLAND.
NGLE 29

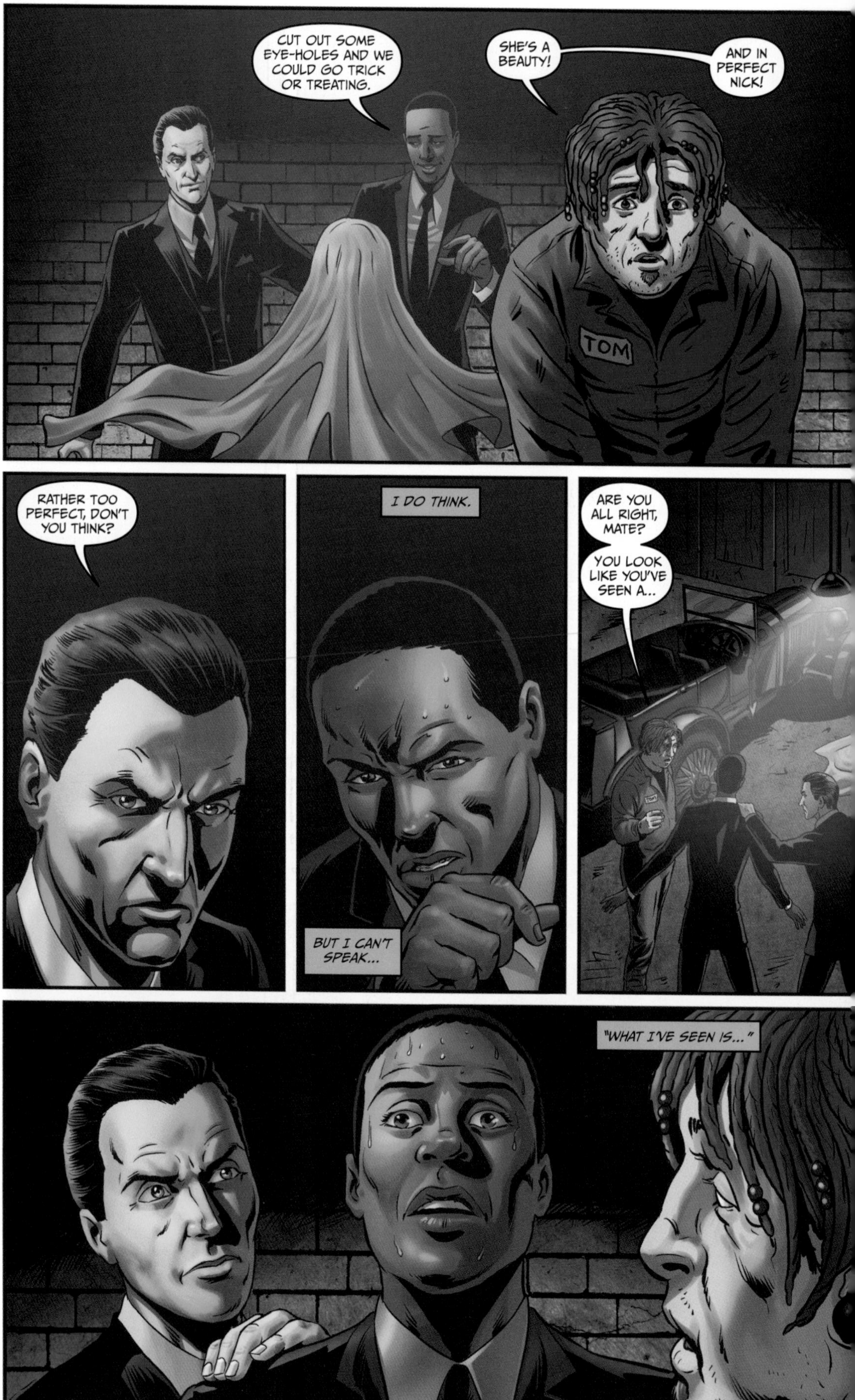
CUT OUT SOME EYE-HOLES AND WE COULD GO TRICK OR TREATING.
SHE'S A BEAUTY!
AND IN PERFECT NICK!
TOM
RATHER TOO PERFECT, DON'T YOU THINK?
I DO THINK.
BUT I CAN'T SPEAK...
ARE YOU ALL RIGHT, MATE?
YOU LOOK LIKE YOU'VE SEEN A...
"WHAT I'VE SEEN IS..."

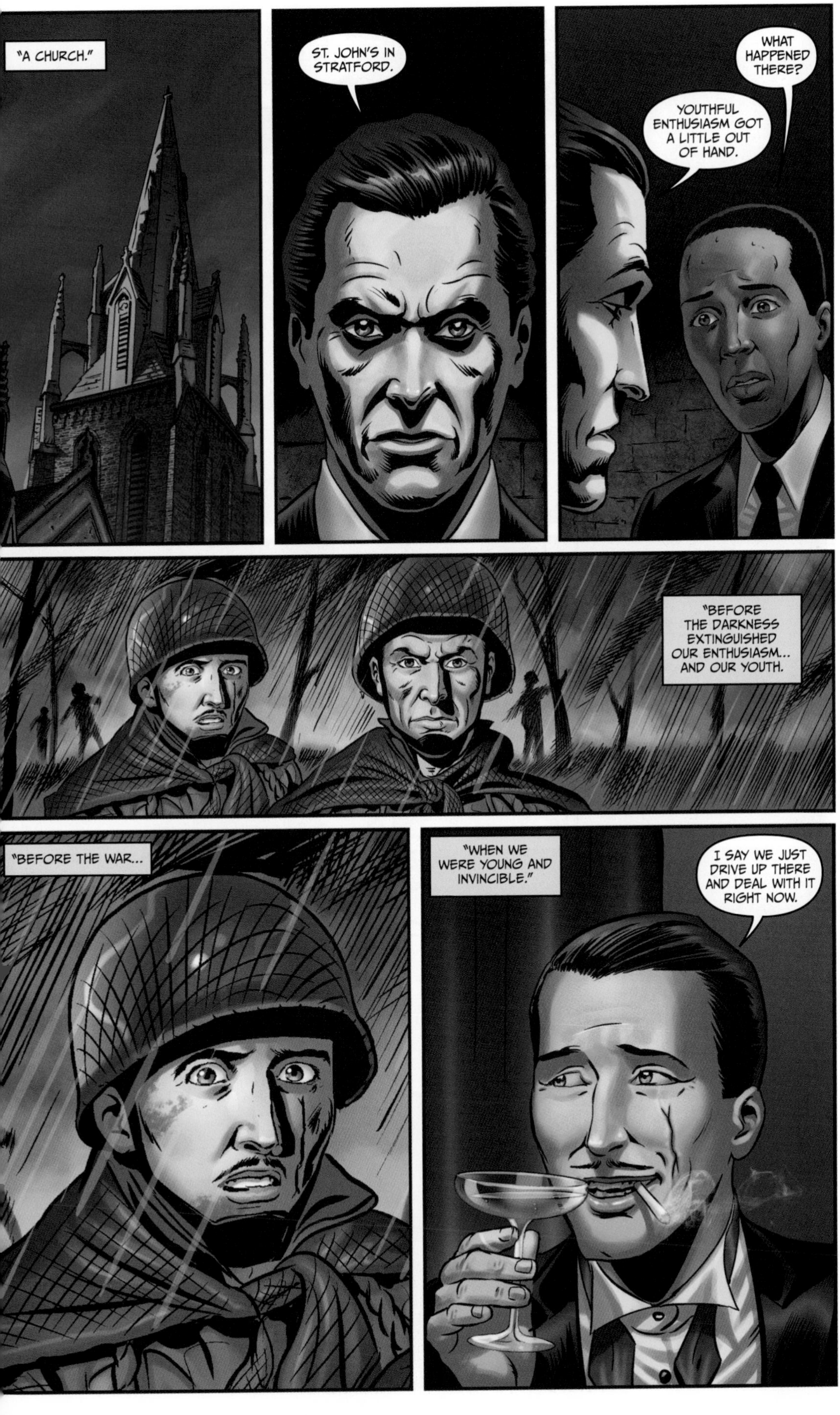
"A CHURCH."
ST. JOHN'S IN STRATFORD.
WHAT HAPPENED THERE?
YOUTHFUL ENTHUSIASM GOT A LITTLE OUT OF HAND.
"BEFORE THE DARKNESS EXTINGUISHED OUR ENTHUSIASM... AND OUR YOUTH.
"BEFORE THE WAR...
"WHEN WE WERE YOUNG AND INVINCIBLE."
I SAY WE JUST DRIVE UP THERE AND DEAL WITH IT RIGHT NOW.

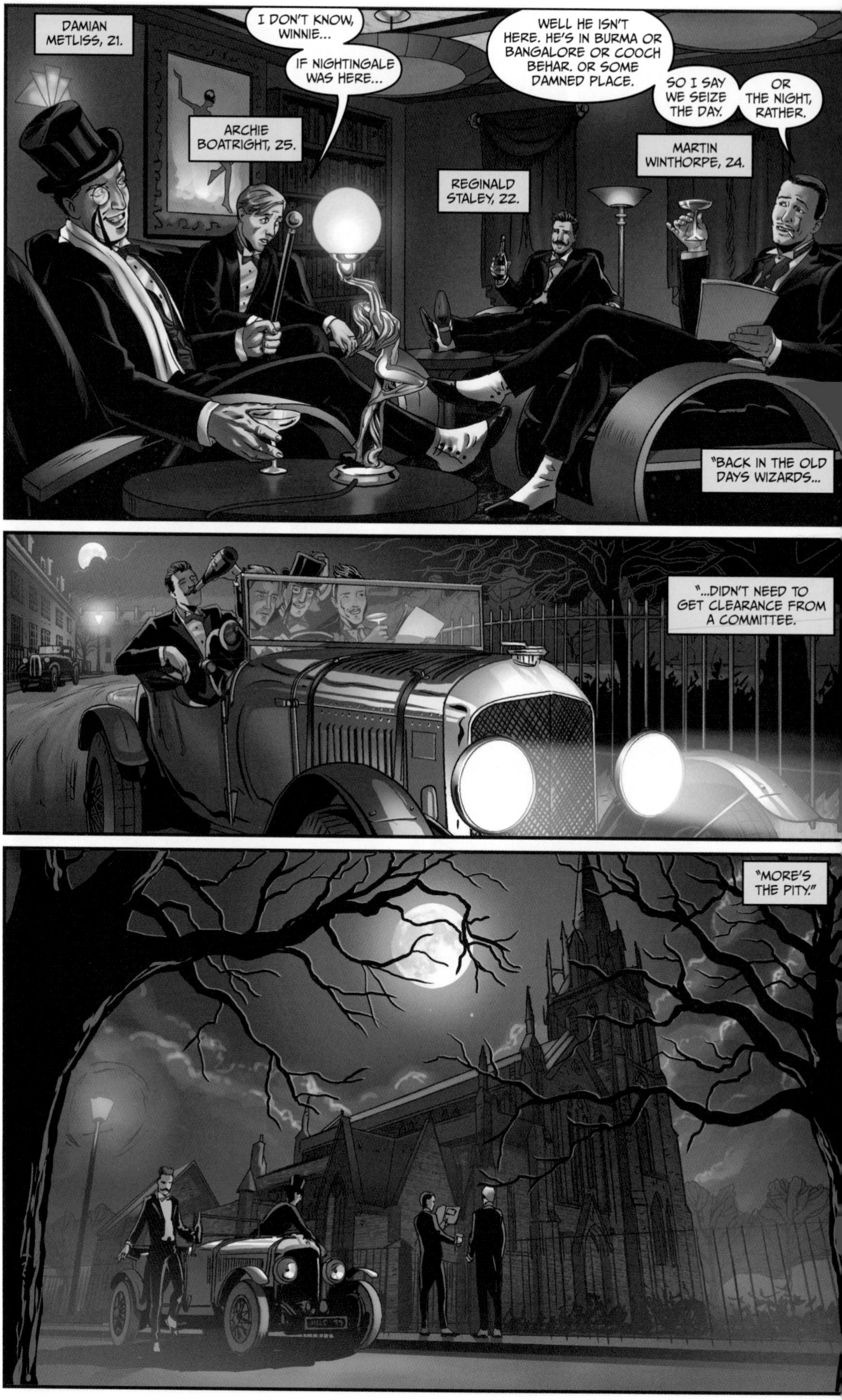
DAMIAN METLISS, 21.
I DON'T KNOW, WINNIE...
IF NIGHTINGALE WAS HERE...
ARCHIE BOATRIGHT, 25.
WELL HE ISN'T HERE. HE'S IN BURMA OR BANGALORE OR COOCH BEHAR. OR SOME DAMNED PLACE.
REGINALD STALEY, 22.
SO I SAY WE SEIZE THE DAY.
OR THE NIGHT, RATHER.
MARTIN WINTHORPE, 24.
"BACK IN THE OLD DAYS WIZARDS...
"...DIDN'T NEED TO GET CLEARANCE FROM A COMMITTEE.
"MORE'S THE PITY."

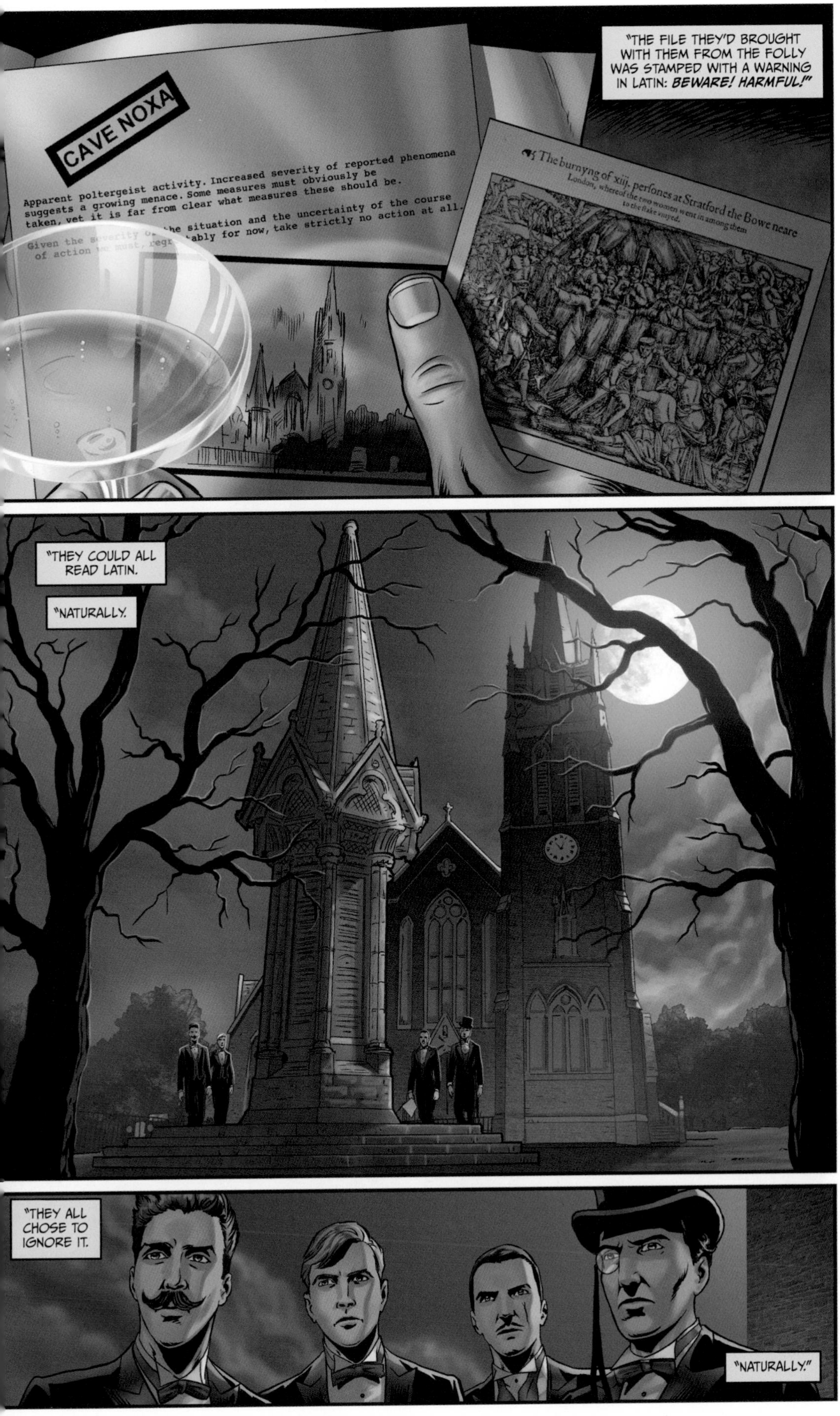
"THE FILE THEY'D BROUGHT WITH THEM FROM THE FOLLY WAS STAMPED WITH A WARNING IN LATIN: *BEWARE! HARMFUL!*"
CAVE NOXA
Apparent poltergeist activity. Increased severity of reported phenomena suggests a growing menace. Some measures must obviously be taken, yet it is far from clear what measures these should be.
the situation and the uncertainty of the course
ably for now, take strictly no action at all.
The burnyng of xiij. persones at Stratford the Bowe neare London, whereof the two women went in among them to the stake vnyed.
"THEY COULD ALL READ LATIN.
"NATURALLY.
"THEY ALL CHOSE TO IGNORE IT.
"NATURALLY."

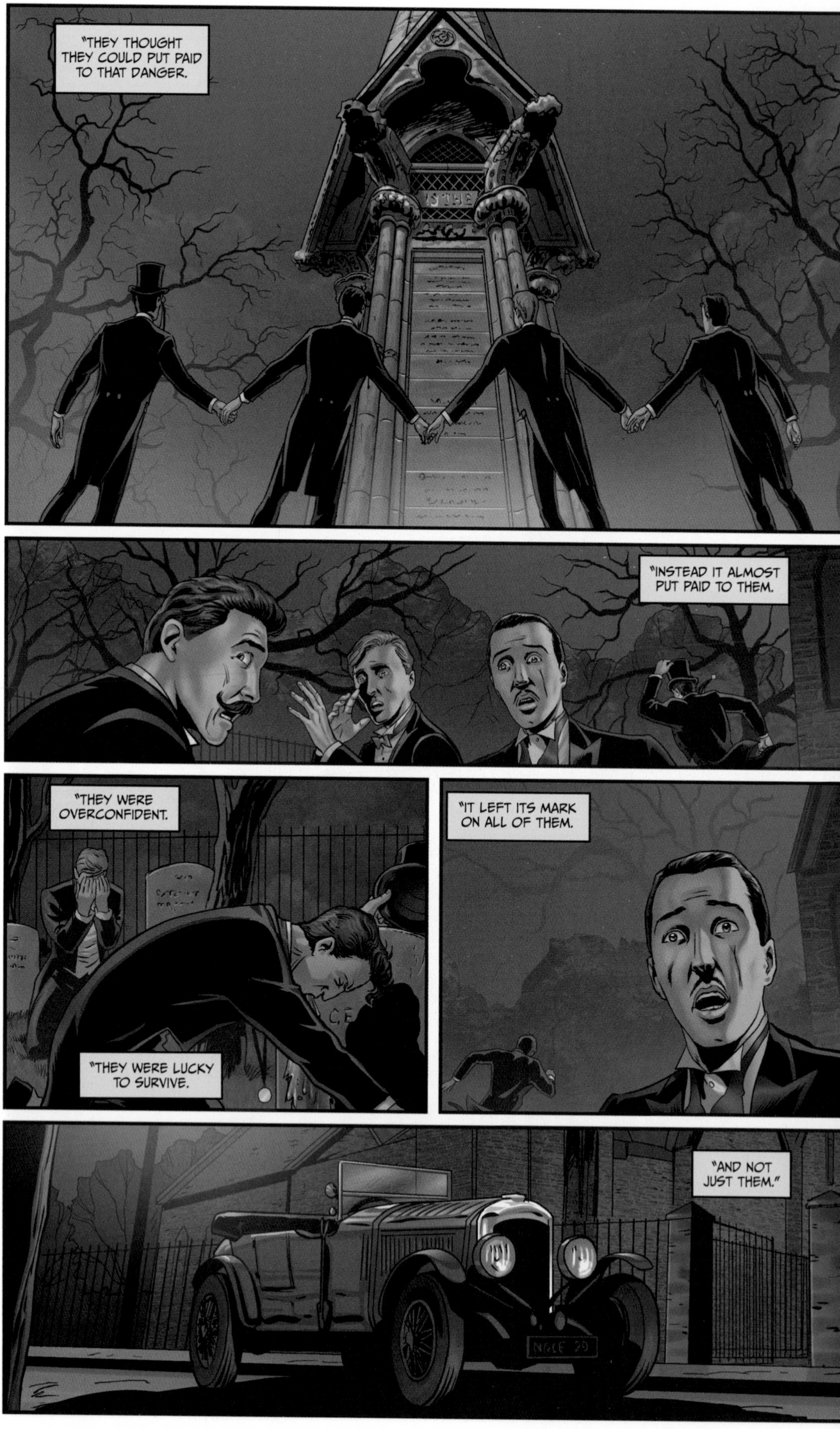
"THEY THOUGHT THEY COULD PUT PAID TO THAT DANGER.
"INSTEAD IT ALMOST PUT PAID TO THEM.
"THEY WERE OVERCONFIDENT.
"THEY WERE LUCKY TO SURVIVE.
"IT LEFT ITS MARK ON ALL OF THEM.
"AND NOT JUST THEM."
NGCE 29

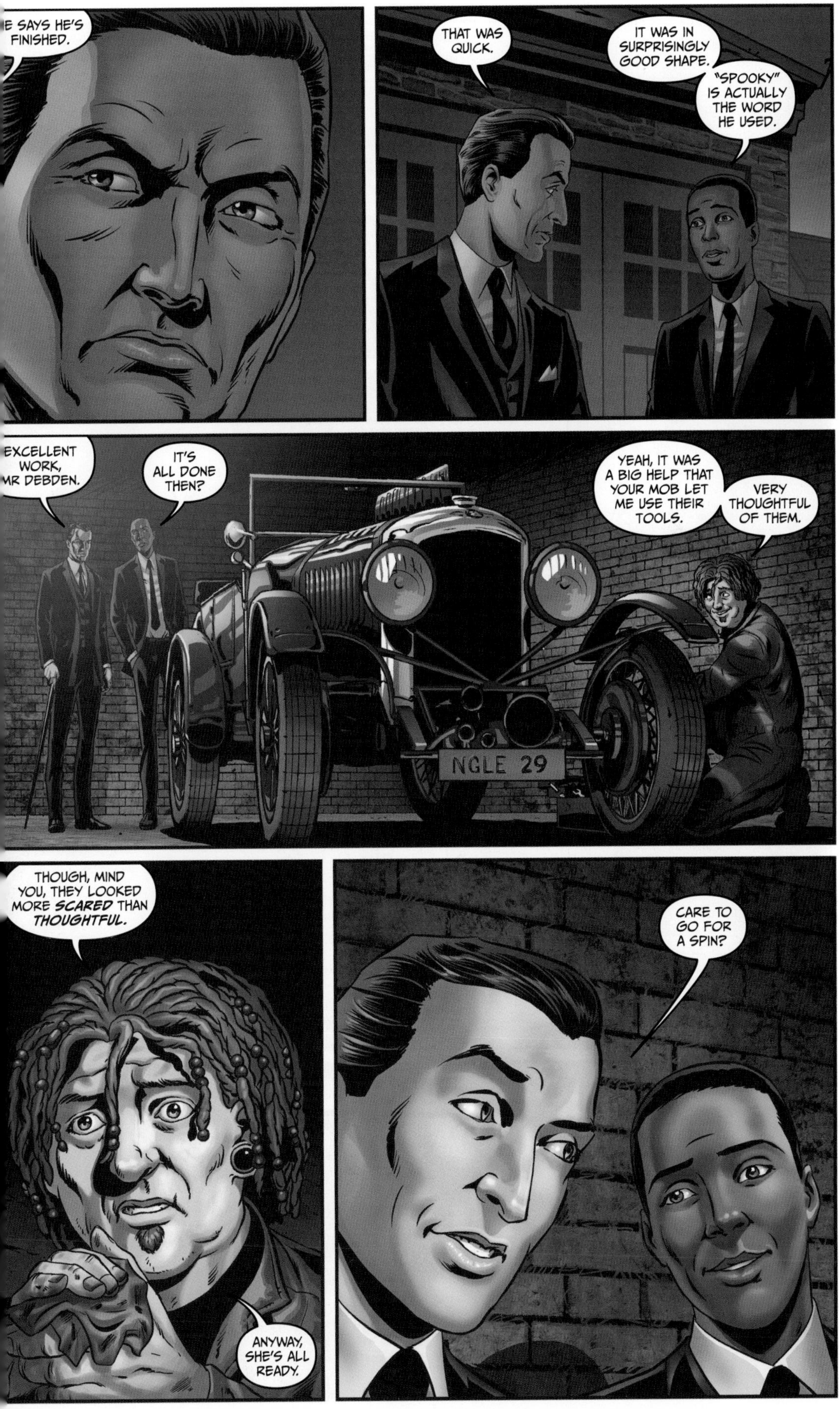
E SAYS HE'S FINISHED.
THAT WAS QUICK.
IT WAS IN SURPRISINGLY GOOD SHAPE.
"SPOOKY" IS ACTUALLY THE WORD HE USED.
EXCELLENT WORK, MR DEBDEN.
IT'S ALL DONE THEN?
NGLE 29
YEAH, IT WAS A BIG HELP THAT YOUR MOB LET ME USE THEIR TOOLS.
VERY THOUGHTFUL OF THEM.
THOUGH, MIND YOU, THEY LOOKED MORE *SCARED* THAN *THOUGHTFUL*.
ANYWAY, SHE'S ALL READY.
CARE TO GO FOR A SPIN?

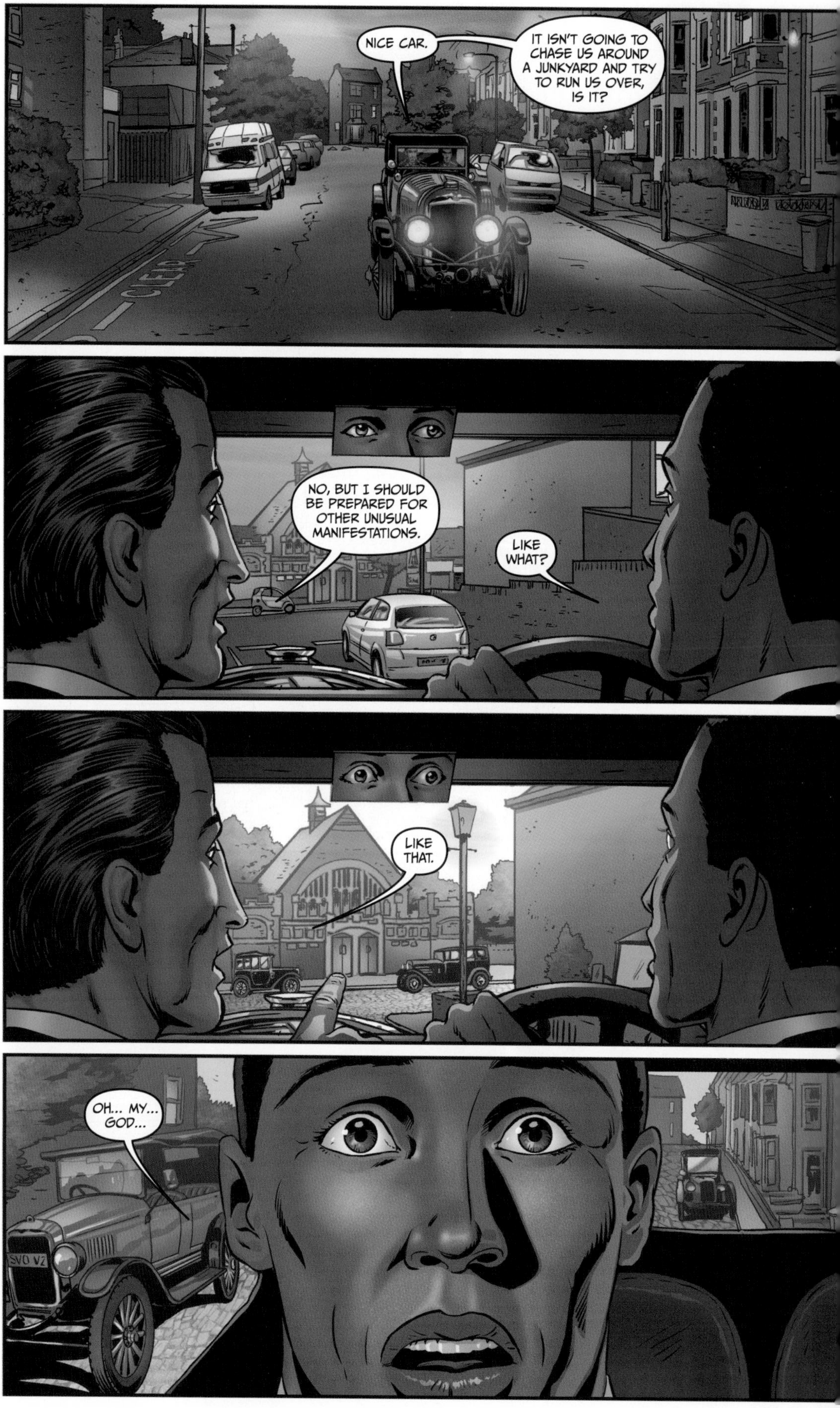
NICE CAR.
IT ISN'T GOING TO CHASE US AROUND A JUNKYARD AND TRY TO RUN US OVER, IS IT?
NO, BUT I SHOULD BE PREPARED FOR OTHER UNUSUAL MANIFESTATIONS.
LIKE WHAT?
LIKE THAT.
OH... MY... GOD...

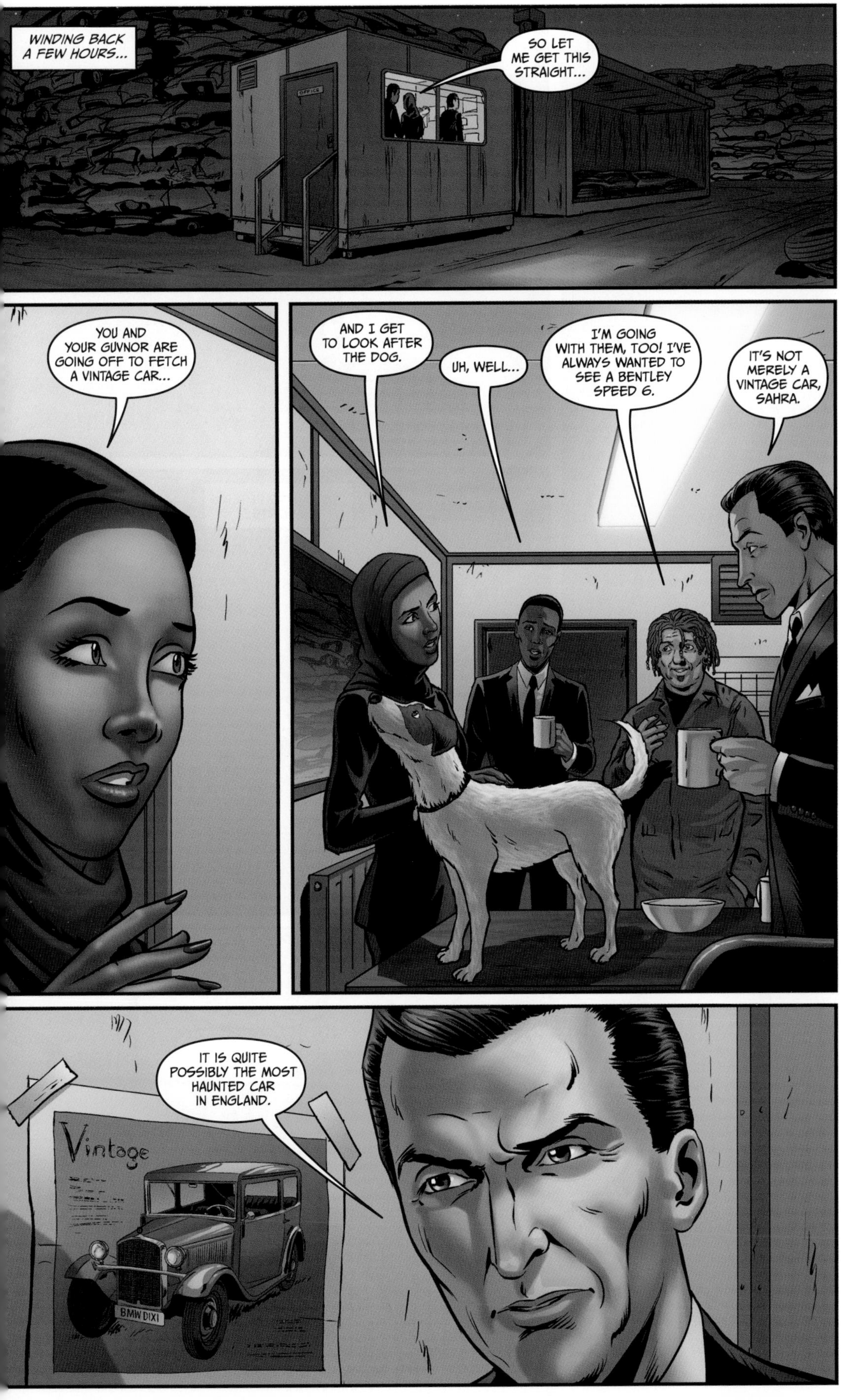
WINDING BACK A FEW HOURS...
OFFICE
SO LET ME GET THIS STRAIGHT...
YOU AND YOUR GUVNOR ARE GOING OFF TO FETCH A VINTAGE CAR...
AND I GET TO LOOK AFTER THE DOG.
UH, WELL...
I'M GOING WITH THEM, TOO! I'VE ALWAYS WANTED TO SEE A BENTLEY SPEED 6.
IT'S NOT MERELY A VINTAGE CAR, SAHRA.
IT IS QUITE POSSIBLY THE MOST HAUNTED CAR IN ENGLAND.
Vintage
BMW DIX1

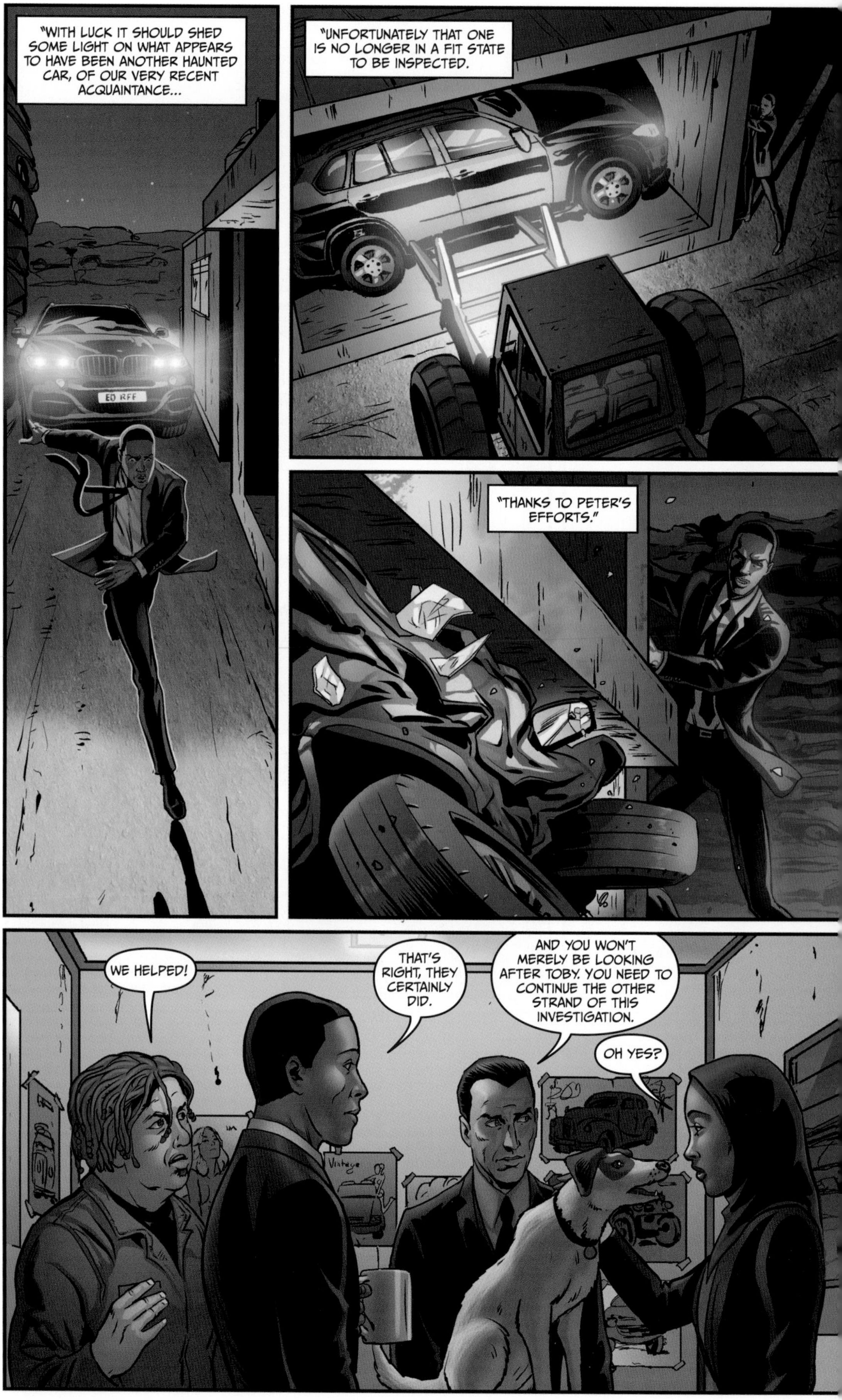
"WITH LUCK IT SHOULD SHED SOME LIGHT ON WHAT APPEARS TO HAVE BEEN ANOTHER HAUNTED CAR, OF OUR VERY RECENT ACQUAINTANCE...
ED RFF
"UNFORTUNATELY THAT ONE IS NO LONGER IN A FIT STATE TO BE INSPECTED.
"THANKS TO PETER'S EFFORTS."
WE HELPED!
THAT'S RIGHT, THEY CERTAINLY DID.
AND YOU WON'T MERELY BE LOOKING AFTER TOBY. YOU NEED TO CONTINUE THE OTHER STRAND OF THIS INVESTIGATION.
OH YES?

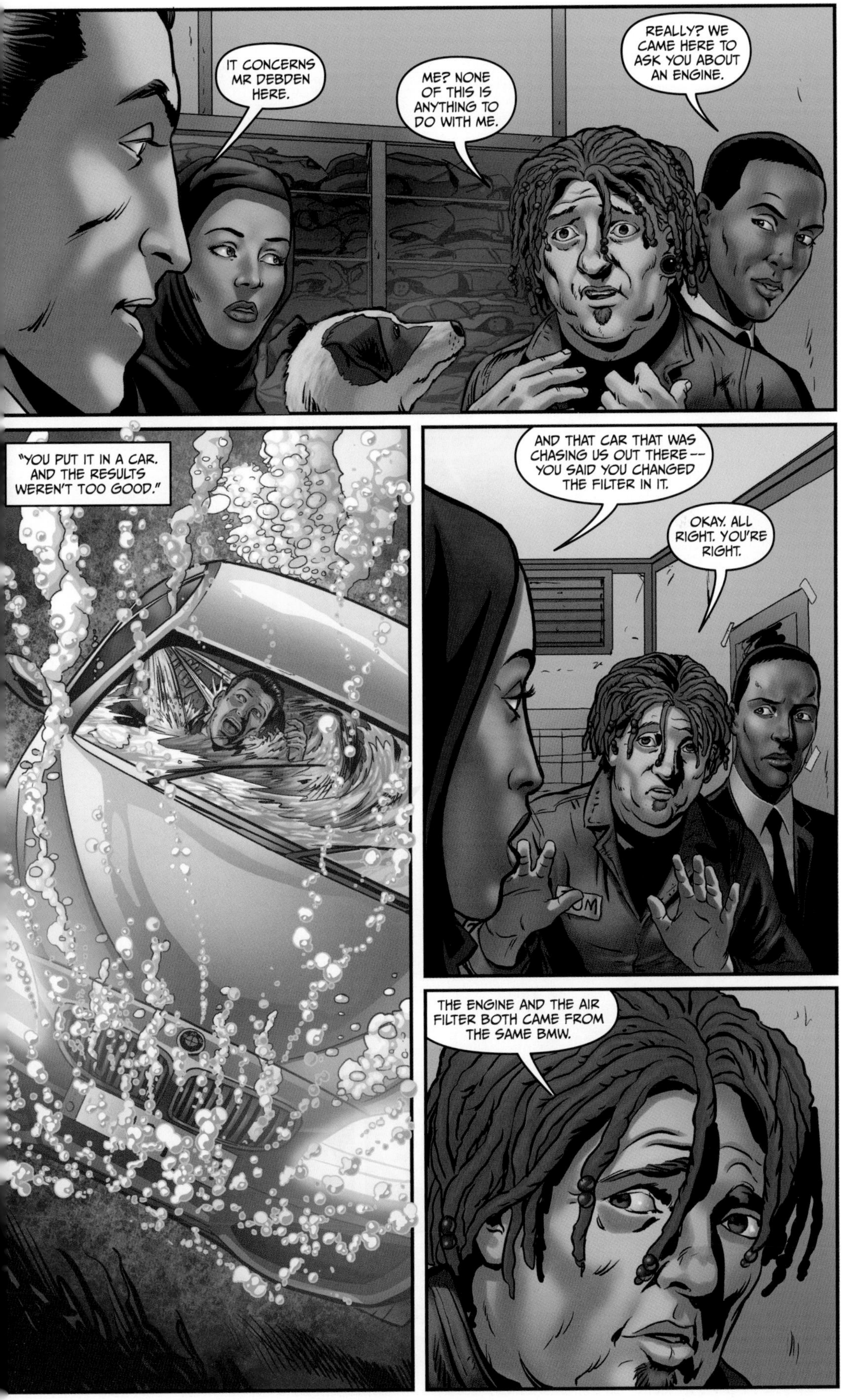
IT CONCERNS MR DEBDEN HERE.
ME? NONE OF THIS IS ANYTHING TO DO WITH ME.
REALLY? WE CAME HERE TO ASK YOU ABOUT AN ENGINE.
"YOU PUT IT IN A CAR. AND THE RESULTS WEREN'T TOO GOOD."
AND THAT CAR THAT WAS CHASING US OUT THERE-- YOU SAID YOU CHANGED THE FILTER IN IT.
OKAY. ALL RIGHT. YOU'RE RIGHT.
THE ENGINE AND THE AIR FILTER BOTH CAME FROM THE SAME BMW.

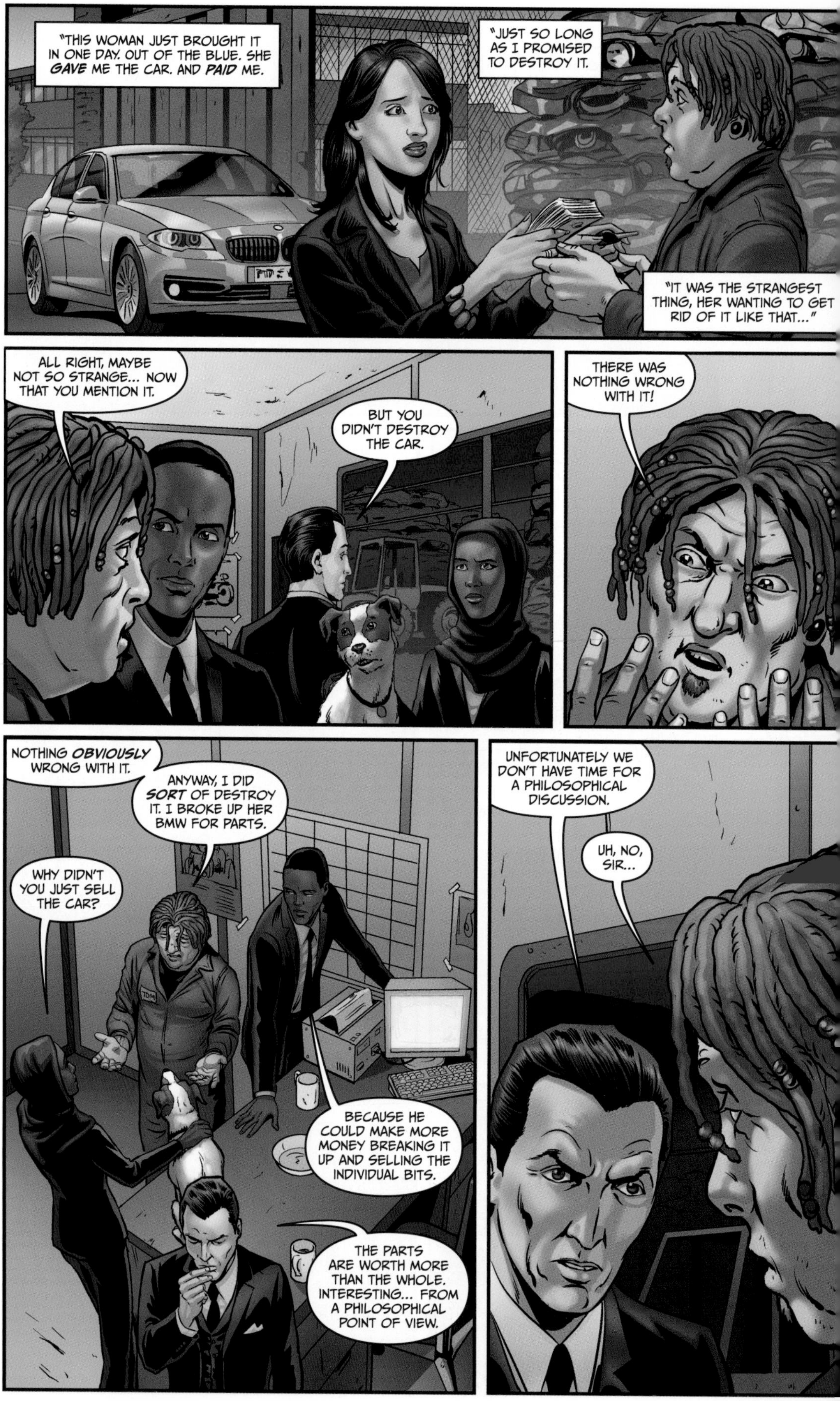

"THIS WOMAN JUST BROUGHT IT IN ONE DAY. OUT OF THE BLUE. SHE *GAVE* ME THE CAR. AND *PAID* ME.
"JUST SO LONG AS I PROMISED TO DESTROY IT.
"IT WAS THE STRANGEST THING, HER WANTING TO GET RID OF IT LIKE THAT..."
ALL RIGHT, MAYBE NOT SO STRANGE... NOW THAT YOU MENTION IT.
BUT YOU DIDN'T DESTROY THE CAR.
THERE WAS NOTHING WRONG WITH IT!
NOTHING *OBVIOUSLY* WRONG WITH IT.
ANYWAY, I DID *SORT* OF DESTROY IT. I BROKE UP HER BMW FOR PARTS.
WHY DIDN'T YOU JUST SELL THE CAR?
BECAUSE HE COULD MAKE MORE MONEY BREAKING IT UP AND SELLING THE INDIVIDUAL BITS.
THE PARTS ARE WORTH MORE THAN THE WHOLE. INTERESTING... FROM A PHILOSOPHICAL POINT OF VIEW.
UNFORTUNATELY WE DON'T HAVE TIME FOR A PHILOSOPHICAL DISCUSSION.
UH, NO, SIR...

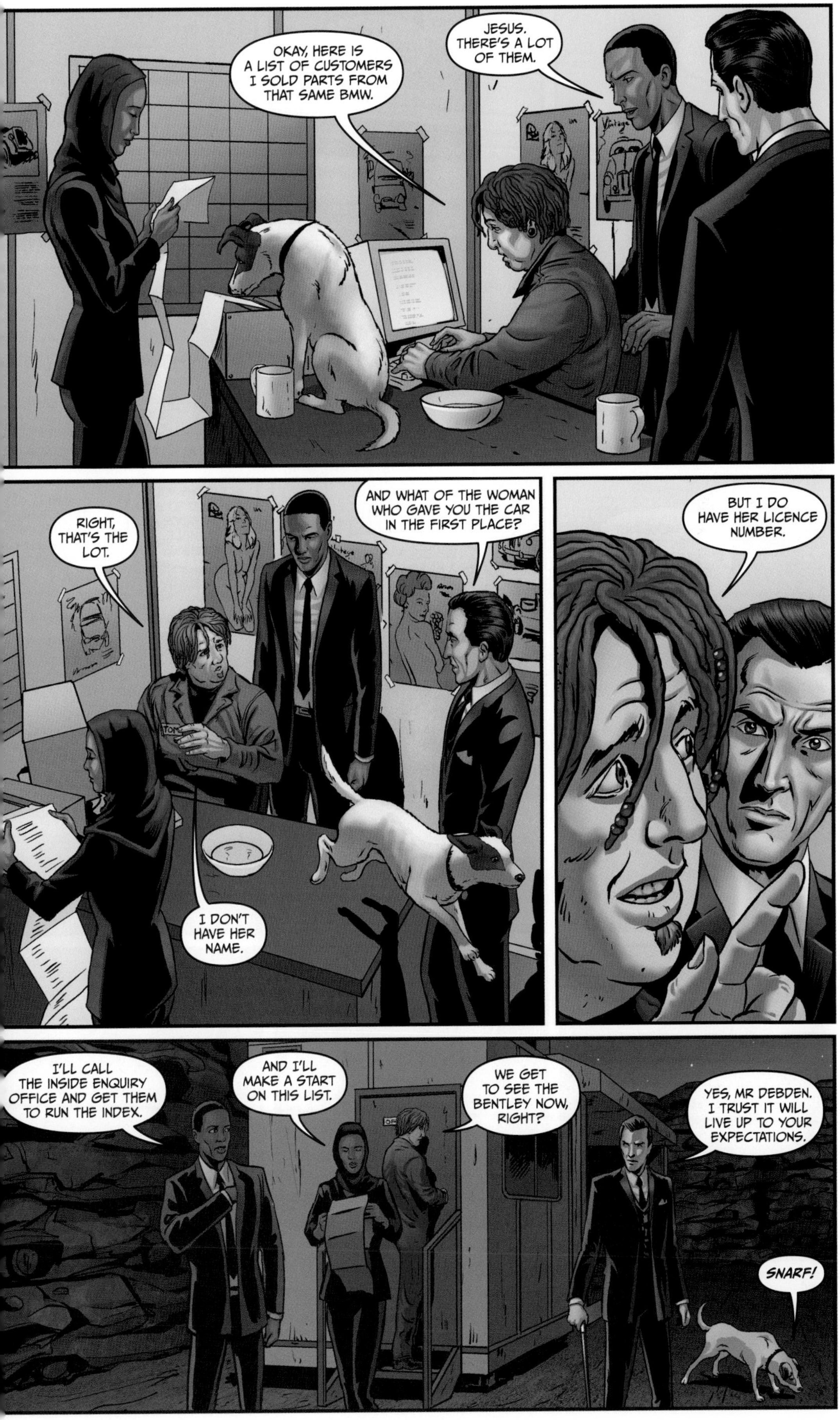
OKAY, HERE IS A LIST OF CUSTOMERS I SOLD PARTS FROM THAT SAME BMW.
JESUS. THERE'S A LOT OF THEM.
RIGHT, THAT'S THE LOT.
AND WHAT OF THE WOMAN WHO GAVE YOU THE CAR IN THE FIRST PLACE?
I DON'T HAVE HER NAME.
BUT I DO HAVE HER LICENCE NUMBER.
I'LL CALL THE INSIDE ENQUIRY OFFICE AND GET THEM TO RUN THE INDEX.
AND I'LL MAKE A START ON THIS LIST.
WE GET TO SEE THE BENTLEY NOW, RIGHT?
YES, MR DEBDEN. I TRUST IT WILL LIVE UP TO YOUR EXPECTATIONS.
SNARF!

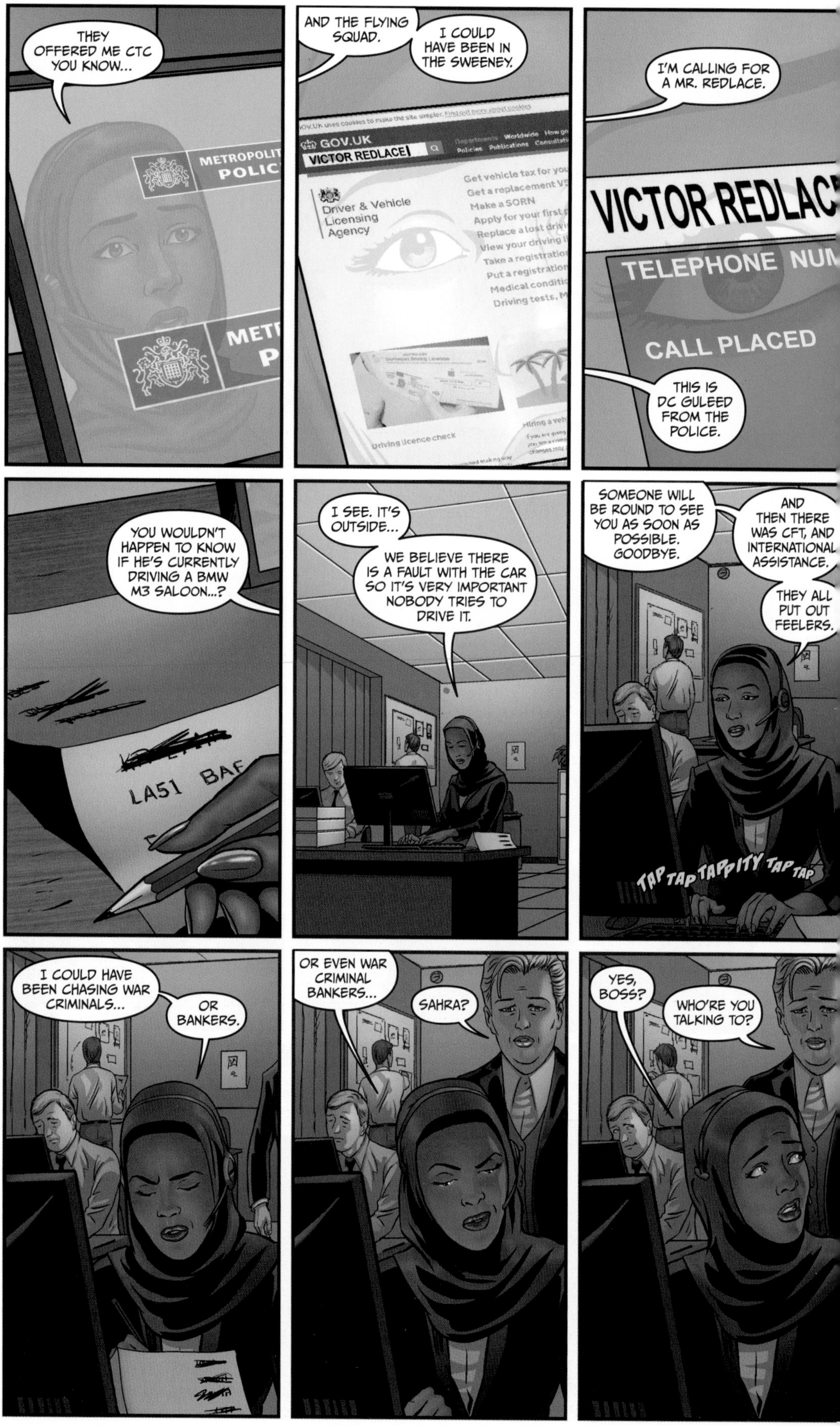
THEY OFFERED ME CTC YOU KNOW...
METROPOLIT
POLIC
METI
P
AND THE FLYING SQUAD.
I COULD HAVE BEEN IN THE SWEENEY.
GOV.UK
VICTOR REDLACE
Driver & Vehicle Licensing Agency
Get vehicle tax for you
Get a replacement V5
Make a SORN
Apply for your first
Replace a lost driv
View your driving
Take a registration
Put a registration
Medical conditio
Driving tests, M
Driving licence check
I'M CALLING FOR A MR. REDLACE.
VICTOR REDLAC
TELEPHONE NUM
CALL PLACED
THIS IS DC GULEED FROM THE POLICE.
YOU WOULDN'T HAPPEN TO KNOW IF HE'S CURRENTLY DRIVING A BMW M3 SALOON...?
LA51 BAF
I SEE. IT'S OUTSIDE...
WE BELIEVE THERE IS A FAULT WITH THE CAR SO IT'S VERY IMPORTANT NOBODY TRIES TO DRIVE IT.
SOMEONE WILL BE ROUND TO SEE YOU AS SOON AS POSSIBLE. GOODBYE.
AND THEN THERE WAS CFT, AND INTERNATIONAL ASSISTANCE.
THEY ALL PUT OUT FEELERS.
TAP TAP TAPPITY TAP TAP
I COULD HAVE BEEN CHASING WAR CRIMINALS...
OR BANKERS.
OR EVEN WAR CRIMINAL BANKERS...
SAHRA?
YES, BOSS?
WHO'RE YOU TALKING TO?

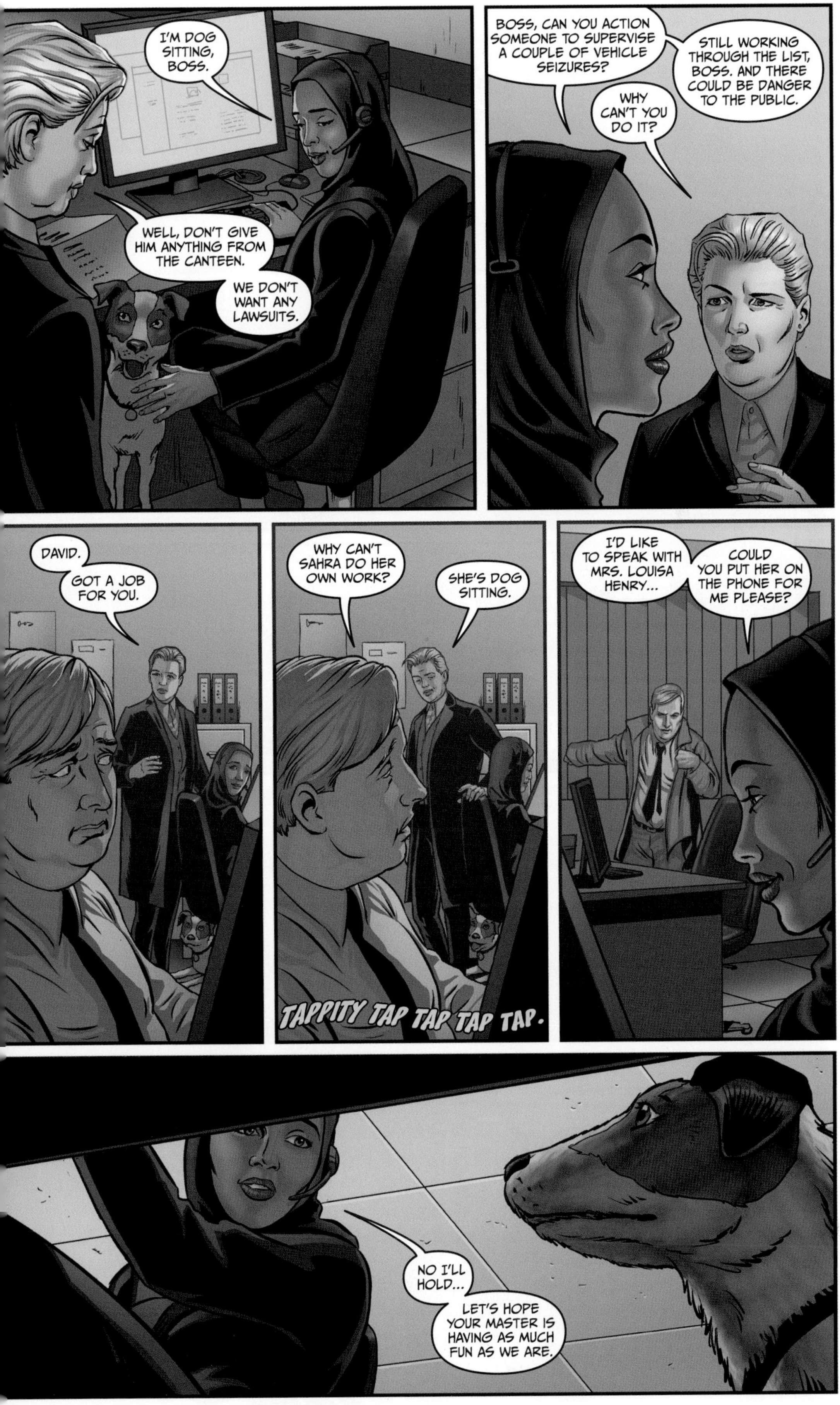

I'M DOG SITTING, BOSS.
WELL, DON'T GIVE HIM ANYTHING FROM THE CANTEEN.
WE DON'T WANT ANY LAWSUITS.
BOSS, CAN YOU ACTION SOMEONE TO SUPERVISE A COUPLE OF VEHICLE SEIZURES?
WHY CAN'T YOU DO IT?
STILL WORKING THROUGH THE LIST, BOSS. AND THERE COULD BE DANGER TO THE PUBLIC.
DAVID.
GOT A JOB FOR YOU.
WHY CAN'T SAHRA DO HER OWN WORK?
SHE'S DOG SITTING.
TAPPITY TAP TAP TAP TAP.
I'D LIKE TO SPEAK WITH MRS. LOUISA HENRY...
COULD YOU PUT HER ON THE PHONE FOR ME PLEASE?
NO I'LL HOLD...
LET'S HOPE YOUR MASTER IS HAVING AS MUCH FUN AS WE ARE.

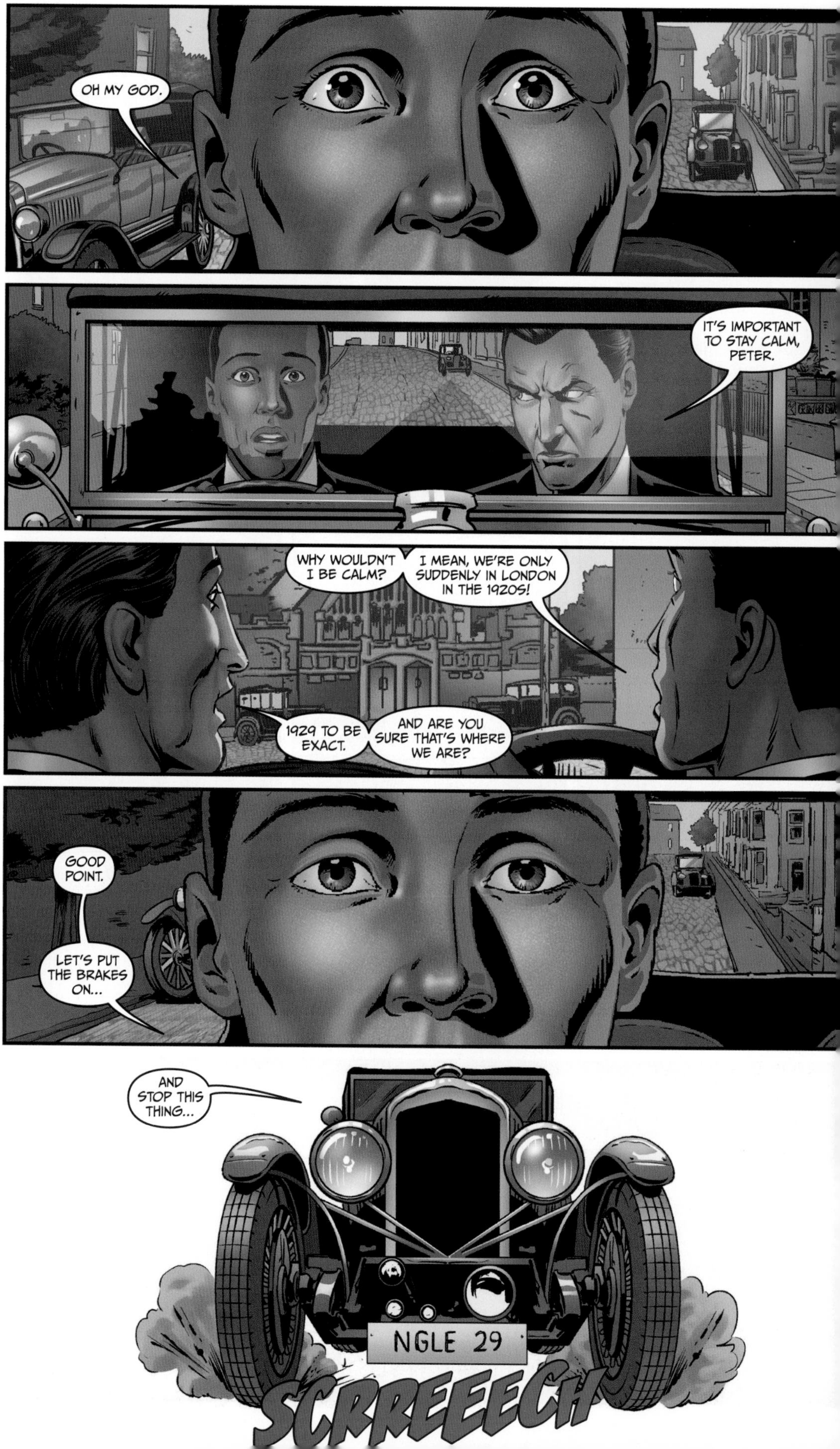
OH MY GOD.
IT'S IMPORTANT TO STAY CALM, PETER.
WHY WOULDN'T I BE CALM?
I MEAN, WE'RE ONLY SUDDENLY IN LONDON IN THE 1920S!
1929 TO BE EXACT.
AND ARE YOU SURE THAT'S WHERE WE ARE?
GOOD POINT.
LET'S PUT THE BRAKES ON...
AND STOP THIS THING...
NGLE 29
SCRREEECH

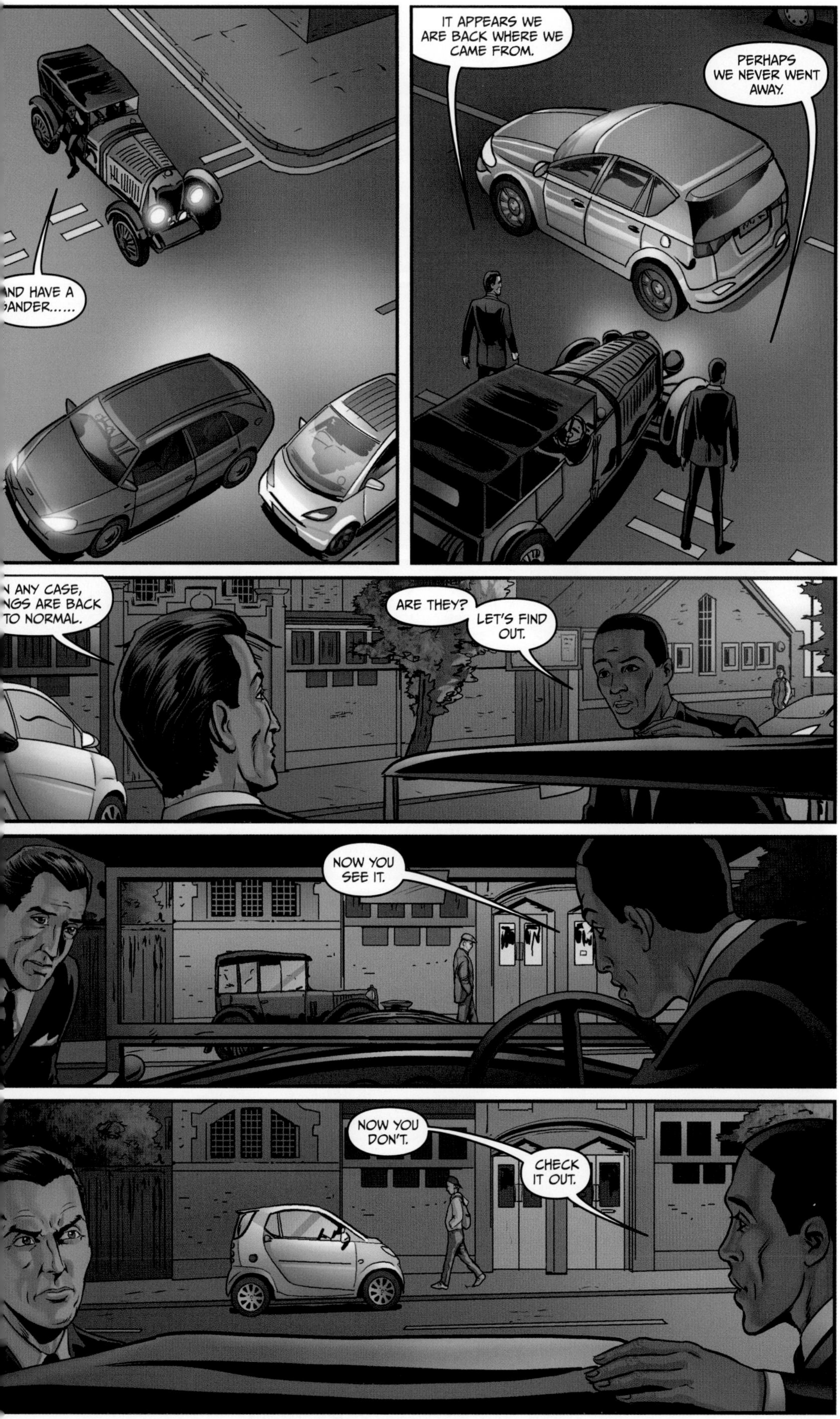
ND HAVE A GANDER......
IT APPEARS WE ARE BACK WHERE WE CAME FROM.
PERHAPS WE NEVER WENT AWAY.
N ANY CASE, NGS ARE BACK TO NORMAL.
ARE THEY?
LET'S FIND OUT.
NOW YOU SEE IT.
NOW YOU DON'T.
CHECK IT OUT.

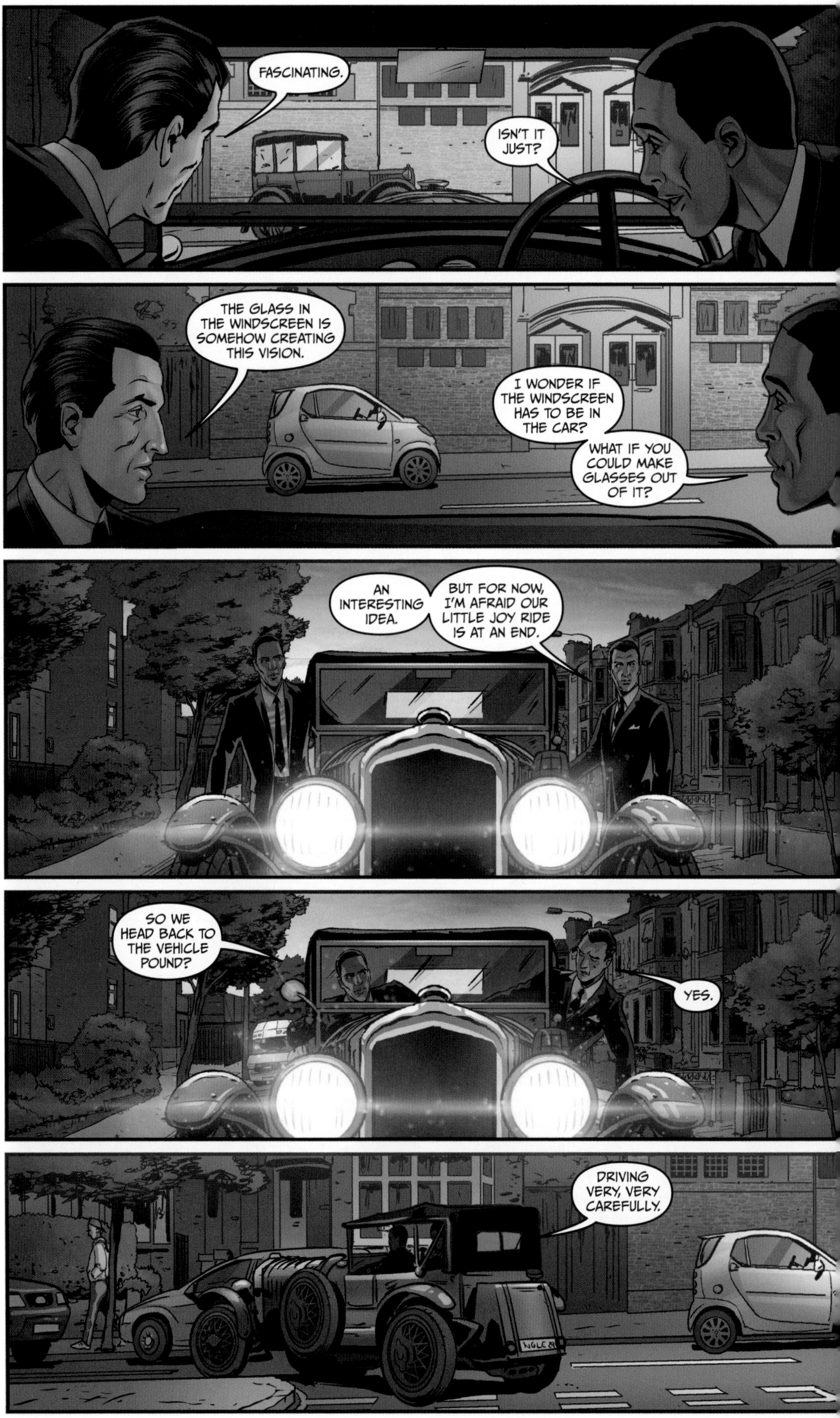
FASCINATING.
ISN'T IT JUST?
THE GLASS IN THE WINDSCREEN IS SOMEHOW CREATING THIS VISION.
I WONDER IF THE WINDSCREEN HAS TO BE IN THE CAR?
WHAT IF YOU COULD MAKE GLASSES OUT OF IT?
AN INTERESTING IDEA.
BUT FOR NOW, I'M AFRAID OUR LITTLE JOY RIDE IS AT AN END.
SO WE HEAD BACK TO THE VEHICLE POUND?
YES.
DRIVING VERY, VERY CAREFULLY.

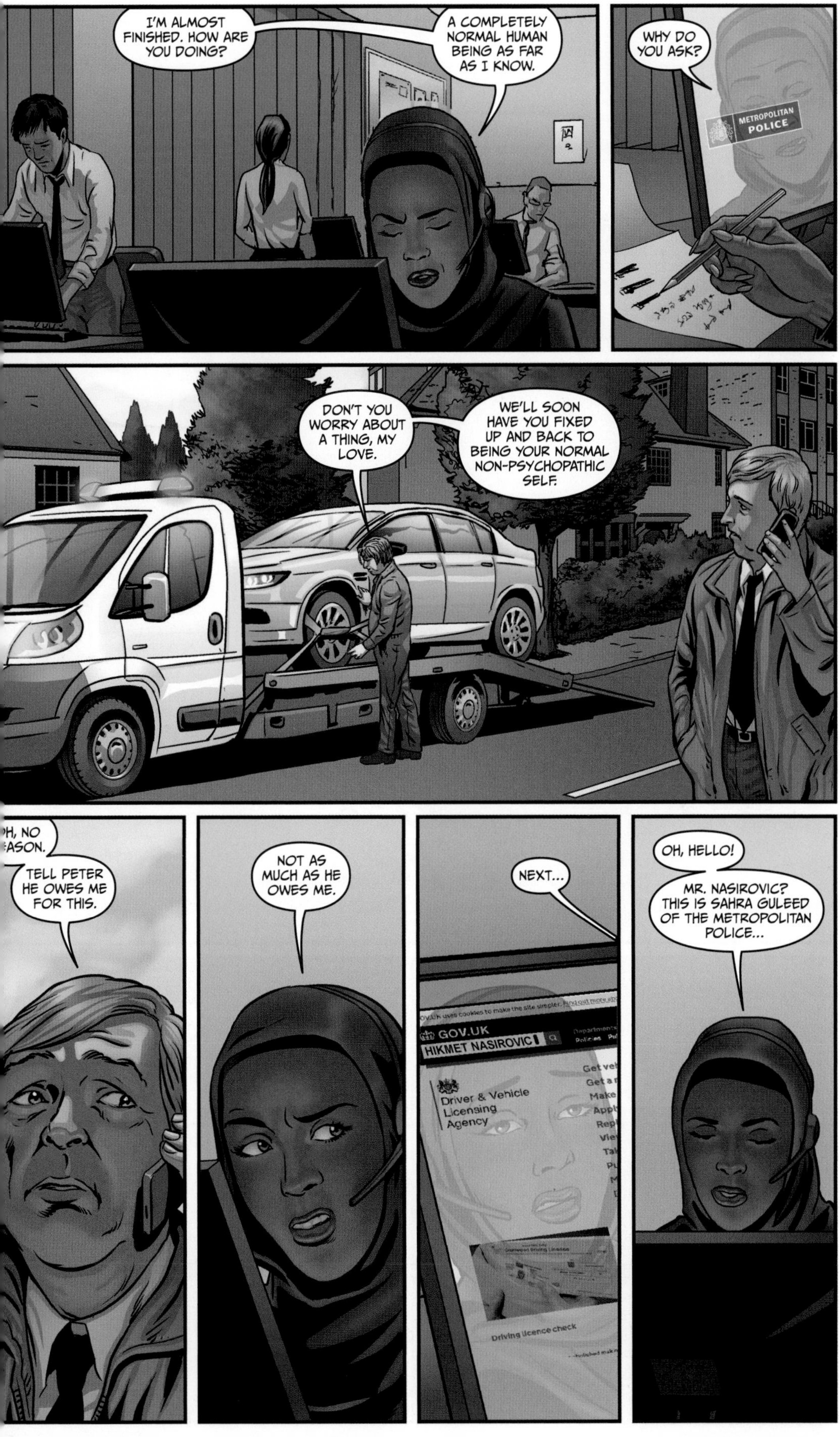
I'M ALMOST FINISHED. HOW ARE YOU DOING?
A COMPLETELY NORMAL HUMAN BEING AS FAR AS I KNOW.
WHY DO YOU ASK?
METROPOLITAN POLICE
DON'T YOU WORRY ABOUT A THING, MY LOVE.
WE'LL SOON HAVE YOU FIXED UP AND BACK TO BEING YOUR NORMAL NON-PSYCHOPATHIC SELF.
H, NO EASON.
TELL PETER HE OWES ME FOR THIS.
NOT AS MUCH AS HE OWES ME.
NEXT...
GOV.UK
HIKMET NASIROVIC
Driver & Vehicle Licensing Agency
Driving licence check
OH, HELLO!
MR. NASIROVIC? THIS IS SAHRA GULEED OF THE METROPOLITAN POLICE...

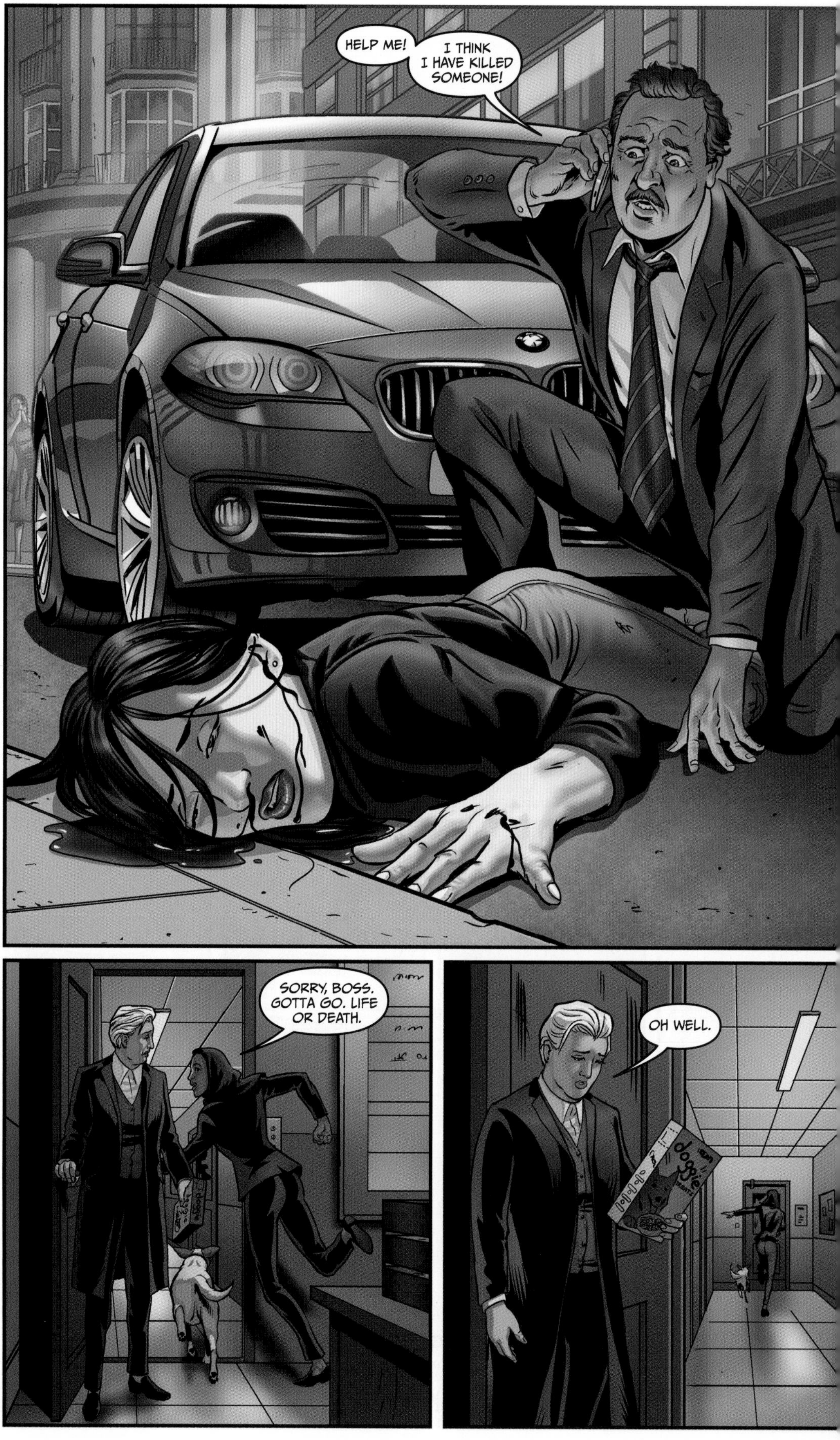
HELP ME!
I THINK I HAVE KILLED SOMEONE!
SORRY, BOSS. GOTTA GO. LIFE OR DEATH.
OH WELL.

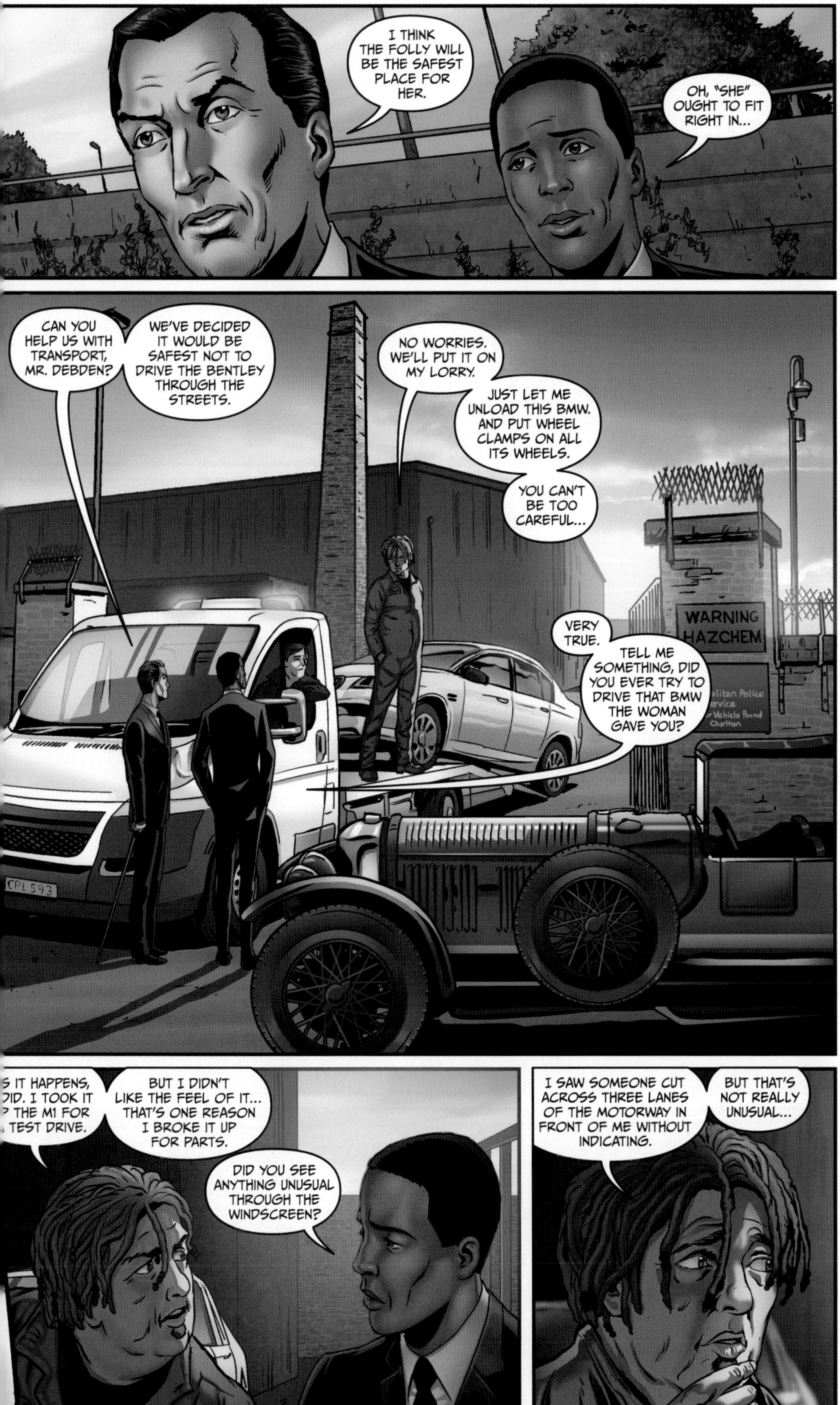

I THINK THE FOLLY WILL BE THE SAFEST PLACE FOR HER.
OH, "SHE" OUGHT TO FIT RIGHT IN...
CAN YOU HELP US WITH TRANSPORT, MR. DEBDEN?
WE'VE DECIDED IT WOULD BE SAFEST NOT TO DRIVE THE BENTLEY THROUGH THE STREETS.
NO WORRIES. WE'LL PUT IT ON MY LORRY.
JUST LET ME UNLOAD THIS BMW. AND PUT WHEEL CLAMPS ON ALL ITS WHEELS.
YOU CAN'T BE TOO CAREFUL...
WARNING HAZCHEM
VERY TRUE.
TELL ME SOMETHING, DID YOU EVER TRY TO DRIVE THAT BMW THE WOMAN GAVE YOU?
S IT HAPPENS, DID. I TOOK IT THE M1 FOR TEST DRIVE.
BUT I DIDN'T LIKE THE FEEL OF IT... THAT'S ONE REASON I BROKE IT UP FOR PARTS.
DID YOU SEE ANYTHING UNUSUAL THROUGH THE WINDSCREEN?
I SAW SOMEONE CUT ACROSS THREE LANES OF THE MOTORWAY IN FRONT OF ME WITHOUT INDICATING.
BUT THAT'S NOT REALLY UNUSUAL...

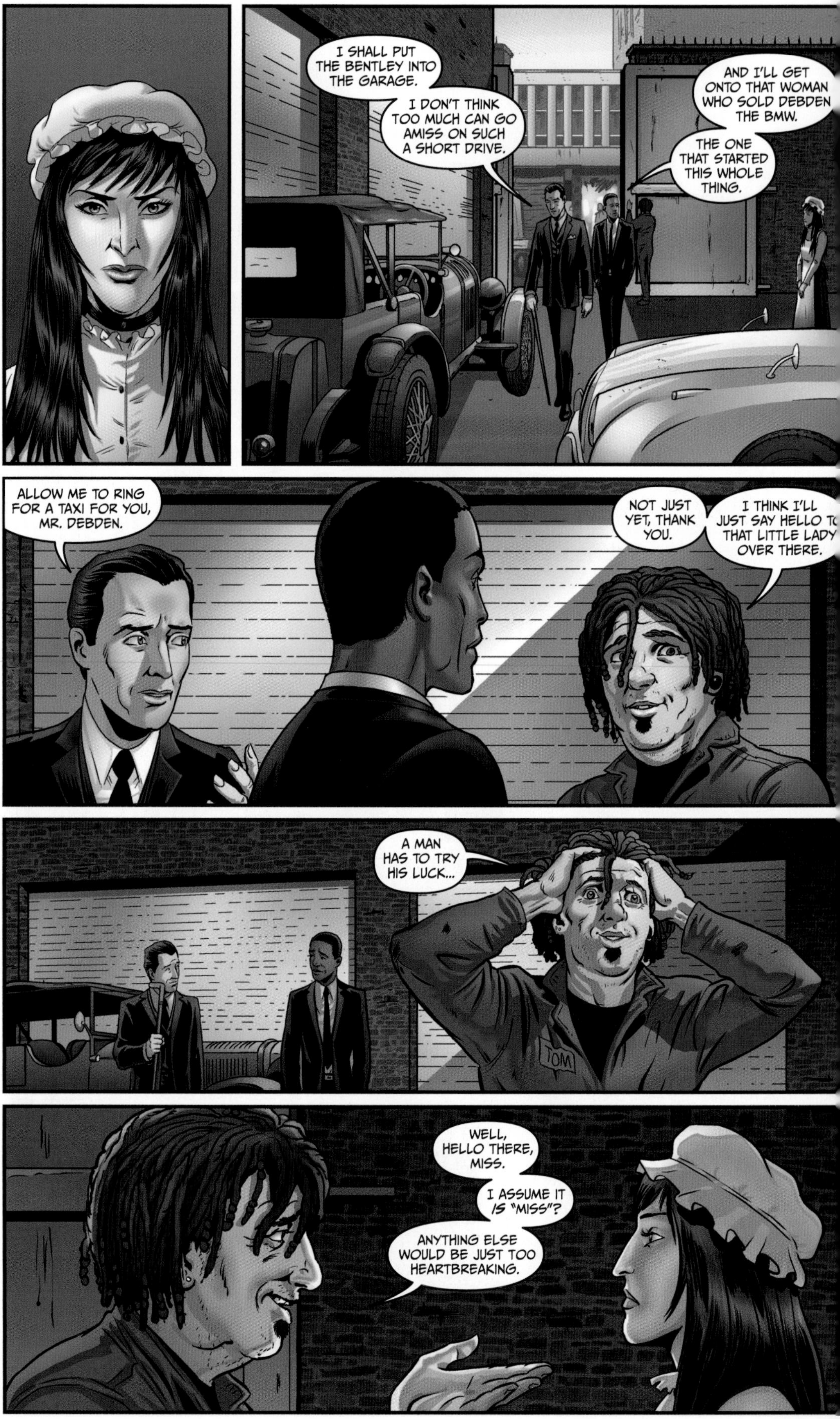
I SHALL PUT THE BENTLEY INTO THE GARAGE.
I DON'T THINK TOO MUCH CAN GO AMISS ON SUCH A SHORT DRIVE.
AND I'LL GET ONTO THAT WOMAN WHO SOLD DEBDEN THE BMW.
THE ONE THAT STARTED THIS WHOLE THING.
ALLOW ME TO RING FOR A TAXI FOR YOU, MR. DEBDEN.
NOT JUST YET, THANK YOU.
I THINK I'LL JUST SAY HELLO TO THAT LITTLE LADY OVER THERE.
A MAN HAS TO TRY HIS LUCK...
TOM
WELL, HELLO THERE, MISS.
I ASSUME IT *IS* "MISS"?
ANYTHING ELSE WOULD BE JUST TOO HEARTBREAKING.

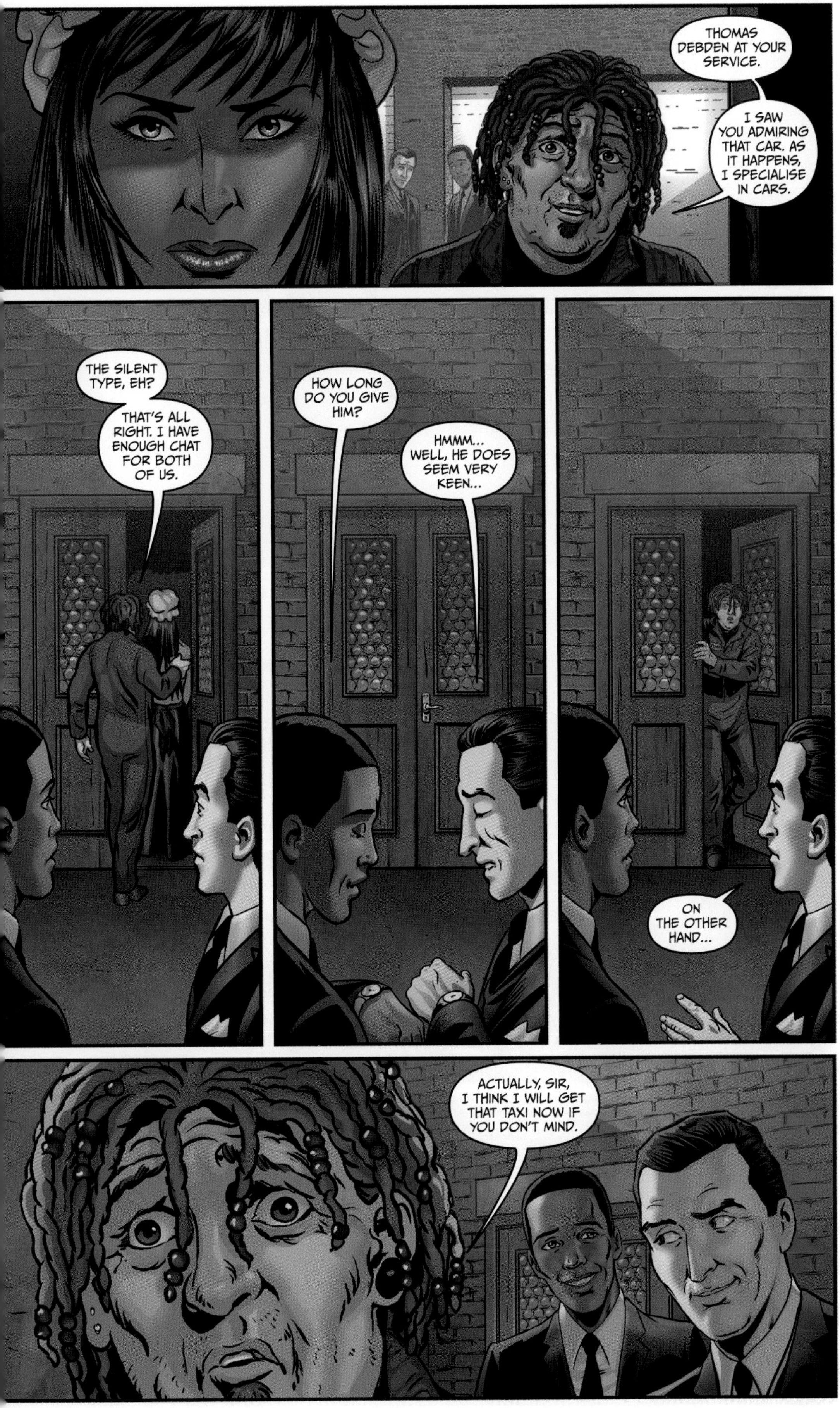
THOMAS DEBDEN AT YOUR SERVICE.
I SAW YOU ADMIRING THAT CAR. AS IT HAPPENS, I SPECIALISE IN CARS.
THE SILENT TYPE, EH?
THAT'S ALL RIGHT. I HAVE ENOUGH CHAT FOR BOTH OF US.
HOW LONG DO YOU GIVE HIM?
HMMM... WELL, HE DOES SEEM VERY KEEN...
ON THE OTHER HAND...
ACTUALLY, SIR, I THINK I WILL GET THAT TAXI NOW IF YOU DON'T MIND.

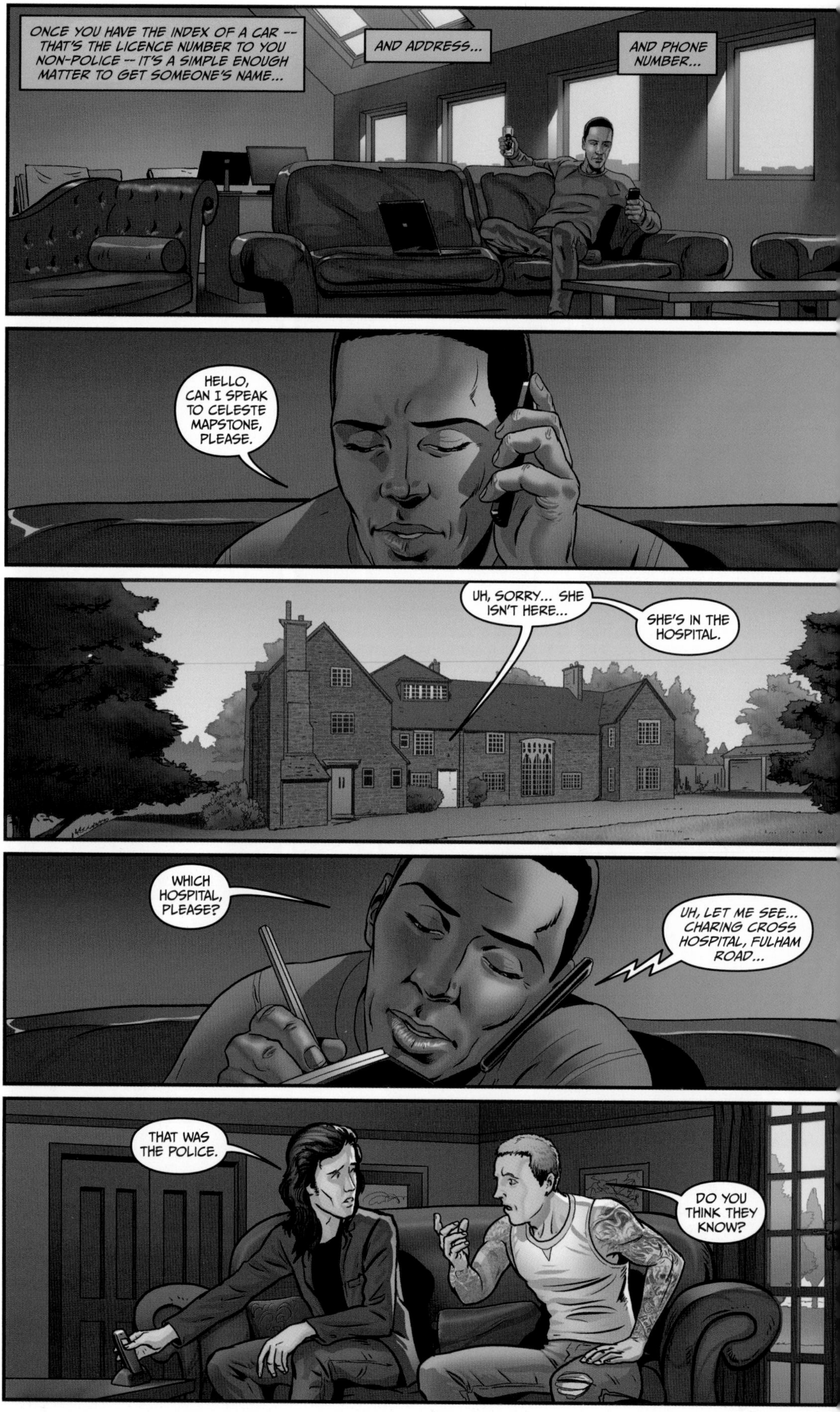
ONCE YOU HAVE THE INDEX OF A CAR -- THAT'S THE LICENCE NUMBER TO YOU NON-POLICE -- IT'S A SIMPLE ENOUGH MATTER TO GET SOMEONE'S NAME...
AND ADDRESS...
AND PHONE NUMBER...
HELLO, CAN I SPEAK TO CELESTE MAPSTONE, PLEASE.
UH, SORRY... SHE ISN'T HERE...
SHE'S IN THE HOSPITAL.
WHICH HOSPITAL, PLEASE?
UH, LET ME SEE... CHARING CROSS HOSPITAL, FULHAM ROAD...
THAT WAS THE POLICE.
DO YOU THINK THEY KNOW?

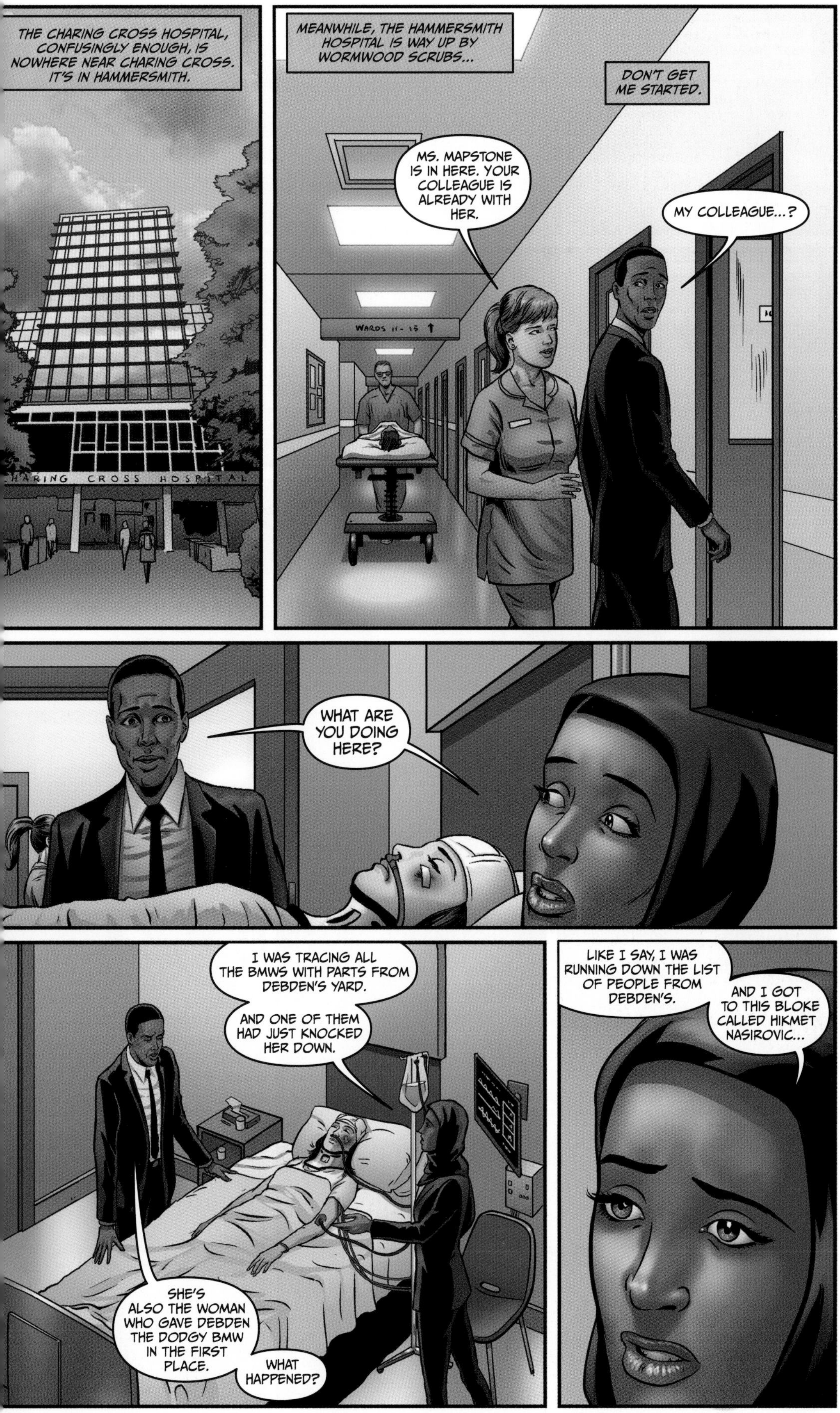
THE CHARING CROSS HOSPITAL, CONFUSINGLY ENOUGH, IS NOWHERE NEAR CHARING CROSS. IT'S IN HAMMERSMITH.
CHARING CROSS HOSPITAL
MEANWHILE, THE HAMMERSMITH HOSPITAL IS WAY UP BY WORMWOOD SCRUBS...
DON'T GET ME STARTED.
MS. MAPSTONE IS IN HERE. YOUR COLLEAGUE IS ALREADY WITH HER.
MY COLLEAGUE...?
WARDS 11 - 15
WHAT ARE YOU DOING HERE?
I WAS TRACING ALL THE BMWS WITH PARTS FROM DEBDEN'S YARD.
AND ONE OF THEM HAD JUST KNOCKED HER DOWN.
SHE'S ALSO THE WOMAN WHO GAVE DEBDEN THE DODGY BMW IN THE FIRST PLACE.
WHAT HAPPENED?
LIKE I SAY, I WAS RUNNING DOWN THE LIST OF PEOPLE FROM DEBDEN'S.
AND I GOT TO THIS BLOKE CALLED HIKMET NASIROVIC...

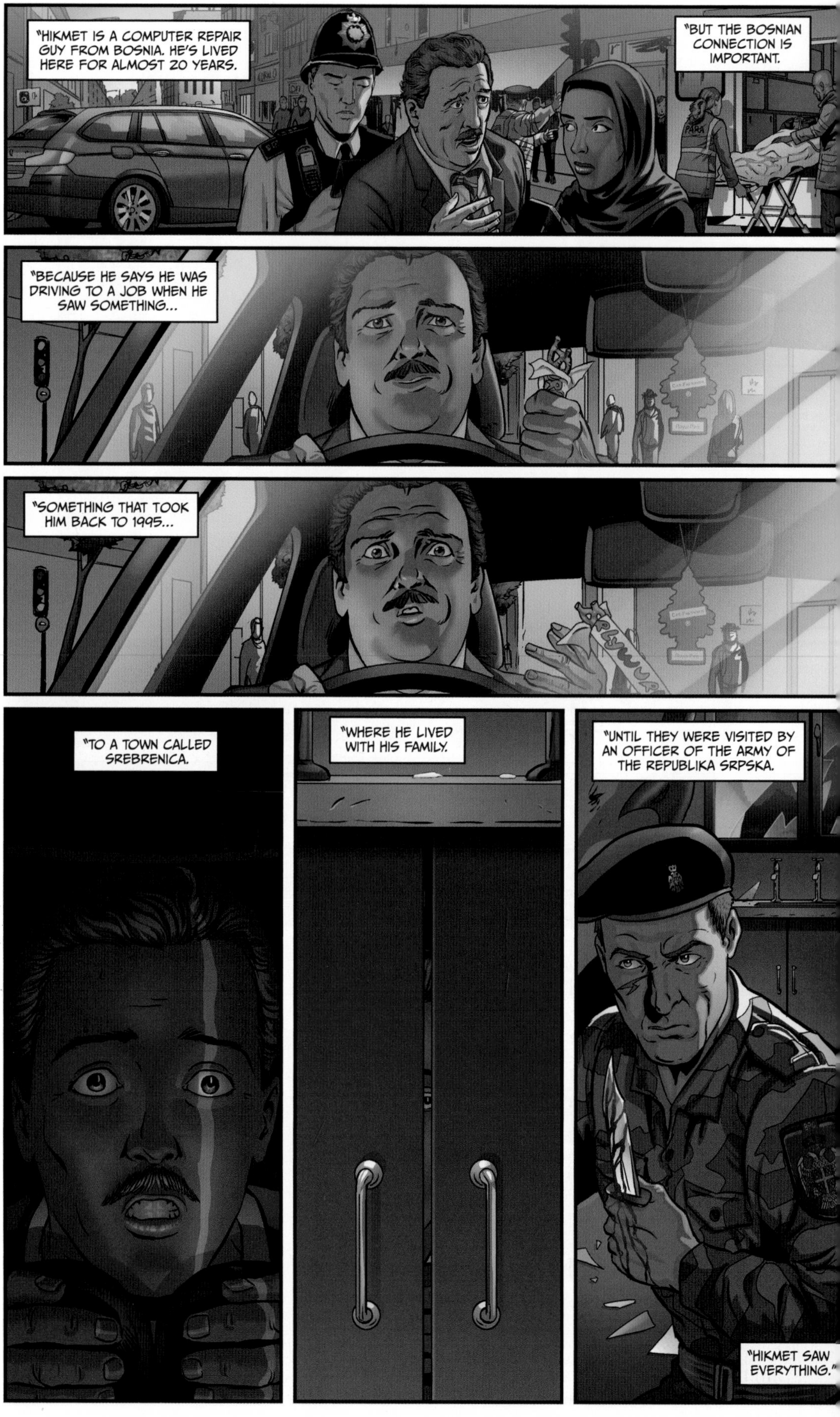
"HIKMET IS A COMPUTER REPAIR GUY FROM BOSNIA. HE'S LIVED HERE FOR ALMOST 20 YEARS.
"BUT THE BOSNIAN CONNECTION IS IMPORTANT.
PARA
"BECAUSE HE SAYS HE WAS DRIVING TO A JOB WHEN HE SAW SOMETHING...
"SOMETHING THAT TOOK HIM BACK TO 1995...
"TO A TOWN CALLED SREBRENICA.
"WHERE HE LIVED WITH HIS FAMILY.
"UNTIL THEY WERE VISITED BY AN OFFICER OF THE ARMY OF THE REPUBLIKA SRPSKA.
"HIKMET SAW EVERYTHING."

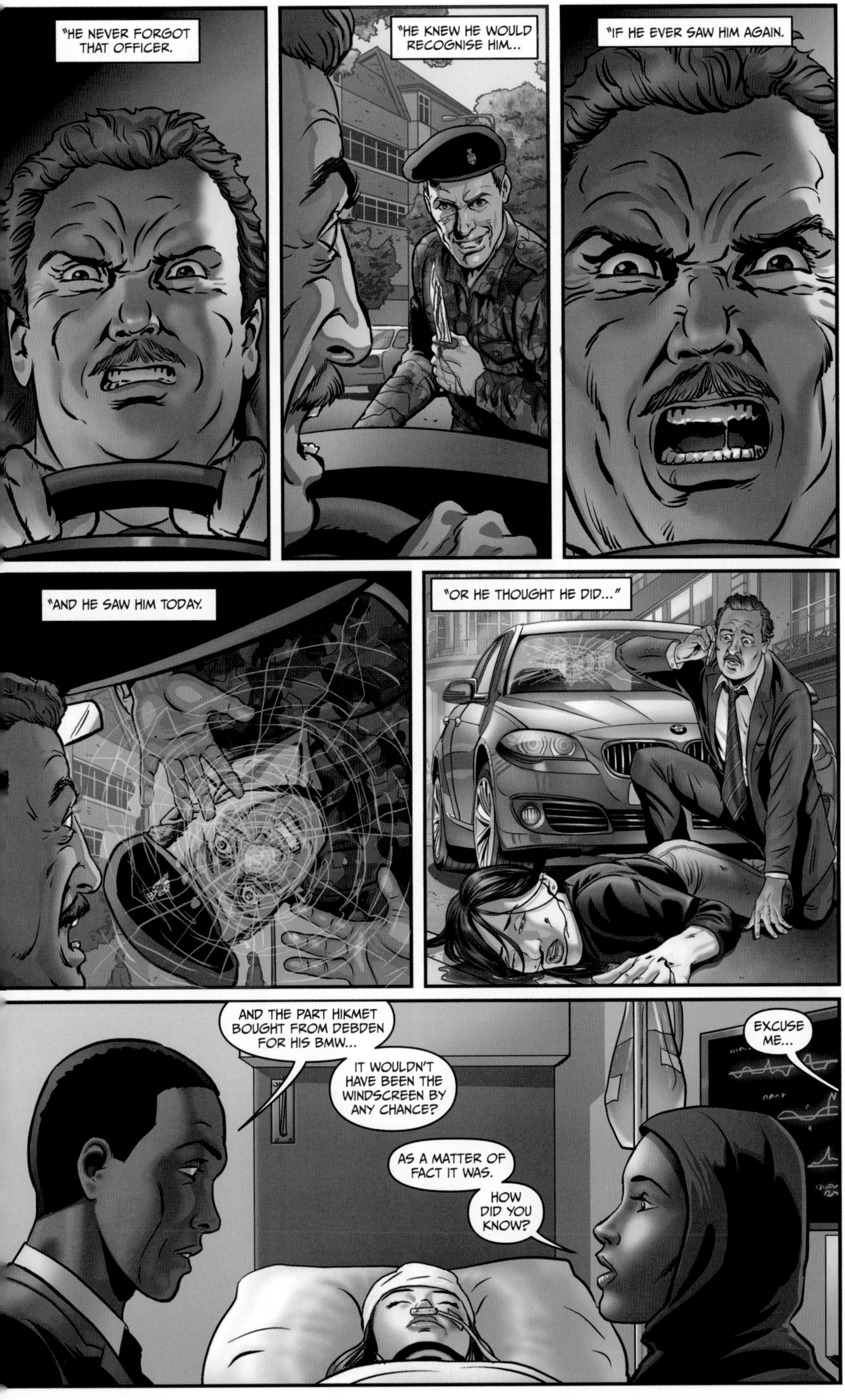
"HE NEVER FORGOT THAT OFFICER.
"HE KNEW HE WOULD RECOGNISE HIM...
"IF HE EVER SAW HIM AGAIN.
"AND HE SAW HIM TODAY.
"OR HE THOUGHT HE DID..."
AND THE PART HIKMET BOUGHT FROM DEBDEN FOR HIS BMW...
IT WOULDN'T HAVE BEEN THE WINDSCREEN BY ANY CHANCE?
EXCUSE ME...
AS A MATTER OF FACT IT WAS.
HOW DID YOU KNOW?

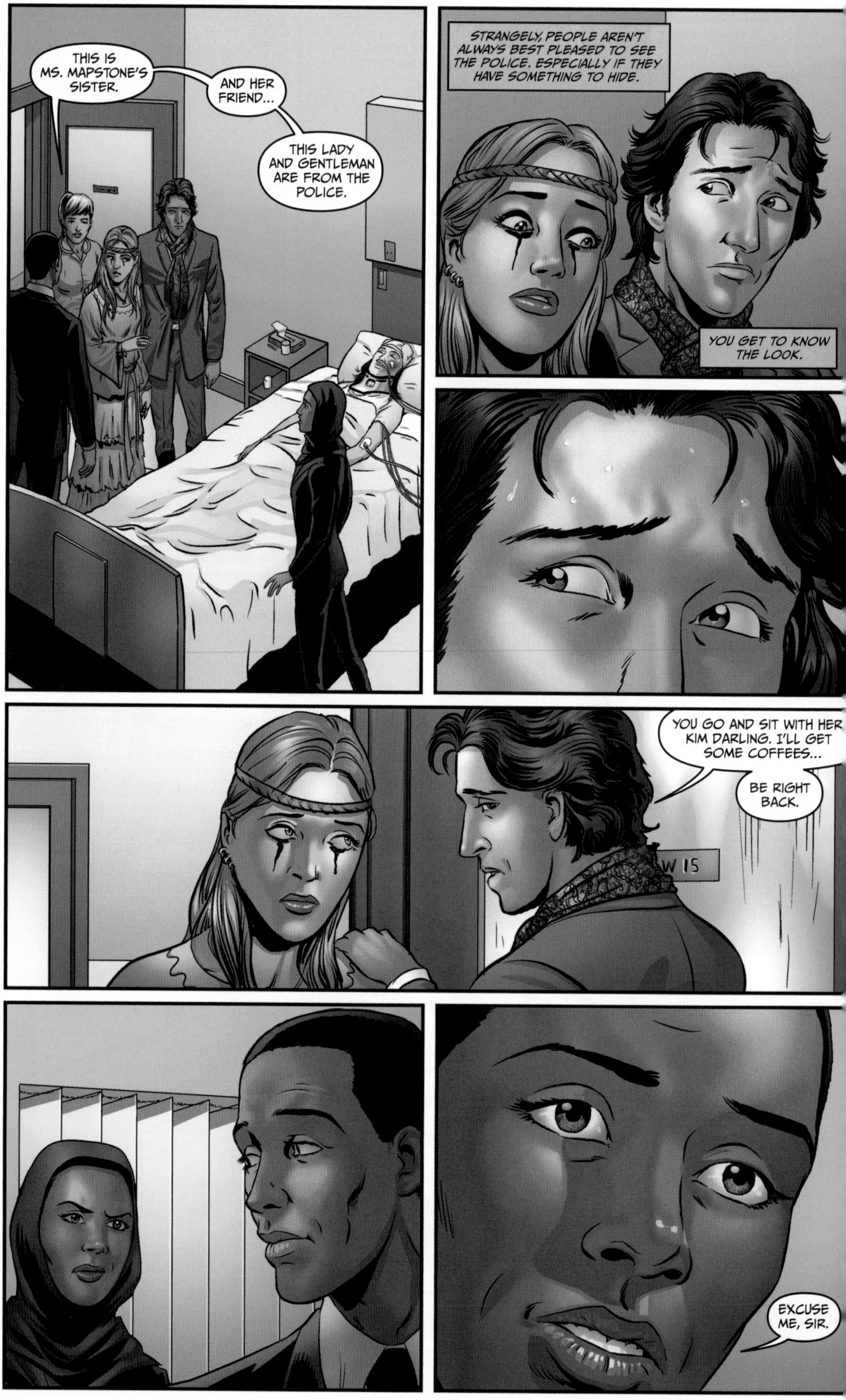

THIS IS MS. MAPSTONE'S SISTER.
AND HER FRIEND...
THIS LADY AND GENTLEMAN ARE FROM THE POLICE.
STRANGELY, PEOPLE AREN'T ALWAYS BEST PLEASED TO SEE THE POLICE. ESPECIALLY IF THEY HAVE SOMETHING TO HIDE.
YOU GET TO KNOW THE LOOK.
W 15
YOU GO AND SIT WITH HER KIM DARLING. I'LL GET SOME COFFEES...
BE RIGHT BACK.
EXCUSE ME, SIR.

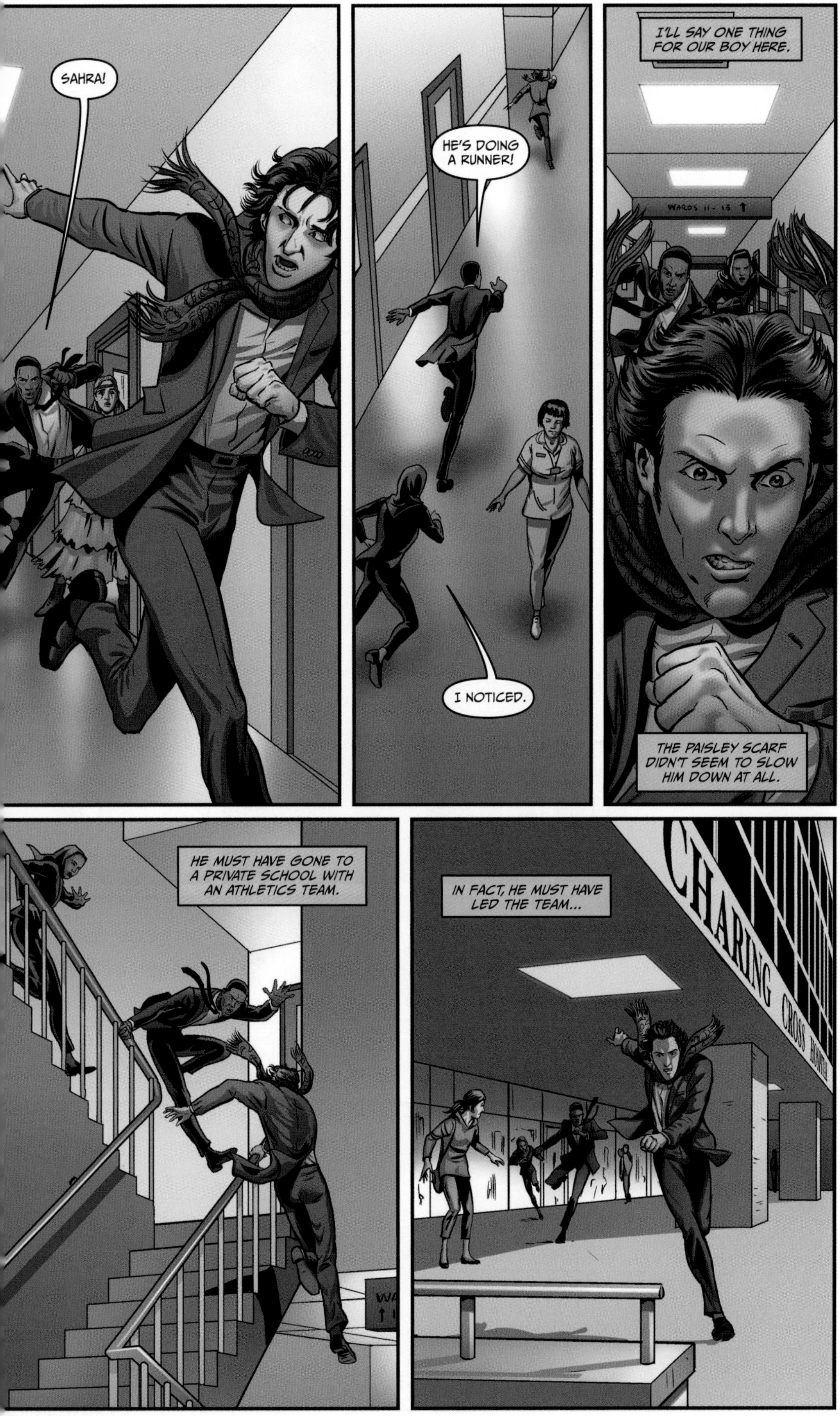
SAHRA!
HE'S DOING A RUNNER!
I NOTICED.
I'LL SAY ONE THING FOR OUR BOY HERE.
THE PAISLEY SCARF DIDN'T SEEM TO SLOW HIM DOWN AT ALL.
HE MUST HAVE GONE TO A PRIVATE SCHOOL WITH AN ATHLETICS TEAM.
IN FACT, HE MUST HAVE LED THE TEAM...
CHARING CROSS

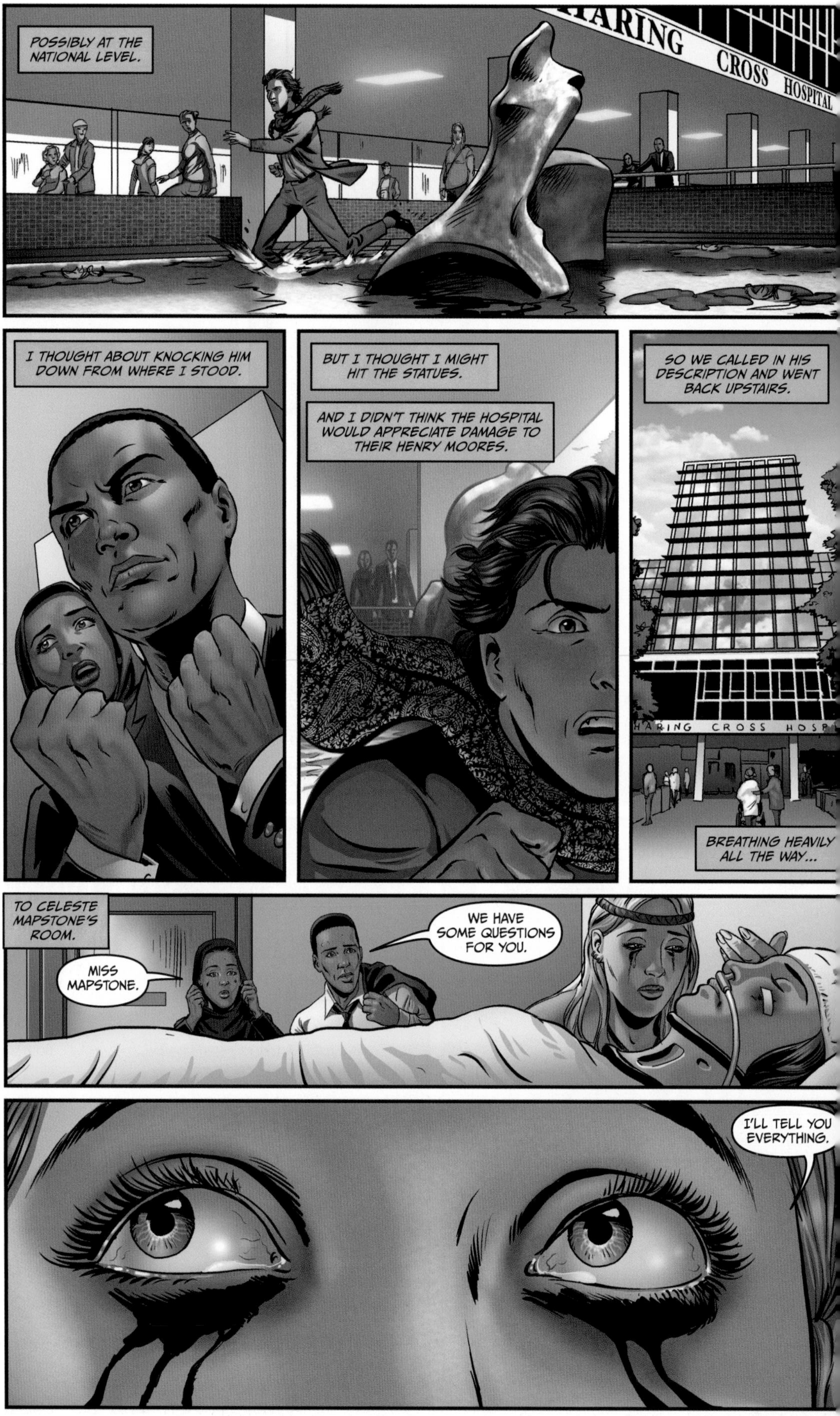
POSSIBLY AT THE NATIONAL LEVEL.
CHARING CROSS HOSPITAL
I THOUGHT ABOUT KNOCKING HIM DOWN FROM WHERE I STOOD.
BUT I THOUGHT I MIGHT HIT THE STATUES.
AND I DIDN'T THINK THE HOSPITAL WOULD APPRECIATE DAMAGE TO THEIR HENRY MOORES.
SO WE CALLED IN HIS DESCRIPTION AND WENT BACK UPSTAIRS.
BREATHING HEAVILY ALL THE WAY...
TO CELESTE MAPSTONE'S ROOM.
MISS MAPSTONE.
WE HAVE SOME QUESTIONS FOR YOU.
I'LL TELL YOU EVERYTHING.

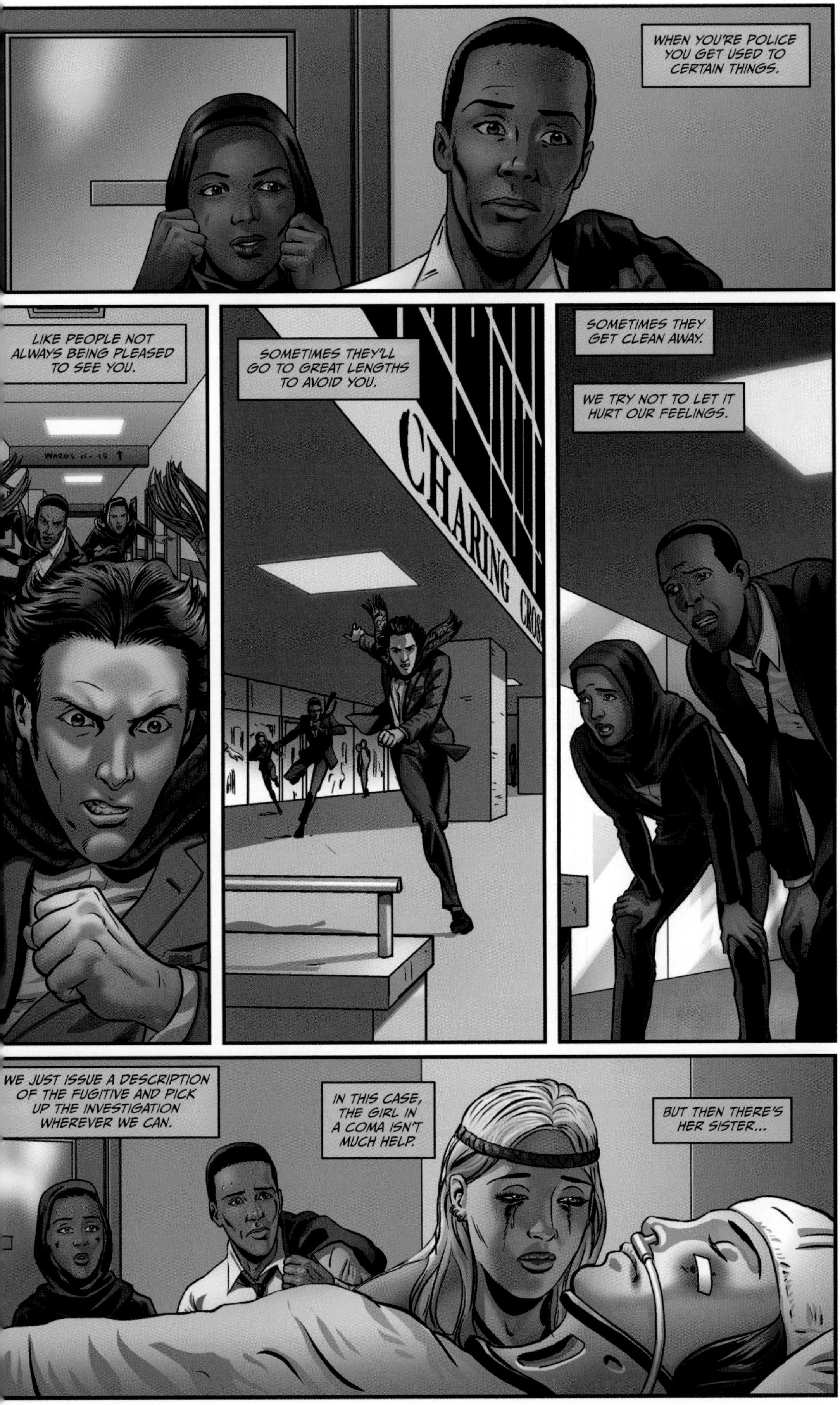
WHEN YOU'RE POLICE YOU GET USED TO CERTAIN THINGS.
LIKE PEOPLE NOT ALWAYS BEING PLEASED TO SEE YOU.
WARDS 11 - 15
SOMETIMES THEY'LL GO TO GREAT LENGTHS TO AVOID YOU.
CHARING CROSS
SOMETIMES THEY GET CLEAN AWAY.
WE TRY NOT TO LET IT HURT OUR FEELINGS.
WE JUST ISSUE A DESCRIPTION OF THE FUGITIVE AND PICK UP THE INVESTIGATION WHEREVER WE CAN.
IN THIS CASE, THE GIRL IN A COMA ISN'T MUCH HELP.
BUT THEN THERE'S HER SISTER...

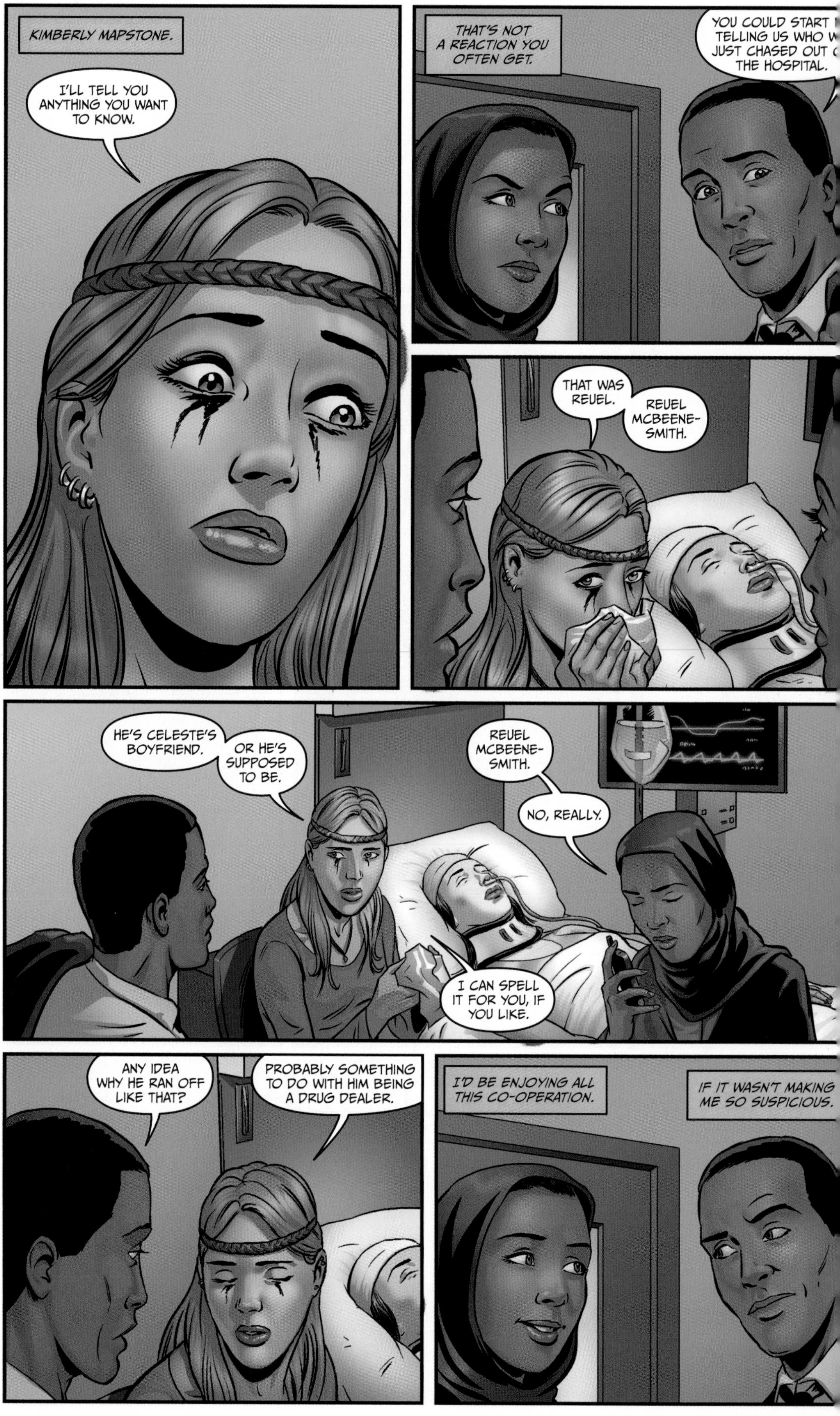
KIMBERLY MAPSTONE.
I'LL TELL YOU ANYTHING YOU WANT TO KNOW.
THAT'S NOT A REACTION YOU OFTEN GET.
YOU COULD START TELLING US WHO JUST CHASED OUT THE HOSPITAL.
THAT WAS REUEL.
REUEL MCBEENE-SMITH.
HE'S CELESTE'S BOYFRIEND.
OR HE'S SUPPOSED TO BE.
REUEL MCBEENE-SMITH.
NO, REALLY.
I CAN SPELL IT FOR YOU, IF YOU LIKE.
ANY IDEA WHY HE RAN OFF LIKE THAT?
PROBABLY SOMETHING TO DO WITH HIM BEING A DRUG DEALER.
I'D BE ENJOYING ALL THIS CO-OPERATION.
IF IT WASN'T MAKING ME SO SUSPICIOUS.

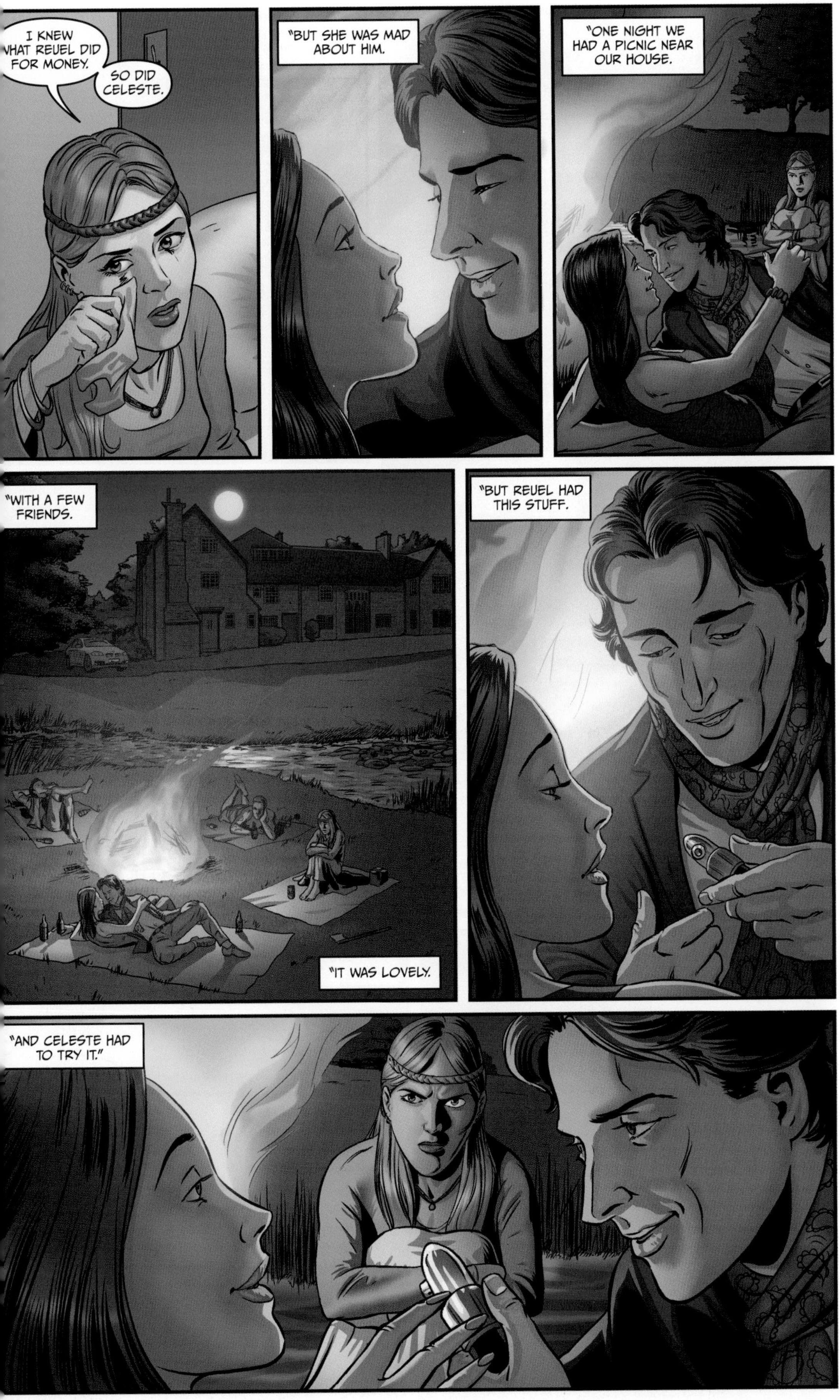
I KNEW WHAT REUEL DID FOR MONEY.
SO DID CELESTE.
"BUT SHE WAS MAD ABOUT HIM.
"ONE NIGHT WE HAD A PICNIC NEAR OUR HOUSE.
"WITH A FEW FRIENDS.
"IT WAS LOVELY.
"BUT REUEL HAD THIS STUFF.
"AND CELESTE HAD TO TRY IT."

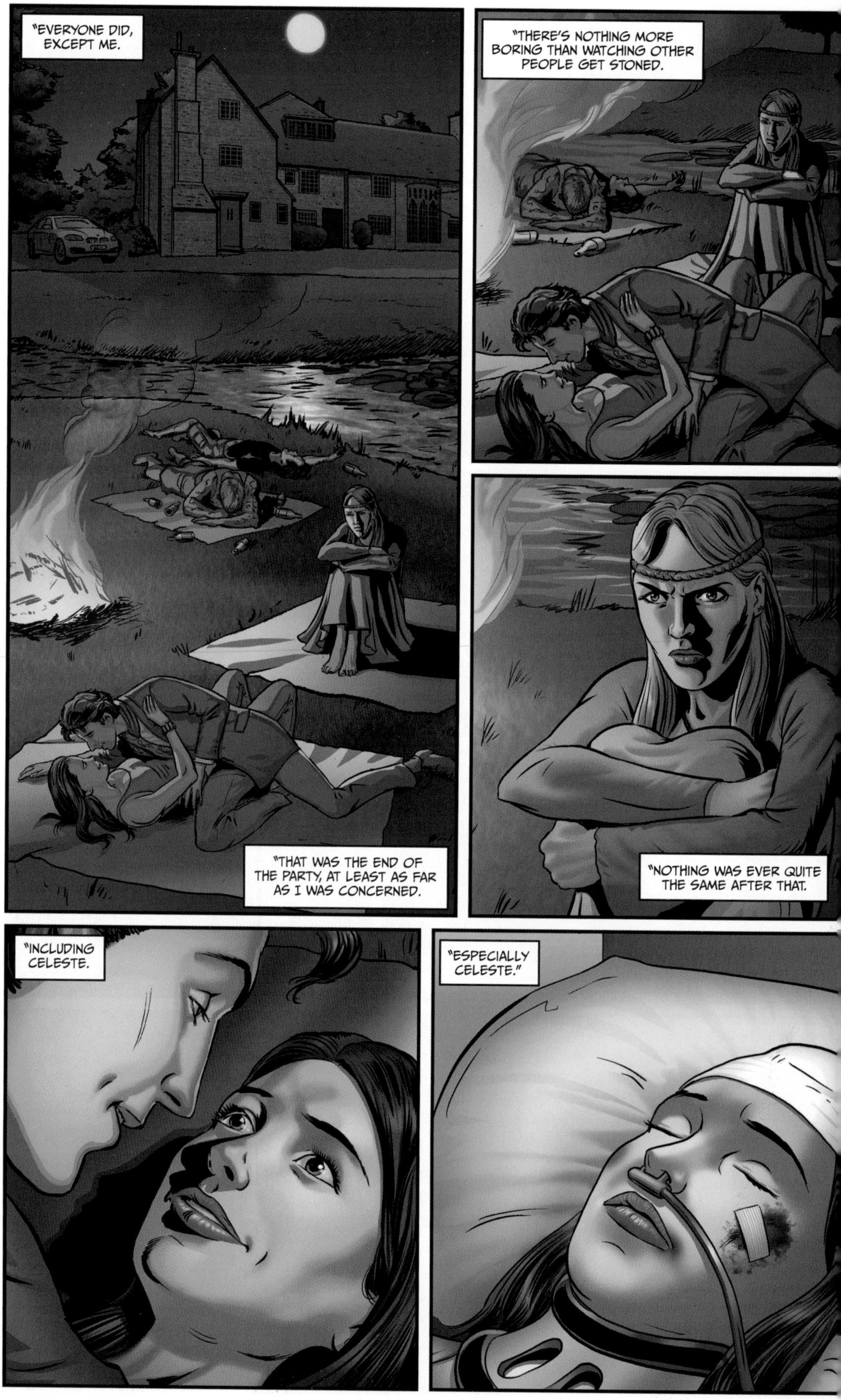
"EVERYONE DID, EXCEPT ME.
"THAT WAS THE END OF THE PARTY, AT LEAST AS FAR AS I WAS CONCERNED.
"THERE'S NOTHING MORE BORING THAN WATCHING OTHER PEOPLE GET STONED.
"NOTHING WAS EVER QUITE THE SAME AFTER THAT.
"INCLUDING CELESTE.
"ESPECIALLY CELESTE."

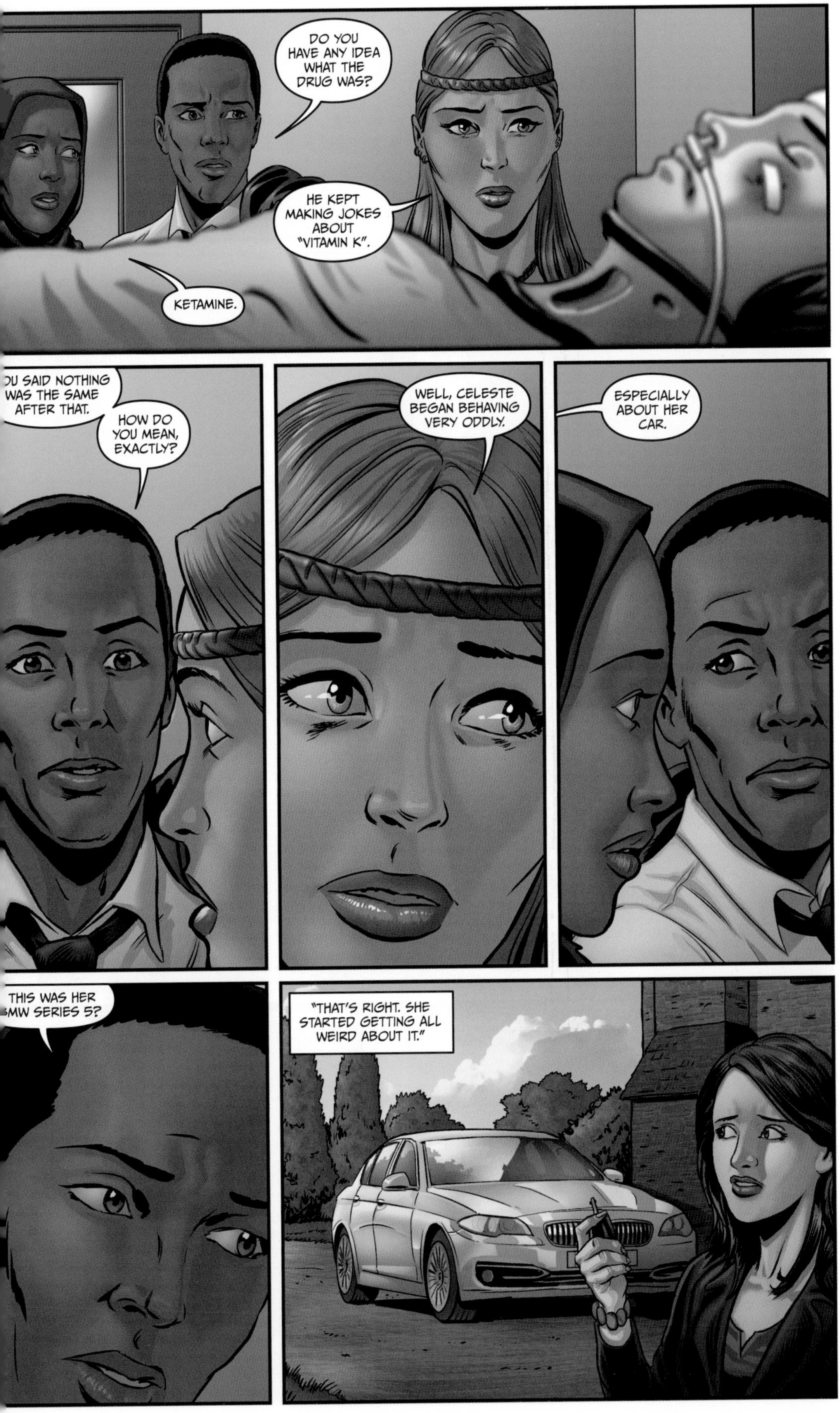
DO YOU HAVE ANY IDEA WHAT THE DRUG WAS?
HE KEPT MAKING JOKES ABOUT "VITAMIN K".
KETAMINE.
OU SAID NOTHING WAS THE SAME AFTER THAT.
HOW DO YOU MEAN, EXACTLY?
WELL, CELESTE BEGAN BEHAVING VERY ODDLY.
ESPECIALLY ABOUT HER CAR.
THIS WAS HER MW SERIES 5?
"THAT'S RIGHT. SHE STARTED GETTING ALL WEIRD ABOUT IT."

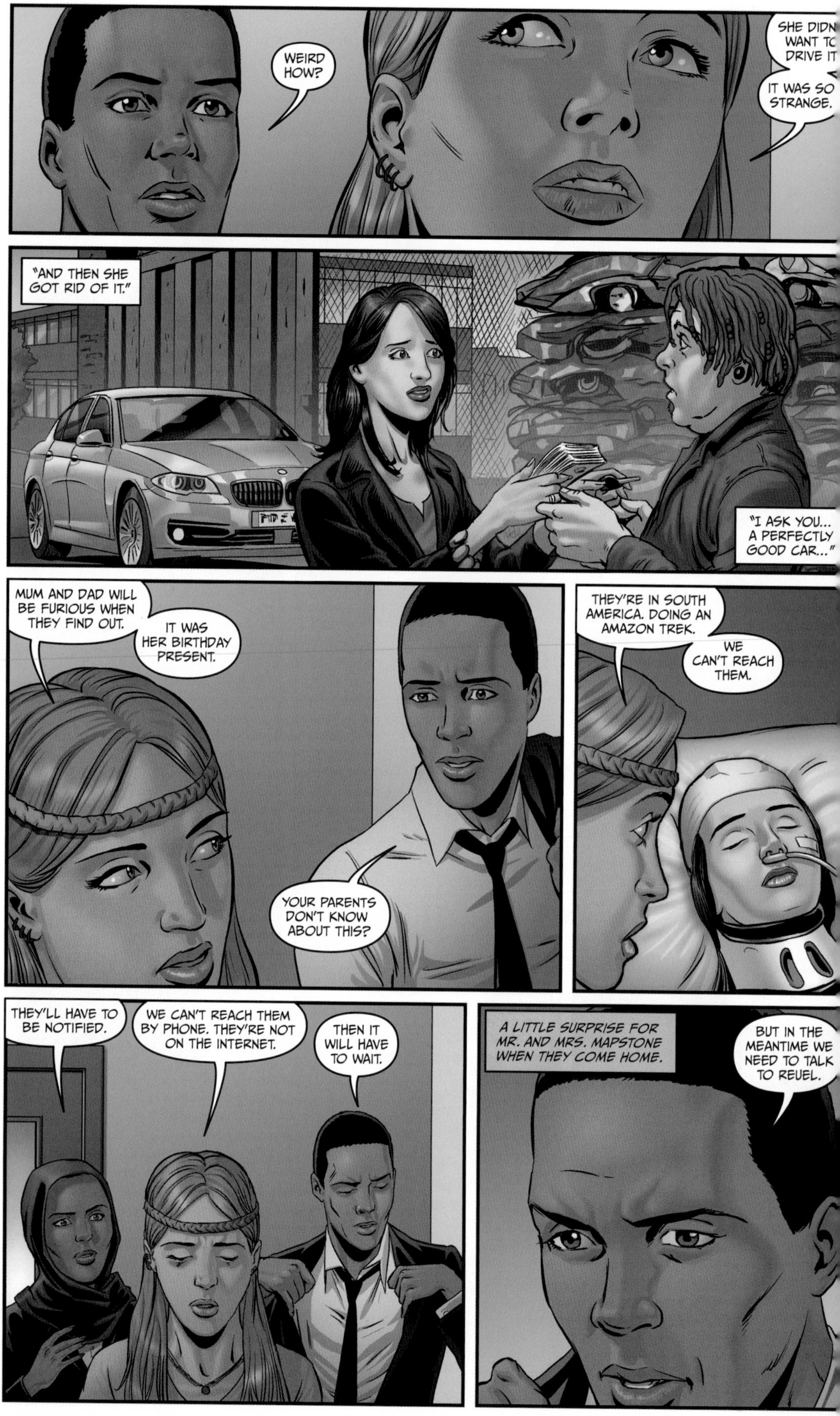
WEIRD HOW?
SHE DIDN WANT TO DRIVE IT
IT WAS SO STRANGE.
"AND THEN SHE GOT RID OF IT."
"I ASK YOU... A PERFECTLY GOOD CAR..."
MUM AND DAD WILL BE FURIOUS WHEN THEY FIND OUT.
IT WAS HER BIRTHDAY PRESENT.
YOUR PARENTS DON'T KNOW ABOUT THIS?
THEY'RE IN SOUTH AMERICA. DOING AN AMAZON TREK.
WE CAN'T REACH THEM.
THEY'LL HAVE TO BE NOTIFIED.
WE CAN'T REACH THEM BY PHONE. THEY'RE NOT ON THE INTERNET.
THEN IT WILL HAVE TO WAIT.
A LITTLE SURPRISE FOR MR. AND MRS. MAPSTONE WHEN THEY COME HOME.
BUT IN THE MEANTIME WE NEED TO TALK TO REUEL.

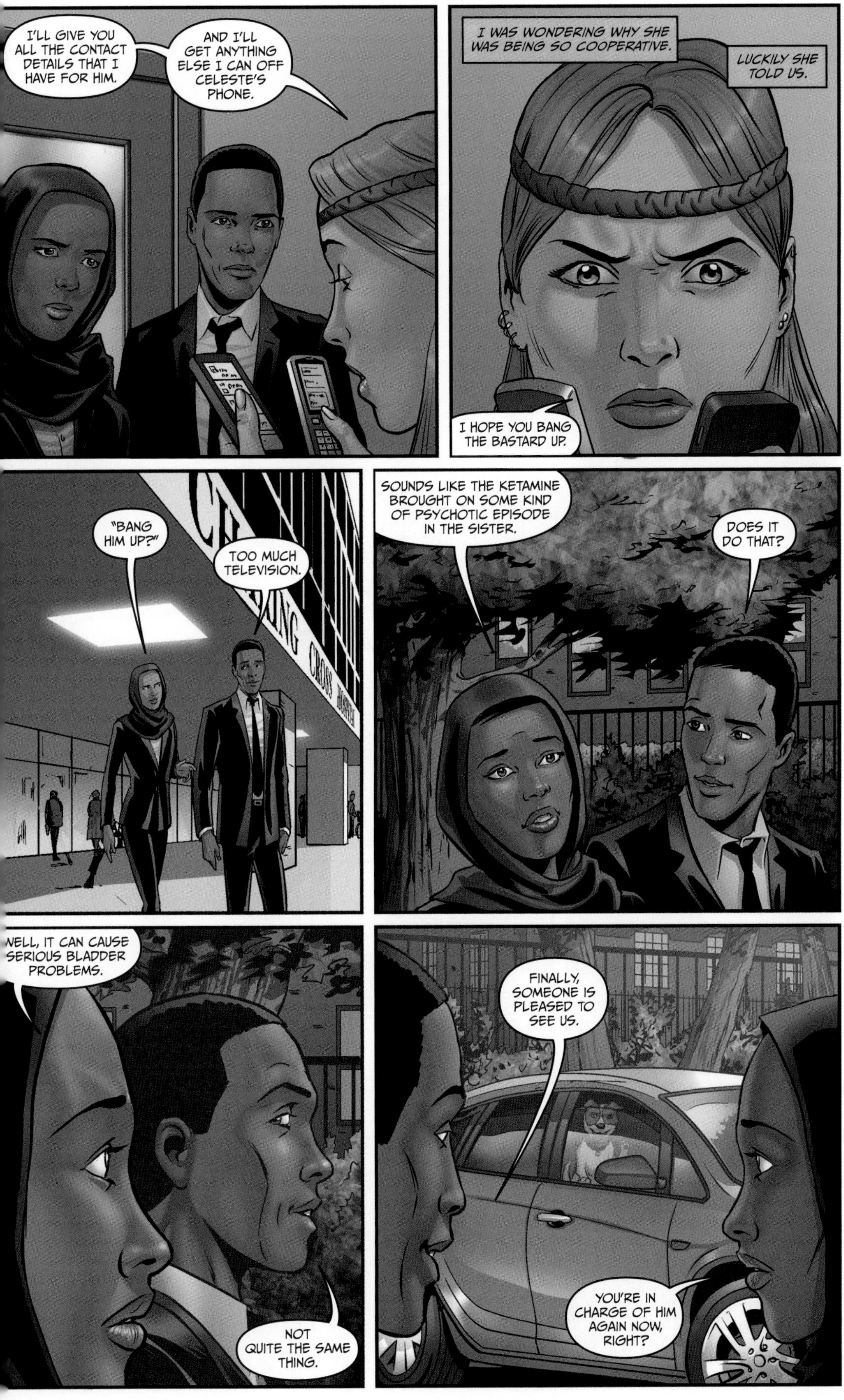
I'LL GIVE YOU ALL THE CONTACT DETAILS THAT I HAVE FOR HIM.
AND I'LL GET ANYTHING ELSE I CAN OFF CELESTE'S PHONE.
I WAS WONDERING WHY SHE WAS BEING SO COOPERATIVE.
LUCKILY SHE TOLD US.
I HOPE YOU BANG THE BASTARD UP.
"BANG HIM UP?"
TOO MUCH TELEVISION.
CROSS
SOUNDS LIKE THE KETAMINE BROUGHT ON SOME KIND OF PSYCHOTIC EPISODE IN THE SISTER.
DOES IT DO THAT?
WELL, IT CAN CAUSE SERIOUS BLADDER PROBLEMS.
NOT QUITE THE SAME THING.
FINALLY, SOMEONE IS PLEASED TO SEE US.
YOU'RE IN CHARGE OF HIM AGAIN NOW, RIGHT?

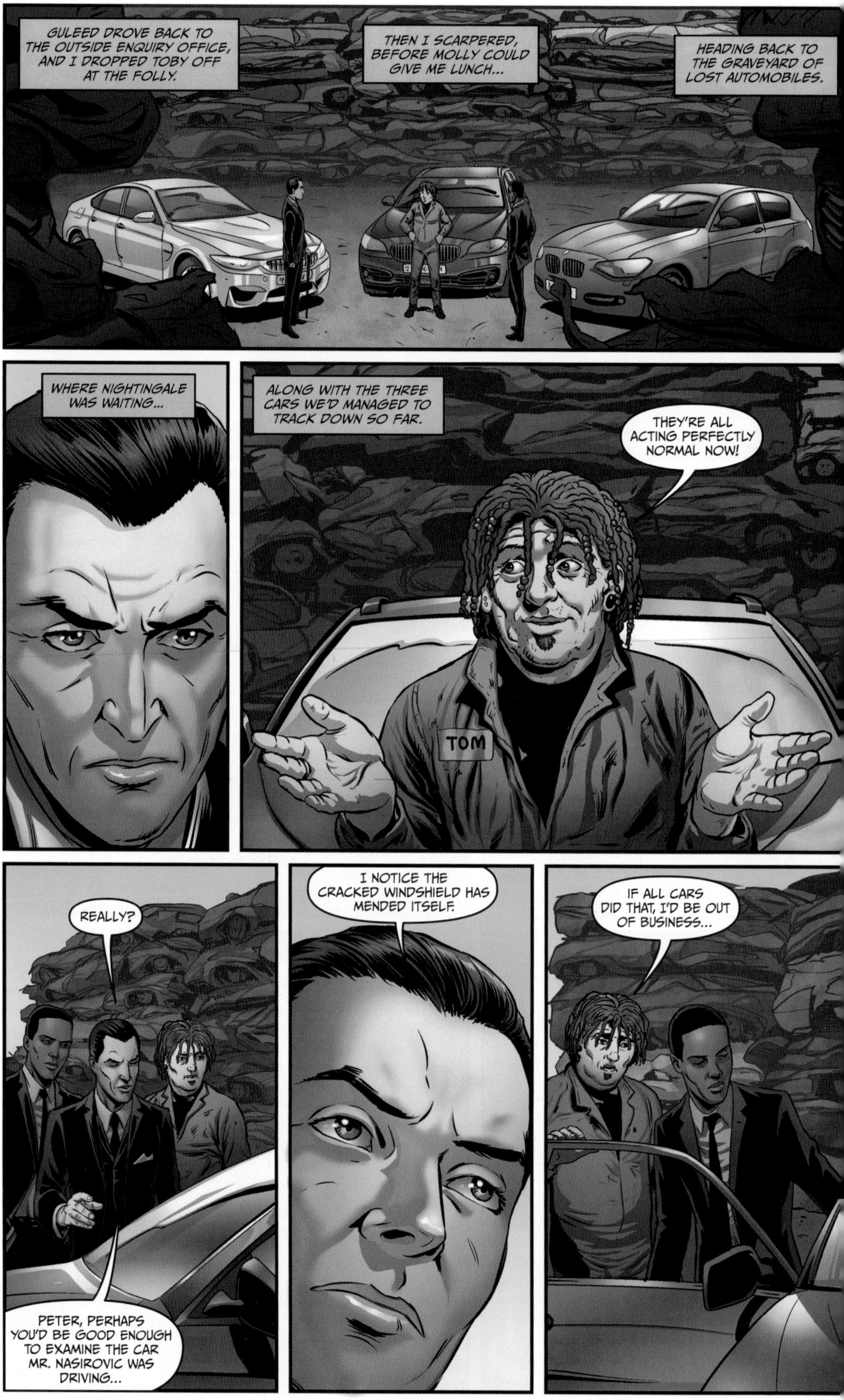
GULEED DROVE BACK TO THE OUTSIDE ENQUIRY OFFICE, AND I DROPPED TOBY OFF AT THE FOLLY.
THEN I SCARPERED, BEFORE MOLLY COULD GIVE ME LUNCH...
HEADING BACK TO THE GRAVEYARD OF LOST AUTOMOBILES.
WHERE NIGHTINGALE WAS WAITING...
ALONG WITH THE THREE CARS WE'D MANAGED TO TRACK DOWN SO FAR.
THEY'RE ALL ACTING PERFECTLY NORMAL NOW!
TOM
REALLY?
PETER, PERHAPS YOU'D BE GOOD ENOUGH TO EXAMINE THE CAR MR. NASIROVIC WAS DRIVING...
I NOTICE THE CRACKED WINDSHIELD HAS MENDED ITSELF.
IF ALL CARS DID THAT, I'D BE OUT OF BUSINESS...

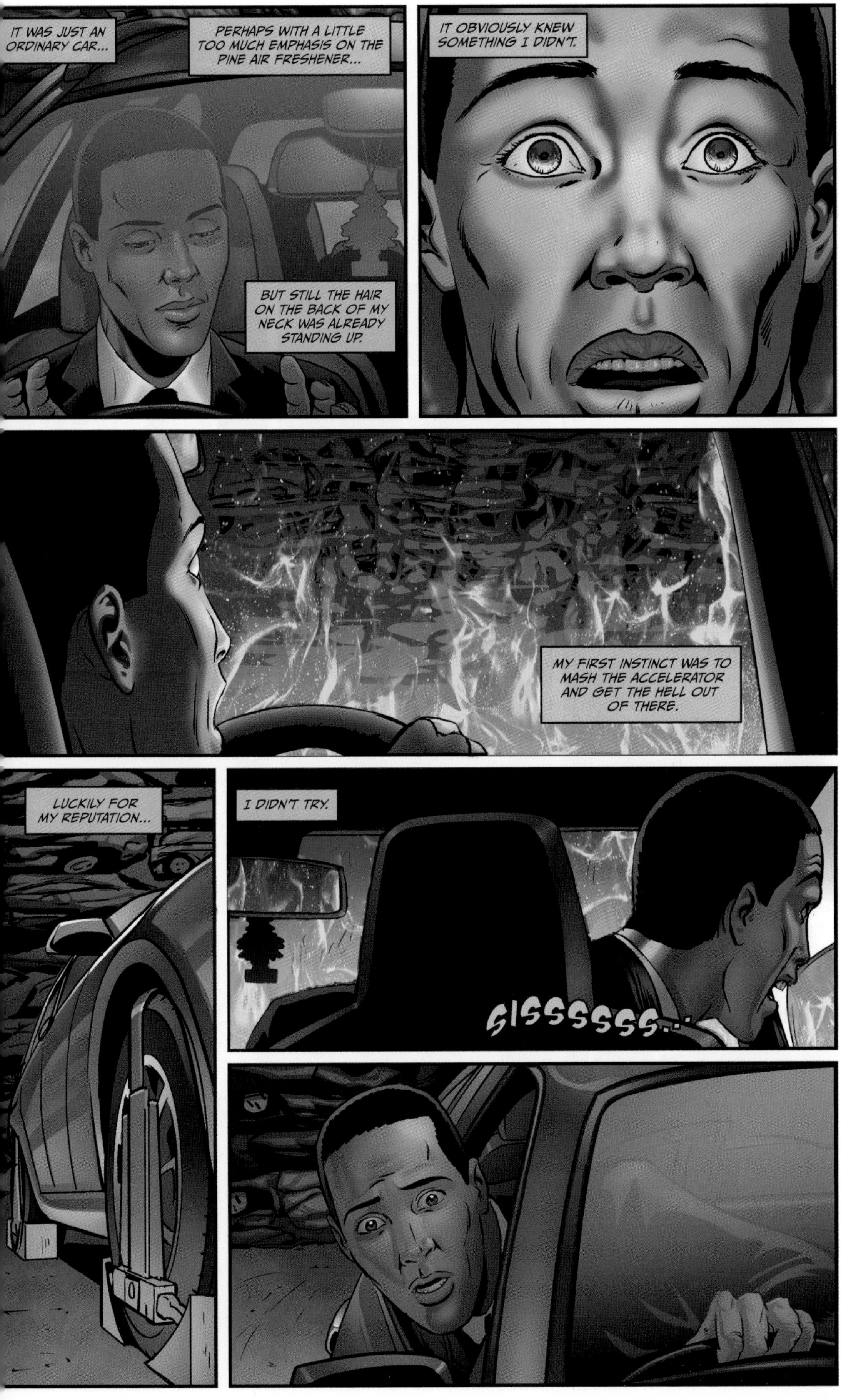
IT WAS JUST AN ORDINARY CAR...
PERHAPS WITH A LITTLE TOO MUCH EMPHASIS ON THE PINE AIR FRESHENER...
BUT STILL THE HAIR ON THE BACK OF MY NECK WAS ALREADY STANDING UP.
IT OBVIOUSLY KNEW SOMETHING I DIDN'T.
MY FIRST INSTINCT WAS TO MASH THE ACCELERATOR AND GET THE HELL OUT OF THERE.
LUCKILY FOR MY REPUTATION...
I DIDN'T TRY.
SISSSSSS...

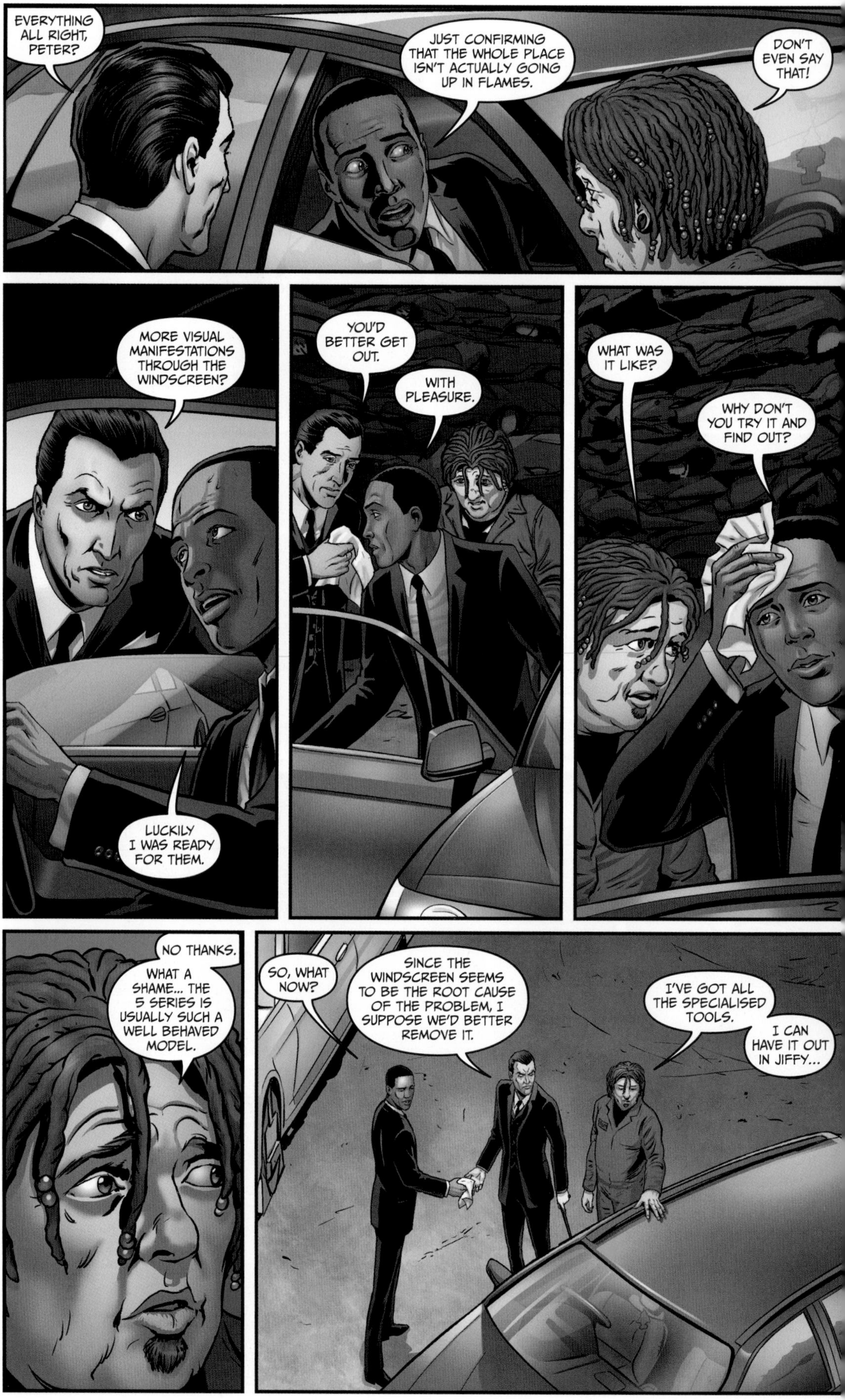

EVERYTHING ALL RIGHT, PETER?
JUST CONFIRMING THAT THE WHOLE PLACE ISN'T ACTUALLY GOING UP IN FLAMES.
DON'T EVEN SAY THAT!
MORE VISUAL MANIFESTATIONS THROUGH THE WINDSCREEN?
LUCKILY I WAS READY FOR THEM.
YOU'D BETTER GET OUT.
WITH PLEASURE.
WHAT WAS IT LIKE?
WHY DON'T YOU TRY IT AND FIND OUT?
NO THANKS.
WHAT A SHAME... THE 5 SERIES IS USUALLY SUCH A WELL BEHAVED MODEL.
SO, WHAT NOW?
SINCE THE WINDSCREEN SEEMS TO BE THE ROOT CAUSE OF THE PROBLEM, I SUPPOSE WE'D BETTER REMOVE IT.
I'VE GOT ALL THE SPECIALISED TOOLS.
I CAN HAVE IT OUT IN JIFFY...

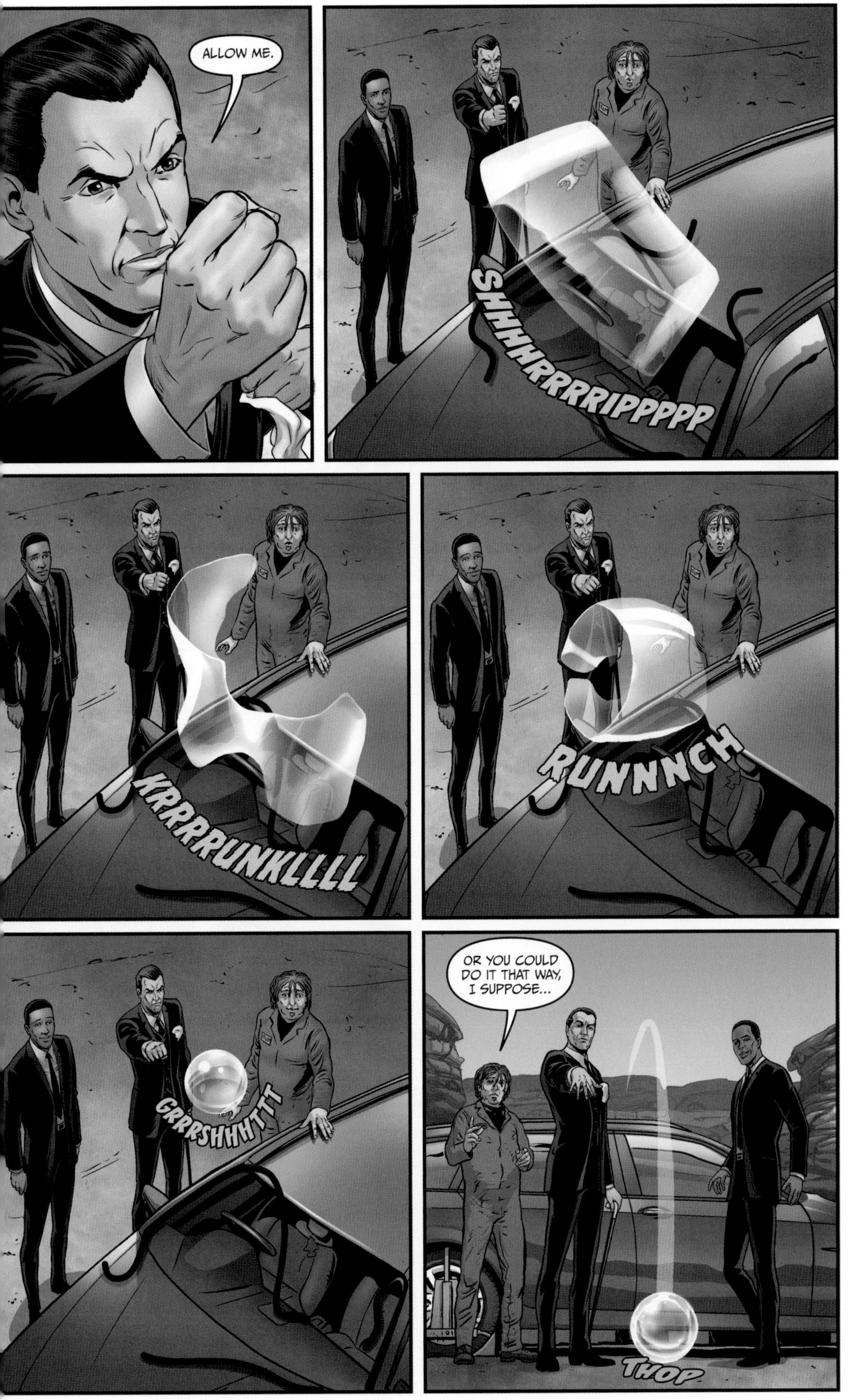
ALLOW ME.
SHHHHRRRRRIPPPPPP
KRRRRRUNKLLLLL
RUNNNCH
GRRRSHHHTTT
OR YOU COULD DO IT THAT WAY, I SUPPOSE...
THOP

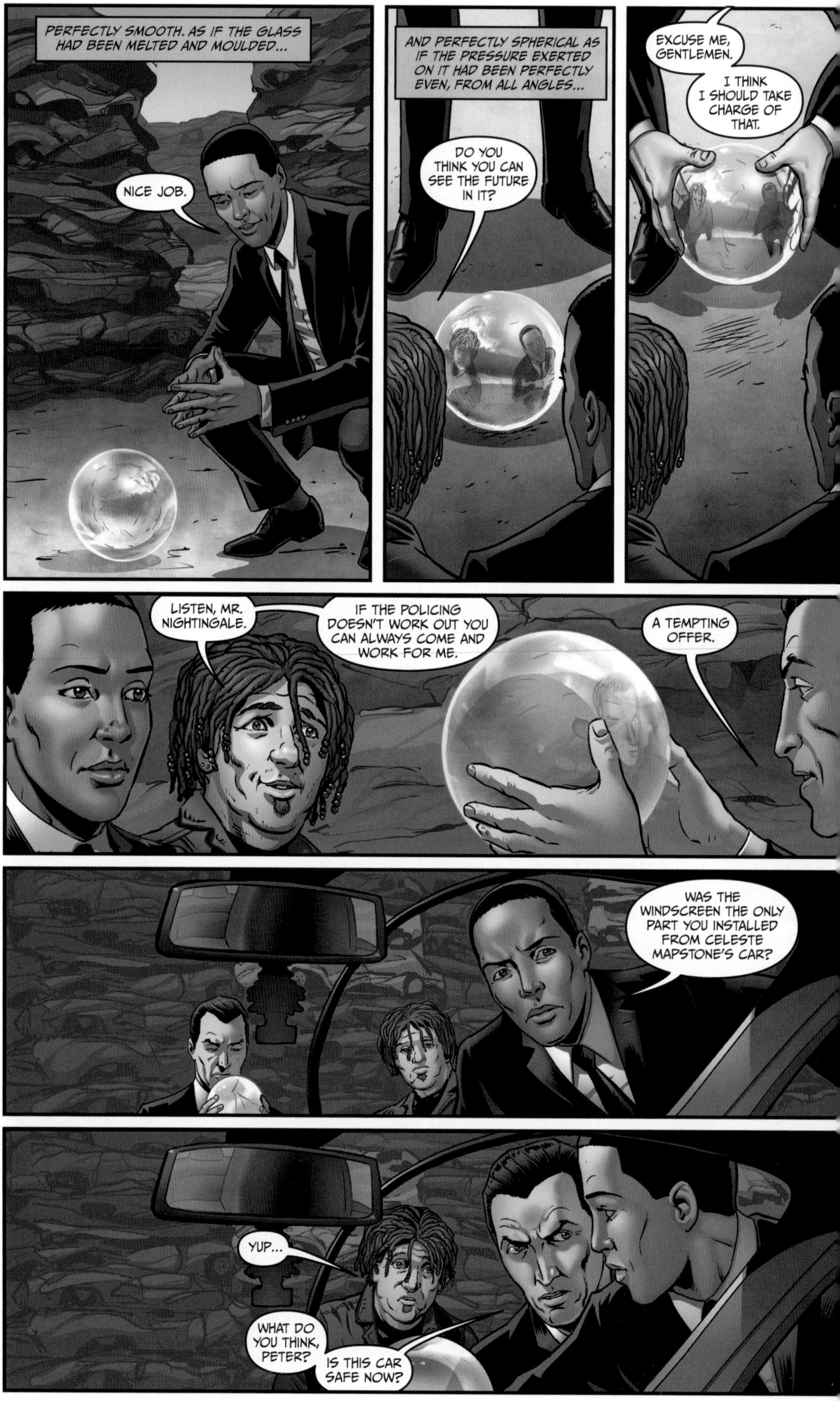
PERFECTLY SMOOTH. AS IF THE GLASS HAD BEEN MELTED AND MOULDED...
NICE JOB.
AND PERFECTLY SPHERICAL AS IF THE PRESSURE EXERTED ON IT HAD BEEN PERFECTLY EVEN, FROM ALL ANGLES...
DO YOU THINK YOU CAN SEE THE FUTURE IN IT?
EXCUSE ME, GENTLEMEN.
I THINK I SHOULD TAKE CHARGE OF THAT.
LISTEN, MR. NIGHTINGALE.
IF THE POLICING DOESN'T WORK OUT YOU CAN ALWAYS COME AND WORK FOR ME.
A TEMPTING OFFER.
WAS THE WINDSCREEN THE ONLY PART YOU INSTALLED FROM CELESTE MAPSTONE'S CAR?
YUP...
WHAT DO YOU THINK, PETER?
IS THIS CAR SAFE NOW?

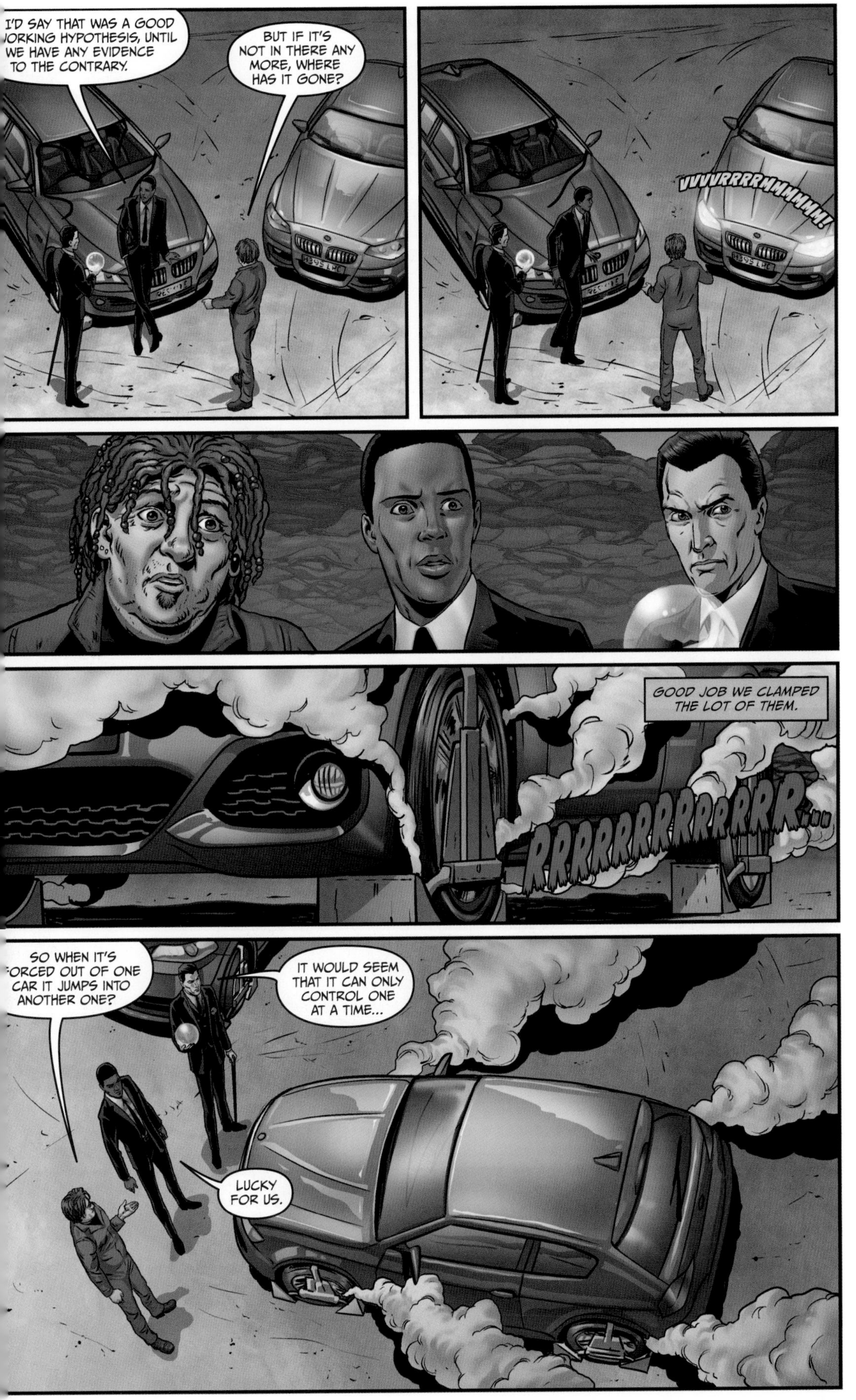
I'D SAY THAT WAS A GOOD WORKING HYPOTHESIS, UNTIL WE HAVE ANY EVIDENCE TO THE CONTRARY.
BUT IF IT'S NOT IN THERE ANY MORE, WHERE HAS IT GONE?
VVVVVRRRRMMMMMMM!
GOOD JOB WE CLAMPED THE LOT OF THEM.
RRRRRRRRRRRRR...
SO WHEN IT'S FORCED OUT OF ONE CAR IT JUMPS INTO ANOTHER ONE?
IT WOULD SEEM THAT IT CAN ONLY CONTROL ONE AT A TIME...
LUCKY FOR US.

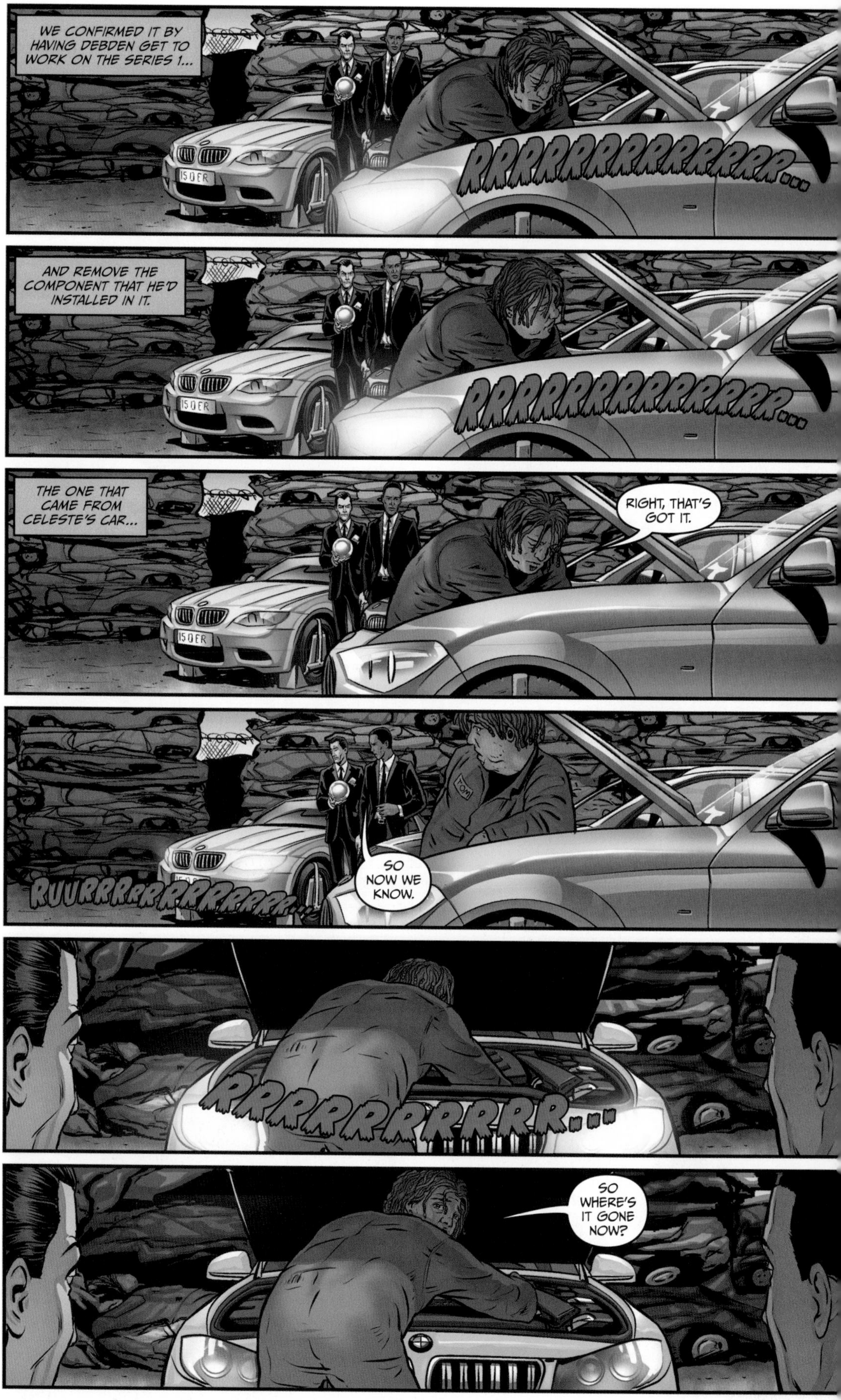
WE CONFIRMED IT BY HAVING DEBDEN GET TO WORK ON THE SERIES 1...
RRRRRRRRRRRRRRRR...
AND REMOVE THE COMPONENT THAT HE'D INSTALLED IN IT.
RRRRRRRRRRRRRRRR...
THE ONE THAT CAME FROM CELESTE'S CAR...
RIGHT, THAT'S GOT IT.
SO NOW WE KNOW.
RUURRRRRRRRRRRRR...
RRRRRRRRRRRR...
SO WHERE'S IT GONE NOW?

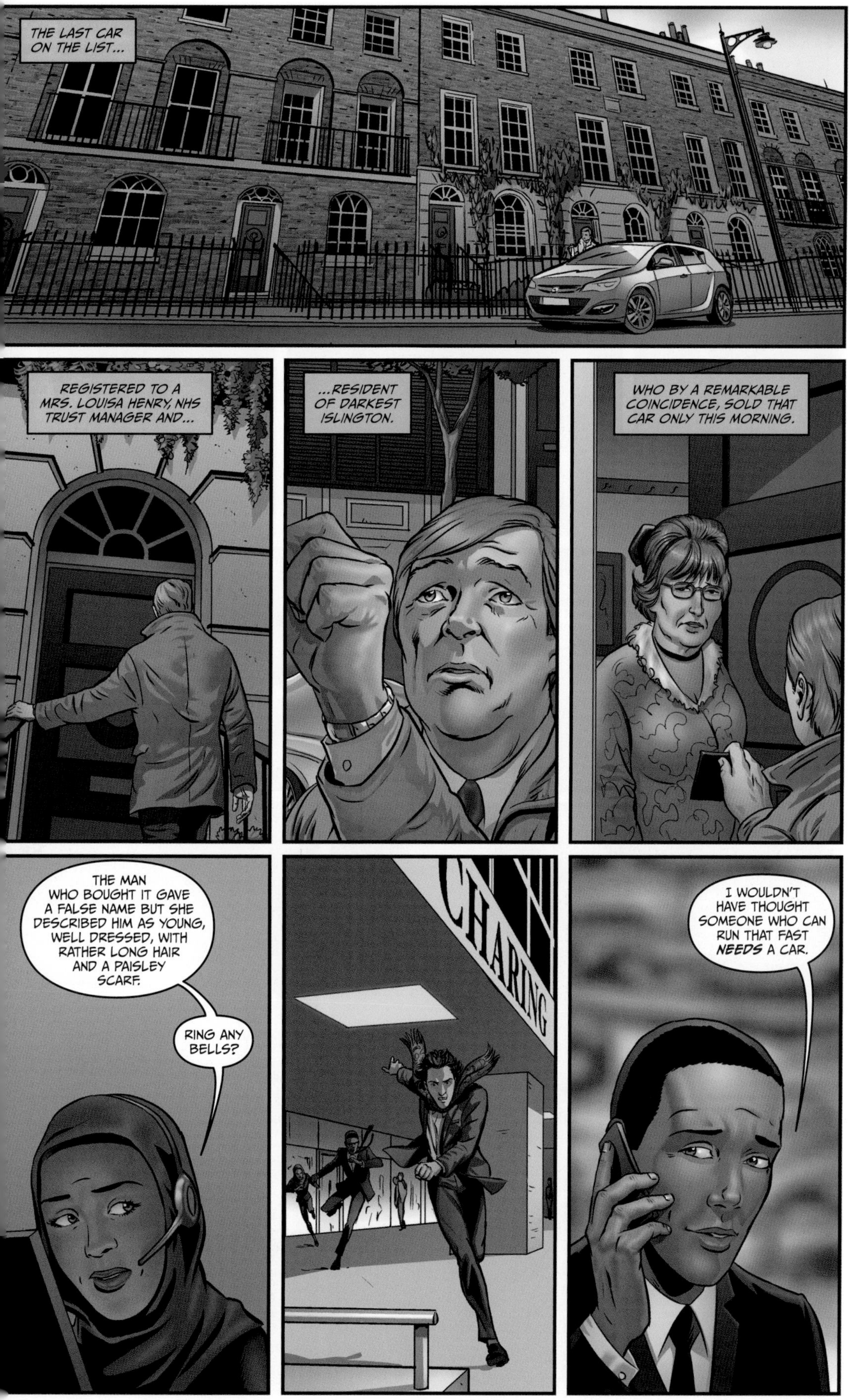
THE LAST CAR ON THE LIST...
REGISTERED TO A MRS. LOUISA HENRY, NHS TRUST MANAGER AND...
...RESIDENT OF DARKEST ISLINGTON.
WHO BY A REMARKABLE COINCIDENCE, SOLD THAT CAR ONLY THIS MORNING.
THE MAN WHO BOUGHT IT GAVE A FALSE NAME BUT SHE DESCRIBED HIM AS YOUNG, WELL DRESSED, WITH RATHER LONG HAIR AND A PAISLEY SCARF.
RING ANY BELLS?
CHARING
I WOULDN'T HAVE THOUGHT SOMEONE WHO CAN RUN THAT FAST NEEDS A CAR.

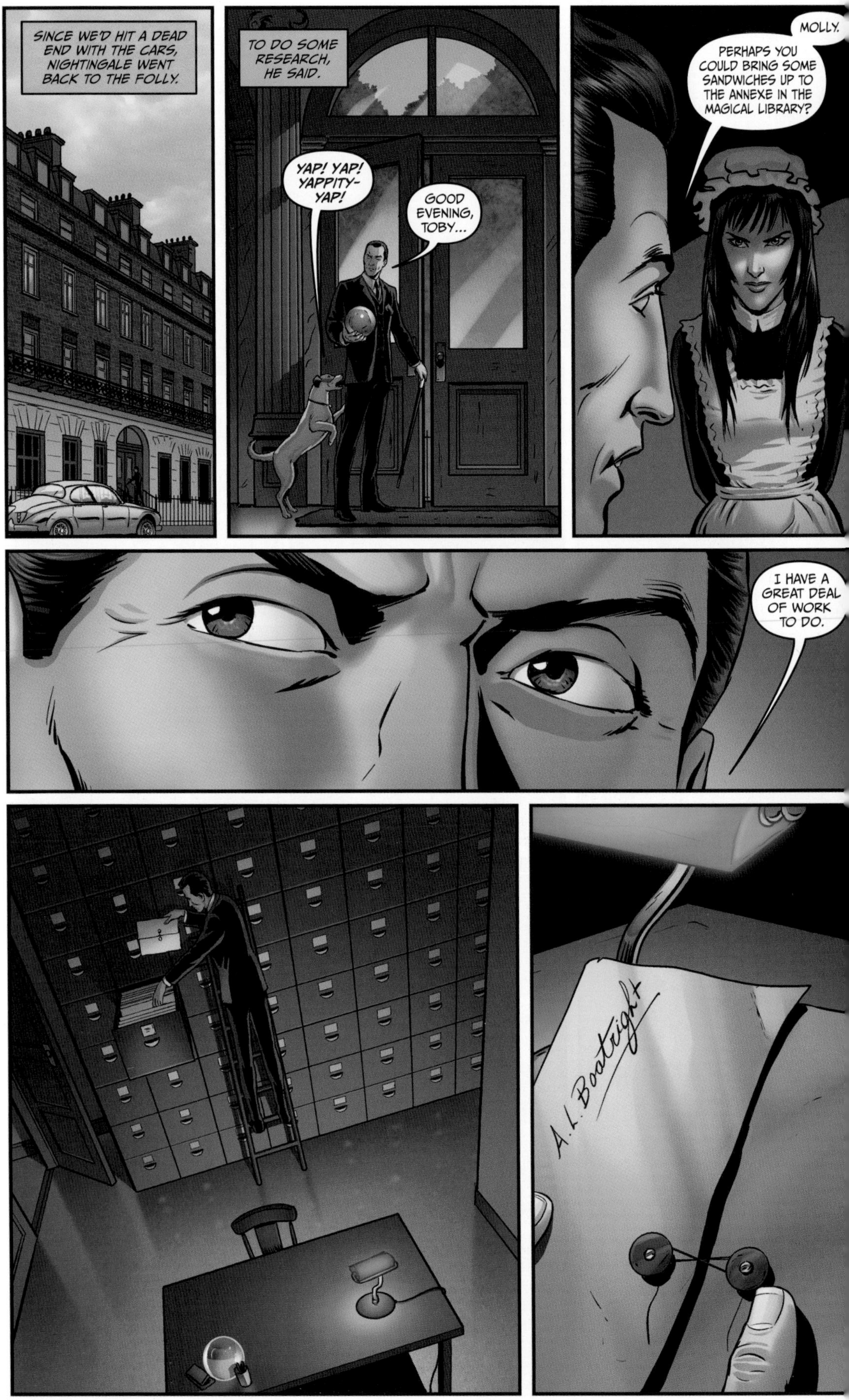
SINCE WE'D HIT A DEAD END WITH THE CARS, NIGHTINGALE WENT BACK TO THE FOLLY.
TO DO SOME RESEARCH, HE SAID.
YAP! YAP! YAPPITY-YAP!
GOOD EVENING, TOBY...
MOLLY.
PERHAPS YOU COULD BRING SOME SANDWICHES UP TO THE ANNEXE IN THE MAGICAL LIBRARY?
I HAVE A GREAT DEAL OF WORK TO DO.
A. L. Boatright

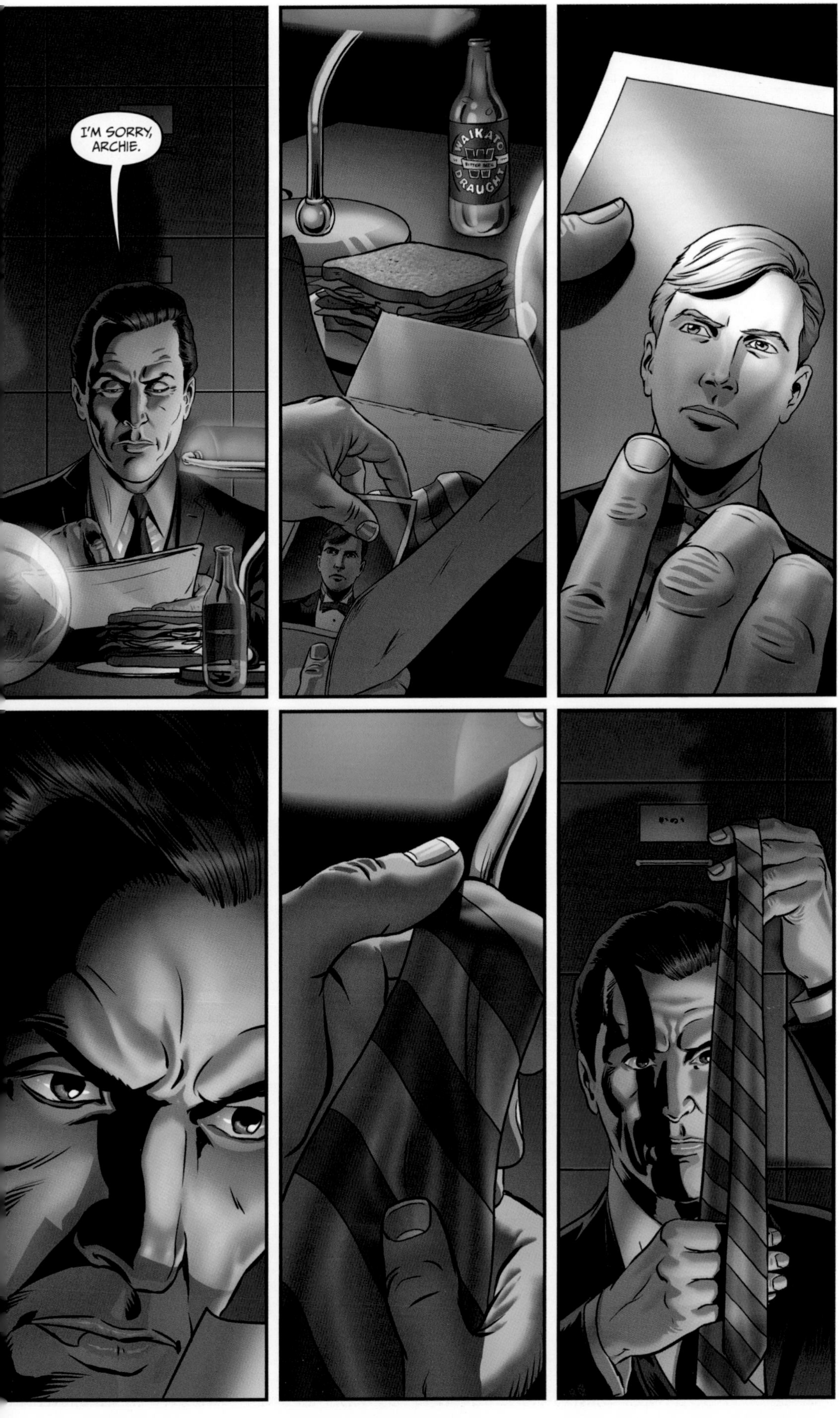
I'M SORRY, ARCHIE.
WAIKATO
DRAUGHT

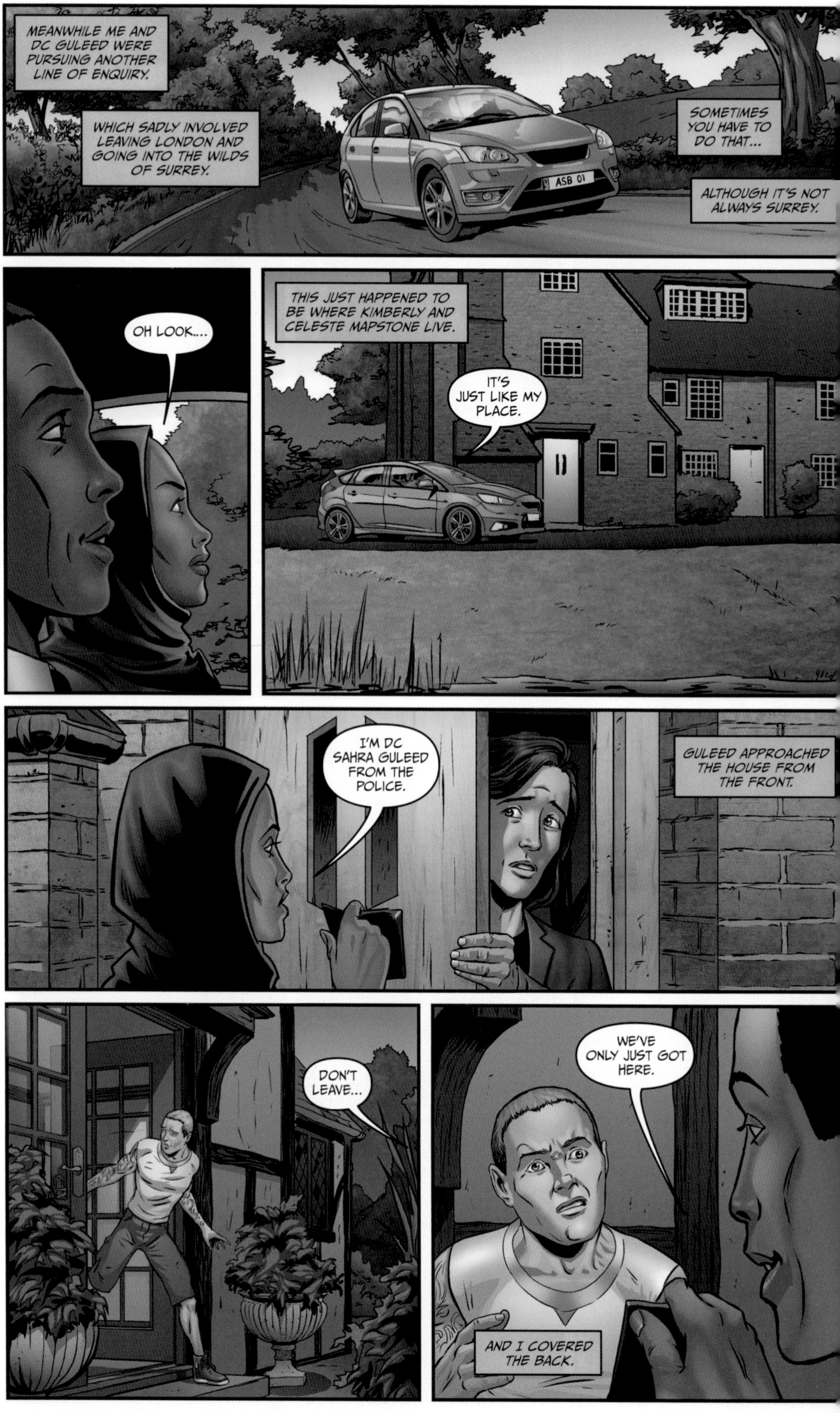
MEANWHILE ME AND DC GULEED WERE PURSUING ANOTHER LINE OF ENQUIRY.
WHICH SADLY INVOLVED LEAVING LONDON AND GOING INTO THE WILDS OF SURREY.
ASB 01
SOMETIMES YOU HAVE TO DO THAT...
ALTHOUGH IT'S NOT ALWAYS SURREY.
OH LOOK....
THIS JUST HAPPENED TO BE WHERE KIMBERLY AND CELESTE MAPSTONE LIVE.
IT'S JUST LIKE MY PLACE.
I'M DC SAHRA GULEED FROM THE POLICE.
GULEED APPROACHED THE HOUSE FROM THE FRONT.
DON'T LEAVE...
WE'VE ONLY JUST GOT HERE.
AND I COVERED THE BACK.

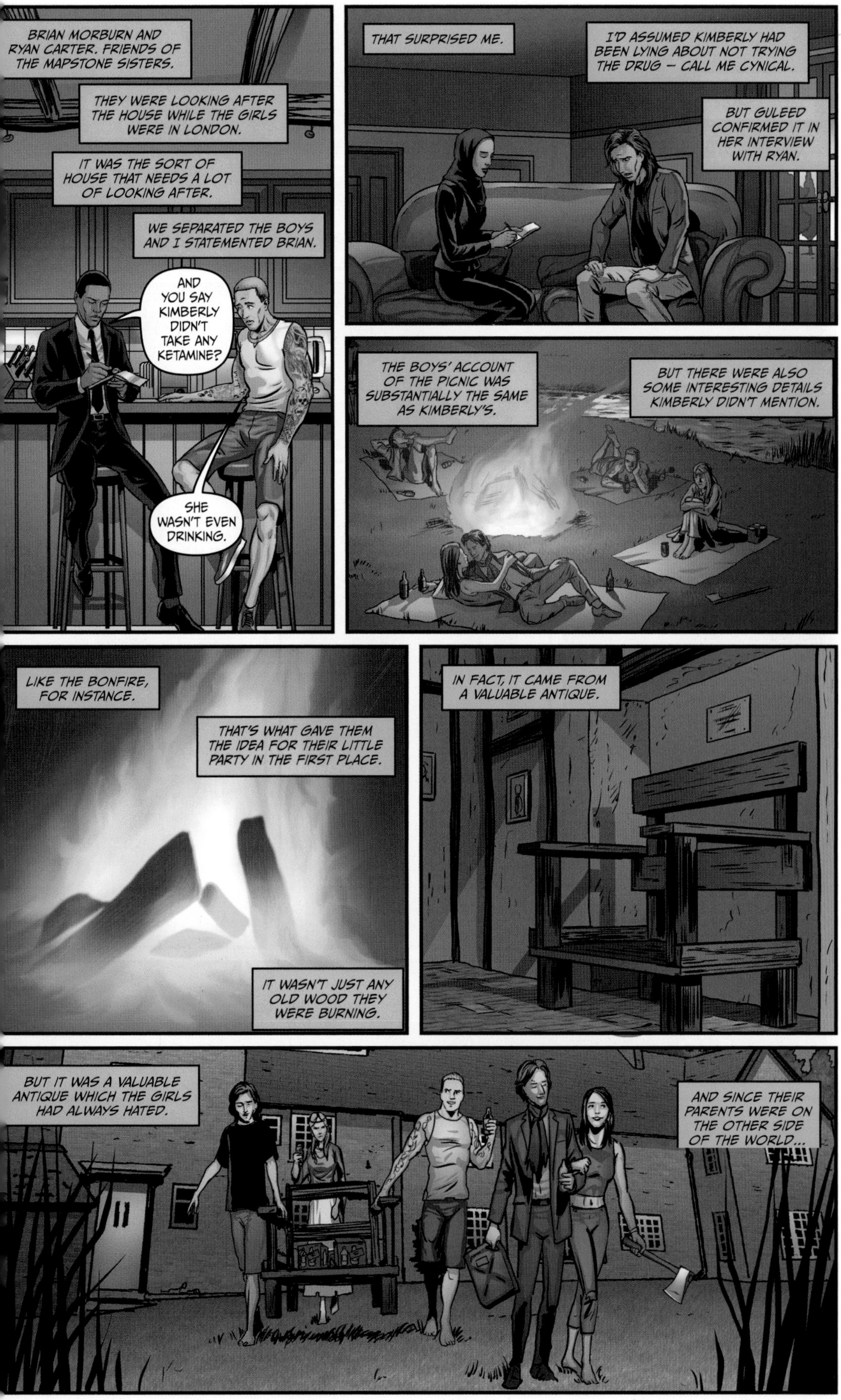
BRIAN MORBURN AND RYAN CARTER. FRIENDS OF THE MAPSTONE SISTERS.
THEY WERE LOOKING AFTER THE HOUSE WHILE THE GIRLS WERE IN LONDON.
IT WAS THE SORT OF HOUSE THAT NEEDS A LOT OF LOOKING AFTER.
WE SEPARATED THE BOYS AND I STATEMENTED BRIAN.
AND YOU SAY KIMBERLY DIDN'T TAKE ANY KETAMINE?
SHE WASN'T EVEN DRINKING.
THAT SURPRISED ME.
I'D ASSUMED KIMBERLY HAD BEEN LYING ABOUT NOT TRYING THE DRUG — CALL ME CYNICAL.
BUT GULEED CONFIRMED IT IN HER INTERVIEW WITH RYAN.
THE BOYS' ACCOUNT OF THE PICNIC WAS SUBSTANTIALLY THE SAME AS KIMBERLY'S.
BUT THERE WERE ALSO SOME INTERESTING DETAILS KIMBERLY DIDN'T MENTION.
LIKE THE BONFIRE, FOR INSTANCE.
THAT'S WHAT GAVE THEM THE IDEA FOR THEIR LITTLE PARTY IN THE FIRST PLACE.
IT WASN'T JUST ANY OLD WOOD THEY WERE BURNING.
IN FACT, IT CAME FROM A VALUABLE ANTIQUE.
BUT IT WAS A VALUABLE ANTIQUE WHICH THE GIRLS HAD ALWAYS HATED.
AND SINCE THEIR PARENTS WERE ON THE OTHER SIDE OF THE WORLD...

THEY SAW THEIR CHANCE.

APPARENTLY IT HAD ALWAYS GIVEN THE GIRLS THE CREEPS.

THERE WAS A PLAQUE ON THE WALL DESCRIBING THIS ITEM OF FURNITURE...

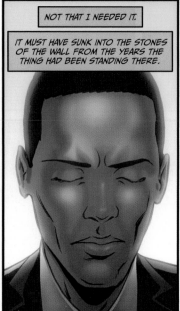

NOT THAT I NEEDED IT.

IT MUST HAVE SUNK INTO THE STONES OF THE WALL FROM THE YEARS THE THING HAD BEEN STANDING THERE.

FLAPFLAPFLAPFLAP...

THE ANGRY MURMURING OF A CROWD...

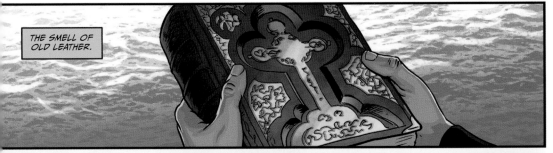

THE SMELL OF OLD LEATHER.

THAT ANGRY MURMURING...

THE REEK OF SWEAT AND RAGE.

THE ICY STINGING IMPACT OF WATER.

THE SUFFOCATING WEIGHT OF IT.

COLD WATER POURING INTO YOUR NOSE, YOUR THROAT, FILLING YOUR LUNGS...

AND THAT RAGE...

BUT ALWAYS THAT RAGE...

I NEED TO TALK TO NIGHTINGALE.

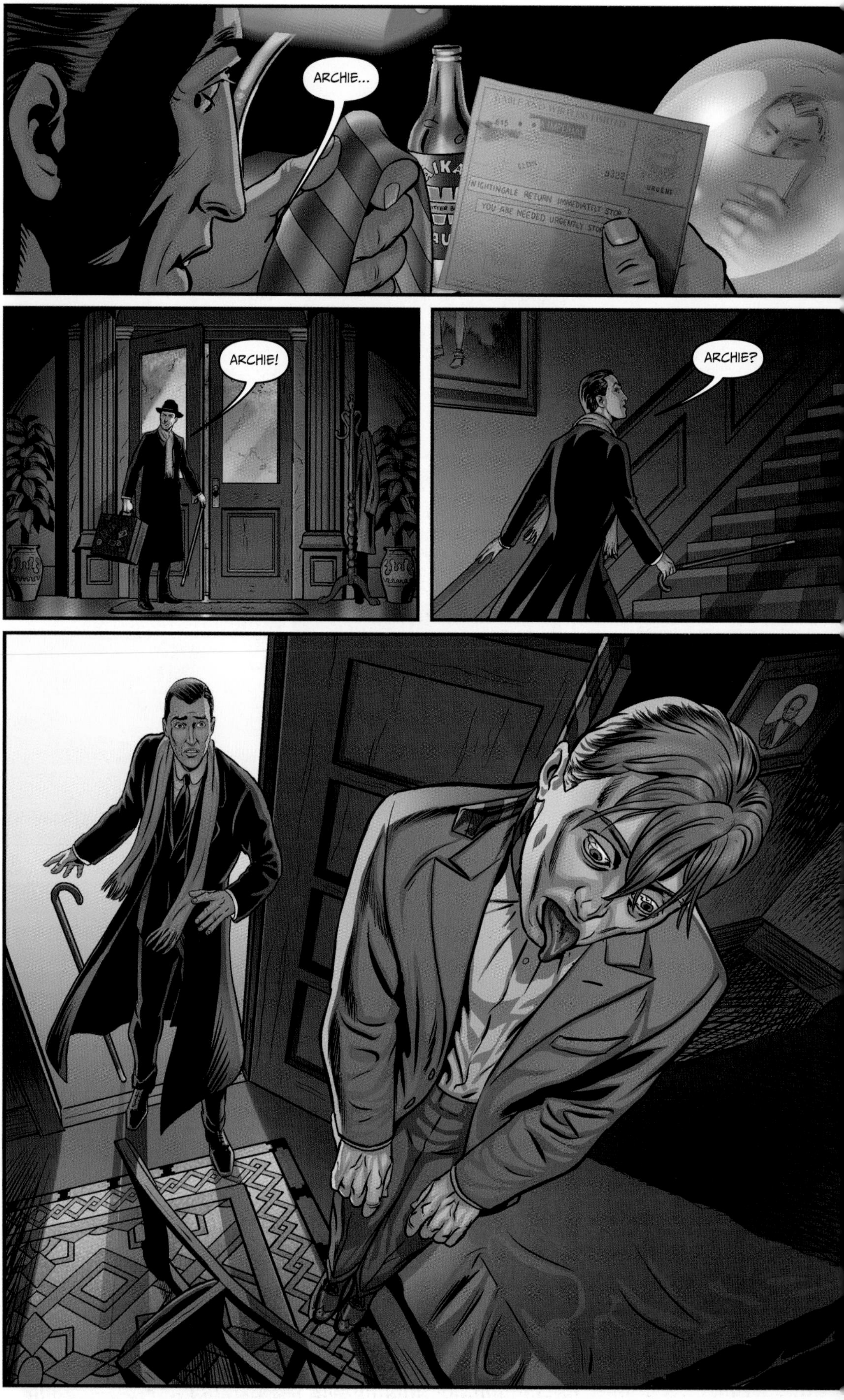
ARCHIE...
CABLE AND WIRELESS LIMITED
615
IMPERIAL
9322
URGENT
NIGHTINGALE RETURN IMMEDIATELY STOP
YOU ARE NEEDED URGENTLY STO
ARCHIE!
ARCHIE?

YOUR FRIENDLY NEIGHBORHOOD LATE MEDIEVAL MANOR HOUSE OFTEN HAD A FISH POND.

IT WAS ALSO HANDY FOR TORTURING ANY LOCAL WOMEN WHO DIDN'T CONFORM TO CURRENT SOCIAL NORMS.

THE GENTRY HAD TO BE KEPT STOCKED UP WITH FISH FOR THOSE MEAT-FREE FRIDAYS.

OF COURSE, IF IT WAS EQUIPPED WITH A DUCKING STOOL...

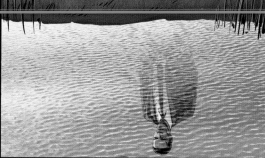

AND SOMETIMES THE WHOLESOME FUN OF TORTURE WENT A LITTLE TOO FAR...

AND SOMEONE ENDED UP DROWNING.

THIS IS ALL STARTING TO MAKE SENSE... SORT OF.

I NEED TO TALK TO NIGHTINGALE.

BUT HE ISN'T ANSWERING.

SOME OF US HAVE TO WORK FOR A LIVING, YOU KNOW.

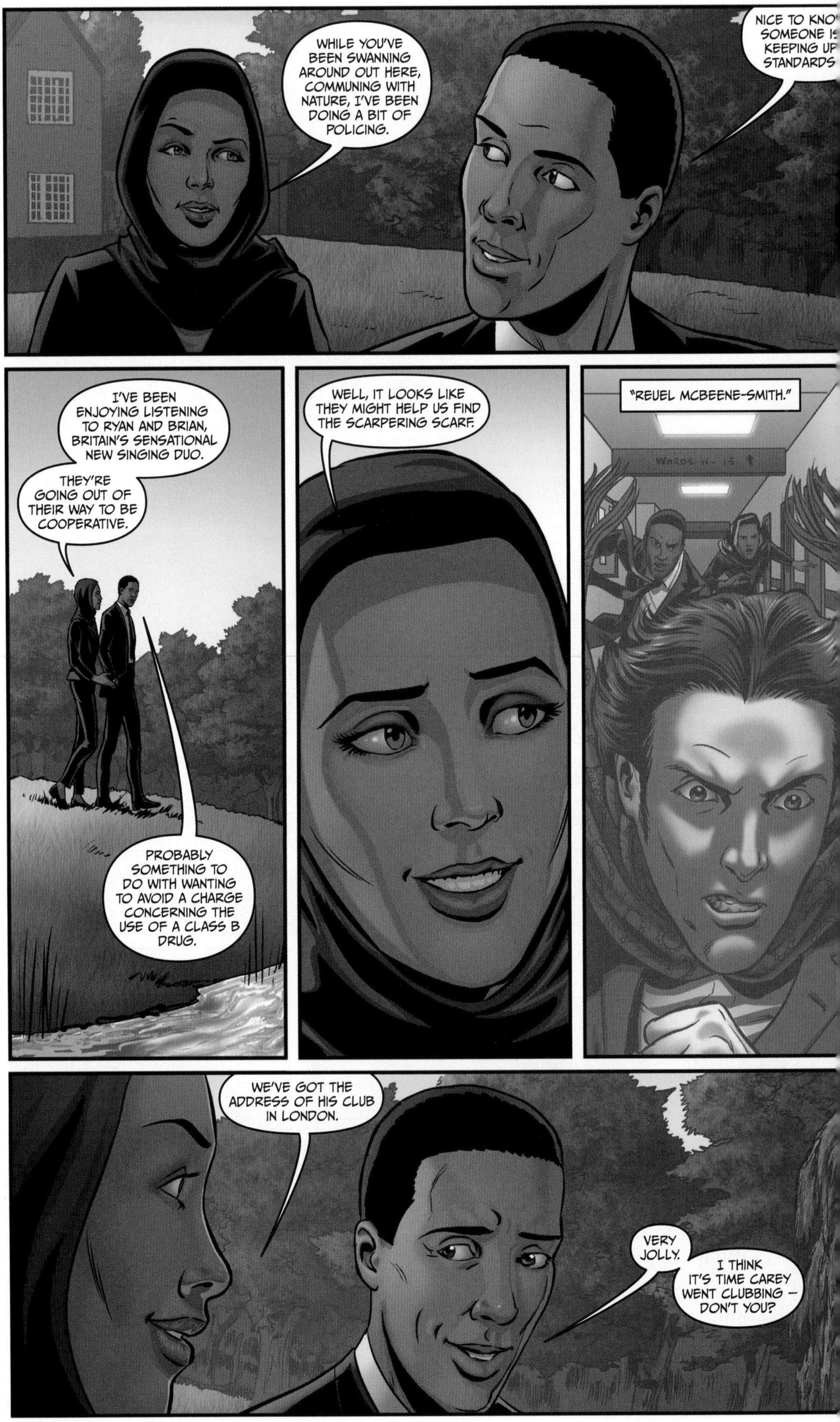
WHILE YOU'VE BEEN SWANNING AROUND OUT HERE, COMMUNING WITH NATURE, I'VE BEEN DOING A BIT OF POLICING.
NICE TO KNO
SOMEONE IS
KEEPING UP
STANDARDS
I'VE BEEN ENJOYING LISTENING TO RYAN AND BRIAN, BRITAIN'S SENSATIONAL NEW SINGING DUO.
THEY'RE GOING OUT OF THEIR WAY TO BE COOPERATIVE.
PROBABLY SOMETHING TO DO WITH WANTING TO AVOID A CHARGE CONCERNING THE USE OF A CLASS B DRUG.
WELL, IT LOOKS LIKE THEY MIGHT HELP US FIND THE SCARPERING SCARF.
"REUEL MCBEENE-SMITH."
WE'VE GOT THE ADDRESS OF HIS CLUB IN LONDON.
VERY JOLLY.
I THINK IT'S TIME CAREY WENT CLUBBING — DON'T YOU?

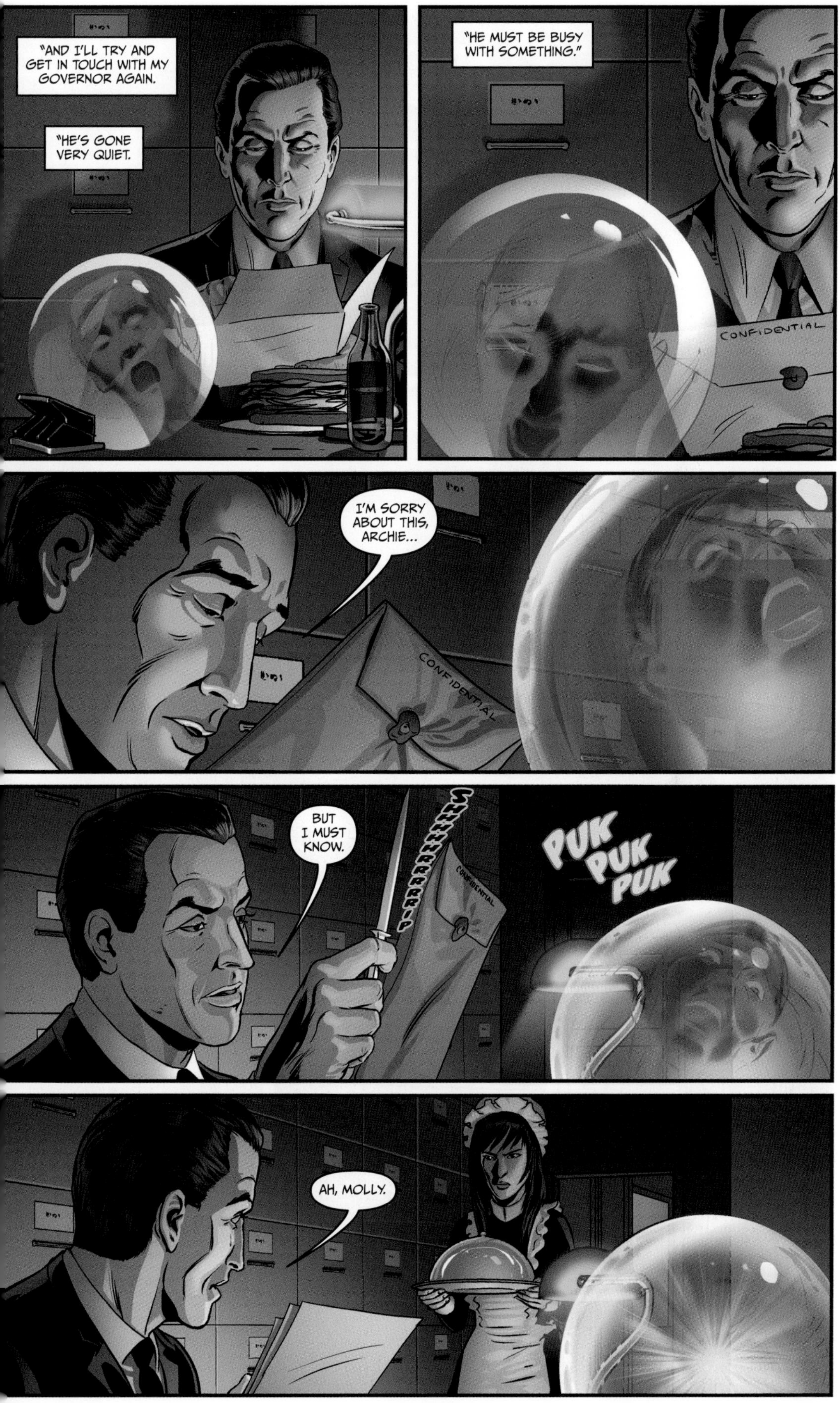
"AND I'LL TRY AND GET IN TOUCH WITH MY GOVERNOR AGAIN.
"HE'S GONE VERY QUIET.
"HE MUST BE BUSY WITH SOMETHING."
CONFIDENTIAL
I'M SORRY ABOUT THIS, ARCHIE...
CONFIDENTIAL
BUT I MUST KNOW.
SHHHHRRRRRIP
CONFIDENTIAL
PUK PUK PUK
AH, MOLLY.

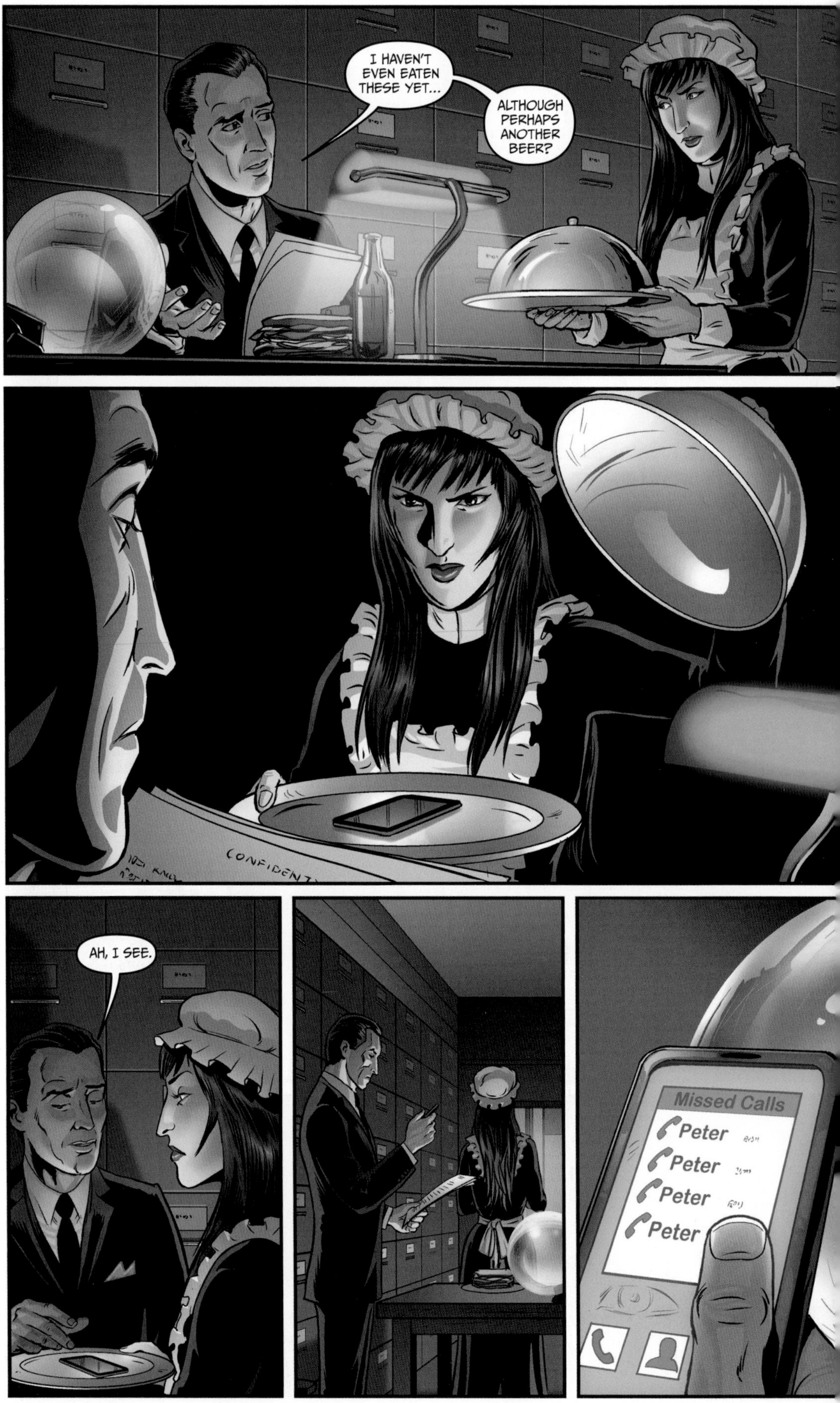
I HAVEN'T EVEN EATEN THESE YET...
ALTHOUGH PERHAPS ANOTHER BEER?
AH, I SEE.
Missed Calls
Peter
Peter
Peter
Peter

I APOLOGIZE FOR MY TARDY RESPONSE. I'D LEFT MY PHONE DOWNSTAIRS.

HAVE YOU LISTENED TO THE MESSAGES I LEFT ON VOICEMAIL?

VOICEMAIL? AH...

LET ME SEE... VOICEMAIL...

NEVER MIND.

WE'VE BEEN LOOKING FOR A CONNECTION, HAVEN'T WE?

"BETWEEN THESE TWO CASES.

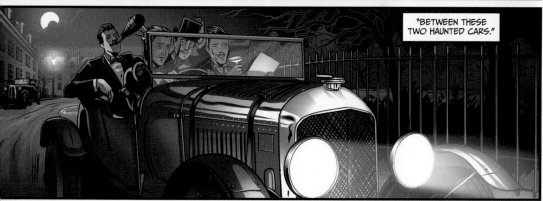

"BETWEEN THESE TWO HAUNTED CARS."

I KNOW I MYSELF USED THE TERM "HAUNTED".

BUT I'M NOT SURE IT'S ENTIRELY...

I THINK I'VE FOUND THE CONNECTION.

THE THING BOTH CASES HAVE IN COMMON.

"WE KNEW THIS BMW BUSINESS ALL STARTED WHEN THESE RICH KIDS HAD A DRUGS PICNIC."

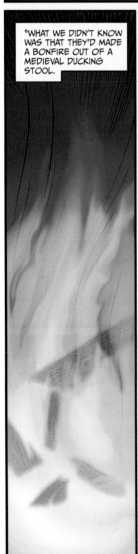

"WHAT WE DIDN'T KNOW WAS THAT THEY'D MADE A BONFIRE OUT OF A MEDIEVAL DUCKING STOOL.

A DUCKING STOOL?

FASCINATING...

THE STOOL WAS BURNED TO ASH.

BUT I INSPECTED THE ALCOVE IN THE HOUSE WHERE IT HAD BEEN STORED...

THE VESTIGIA THERE NEARLY KNOCKED ME OFF MY FEET.

"THERE WAS THIS WOMAN WHO DIED IN THE DUCKING STOOL.

"DROWNED."

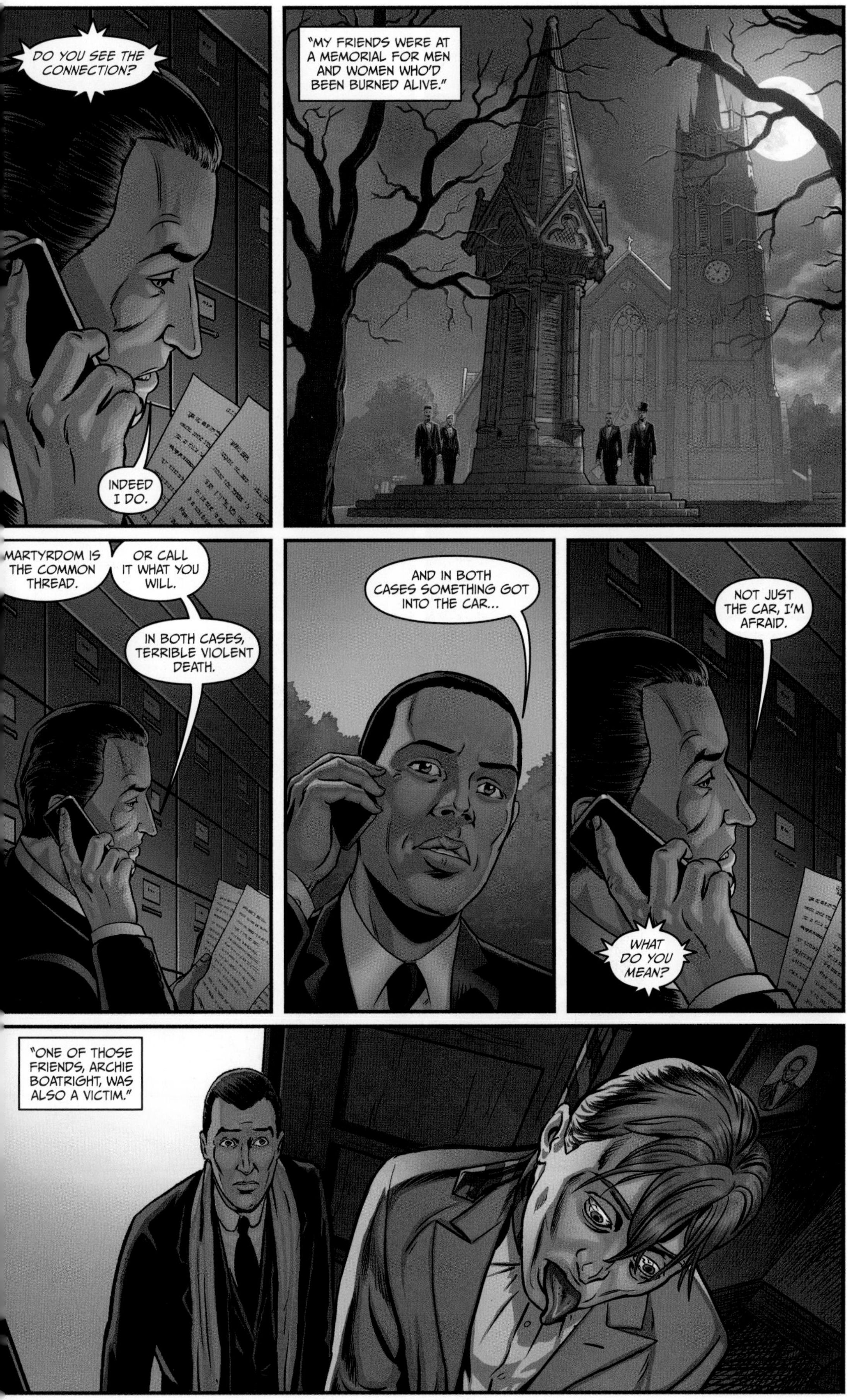
DO YOU SEE THE CONNECTION?
INDEED I DO.
"MY FRIENDS WERE AT A MEMORIAL FOR MEN AND WOMEN WHO'D BEEN BURNED ALIVE."
MARTYRDOM IS THE COMMON THREAD.
OR CALL IT WHAT YOU WILL.
IN BOTH CASES, TERRIBLE VIOLENT DEATH.
AND IN BOTH CASES SOMETHING GOT INTO THE CAR...
NOT JUST THE CAR, I'M AFRAID.
WHAT DO YOU MEAN?
"ONE OF THOSE FRIENDS, ARCHIE BOATRIGHT, WAS ALSO A VICTIM."

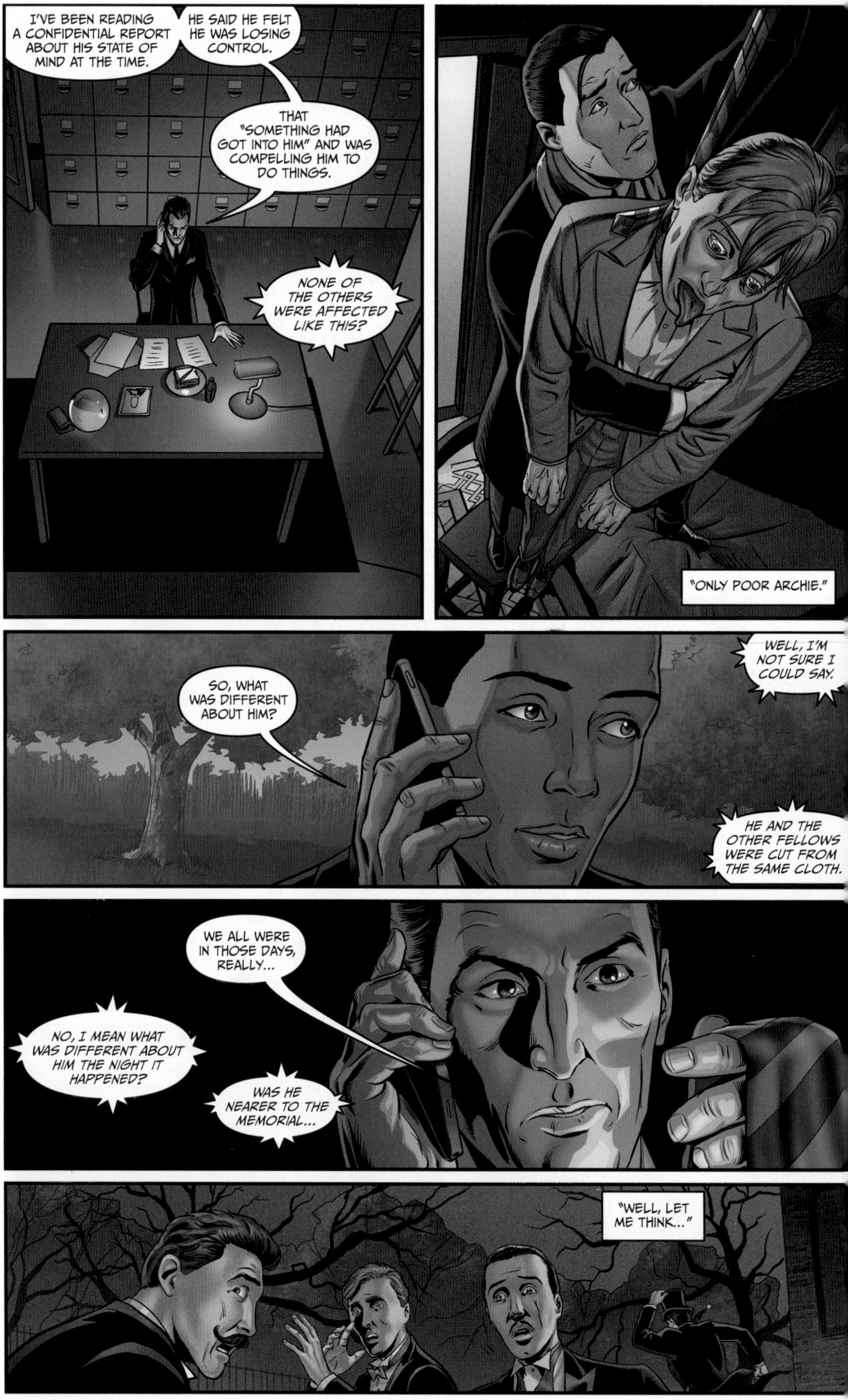
I'VE BEEN READING A CONFIDENTIAL REPORT ABOUT HIS STATE OF MIND AT THE TIME.
HE SAID HE FELT HE WAS LOSING CONTROL.
THAT "SOMETHING HAD GOT INTO HIM" AND WAS COMPELLING HIM TO DO THINGS.
NONE OF THE OTHERS WERE AFFECTED LIKE THIS?
"ONLY POOR ARCHIE."
SO, WHAT WAS DIFFERENT ABOUT HIM?
WELL, I'M NOT SURE I COULD SAY.
HE AND THE OTHER FELLOWS WERE CUT FROM THE SAME CLOTH.
WE ALL WERE IN THOSE DAYS, REALLY...
NO, I MEAN WHAT WAS DIFFERENT ABOUT HIM THE NIGHT IT HAPPENED?
WAS HE NEARER TO THE MEMORIAL...
"WELL, LET ME THINK..."

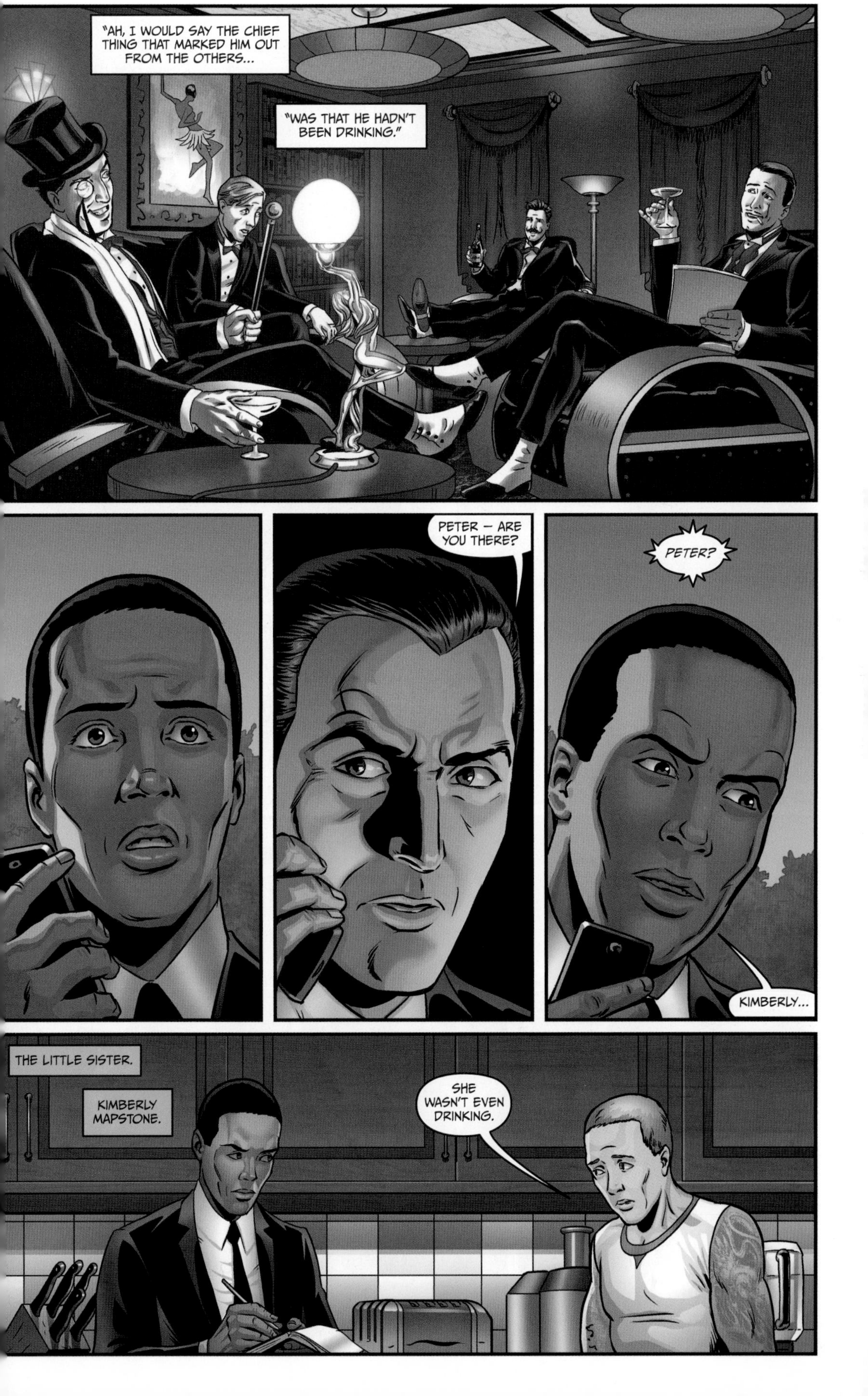
"AH, I WOULD SAY THE CHIEF THING THAT MARKED HIM OUT FROM THE OTHERS...
"WAS THAT HE HADN'T BEEN DRINKING."
PETER – ARE YOU THERE?
PETER?
KIMBERLY...
THE LITTLE SISTER.
KIMBERLY MAPSTONE.
SHE WASN'T EVEN DRINKING.

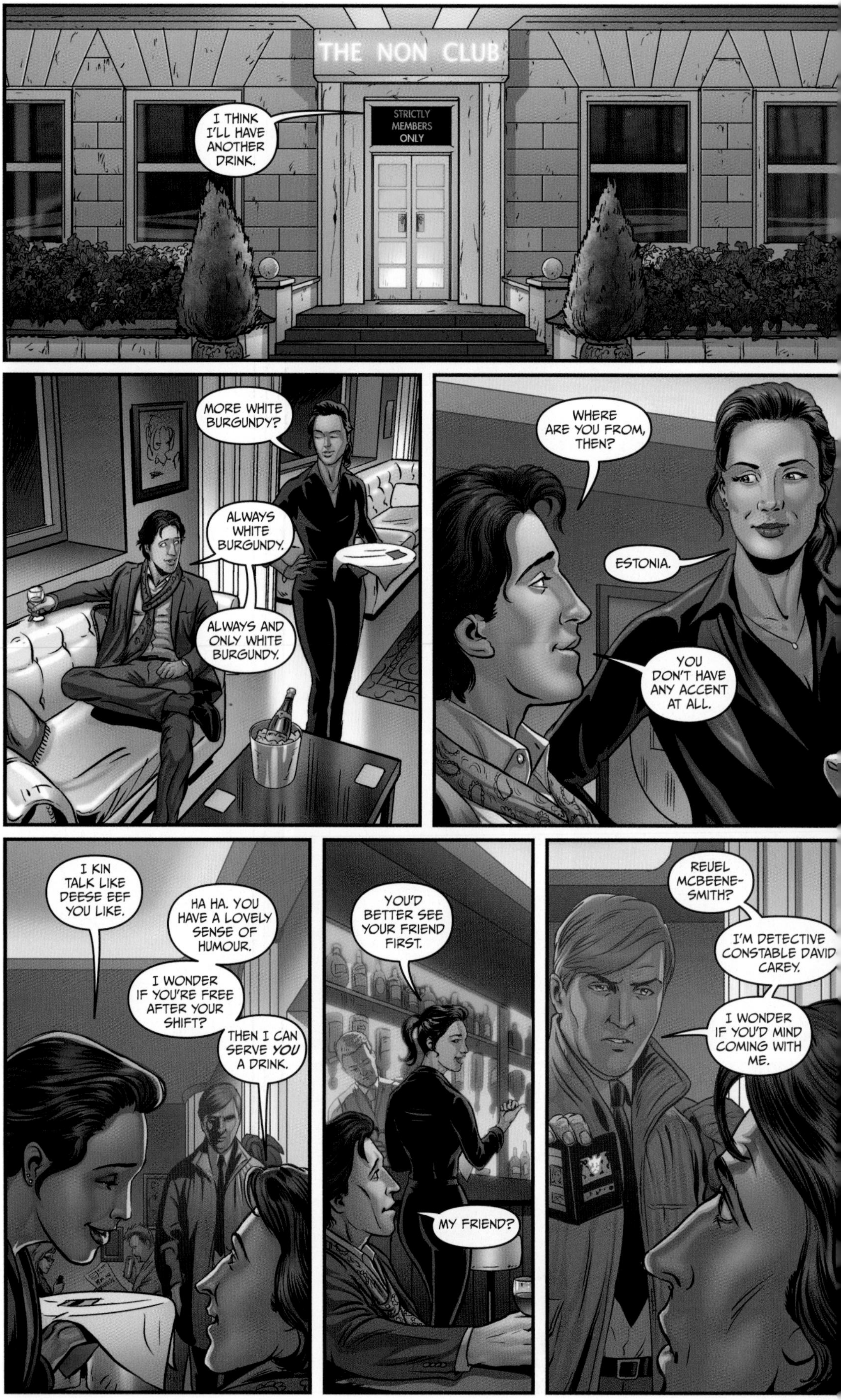
THE NON CLUB
STRICTLY MEMBERS ONLY
I THINK I'LL HAVE ANOTHER DRINK.
MORE WHITE BURGUNDY?
ALWAYS WHITE BURGUNDY.
ALWAYS AND ONLY WHITE BURGUNDY.
WHERE ARE YOU FROM, THEN?
ESTONIA.
YOU DON'T HAVE ANY ACCENT AT ALL.
I KIN TALK LIKE DEESE EEF YOU LIKE.
HA HA. YOU HAVE A LOVELY SENSE OF HUMOUR.
I WONDER IF YOU'RE FREE AFTER YOUR SHIFT?
THEN I CAN SERVE *YOU* A DRINK.
YOU'D BETTER SEE YOUR FRIEND FIRST.
MY FRIEND?
REUEL MCBEENE-SMITH?
I'M DETECTIVE CONSTABLE DAVID CAREY.
I WONDER IF YOU'D MIND COMING WITH ME.

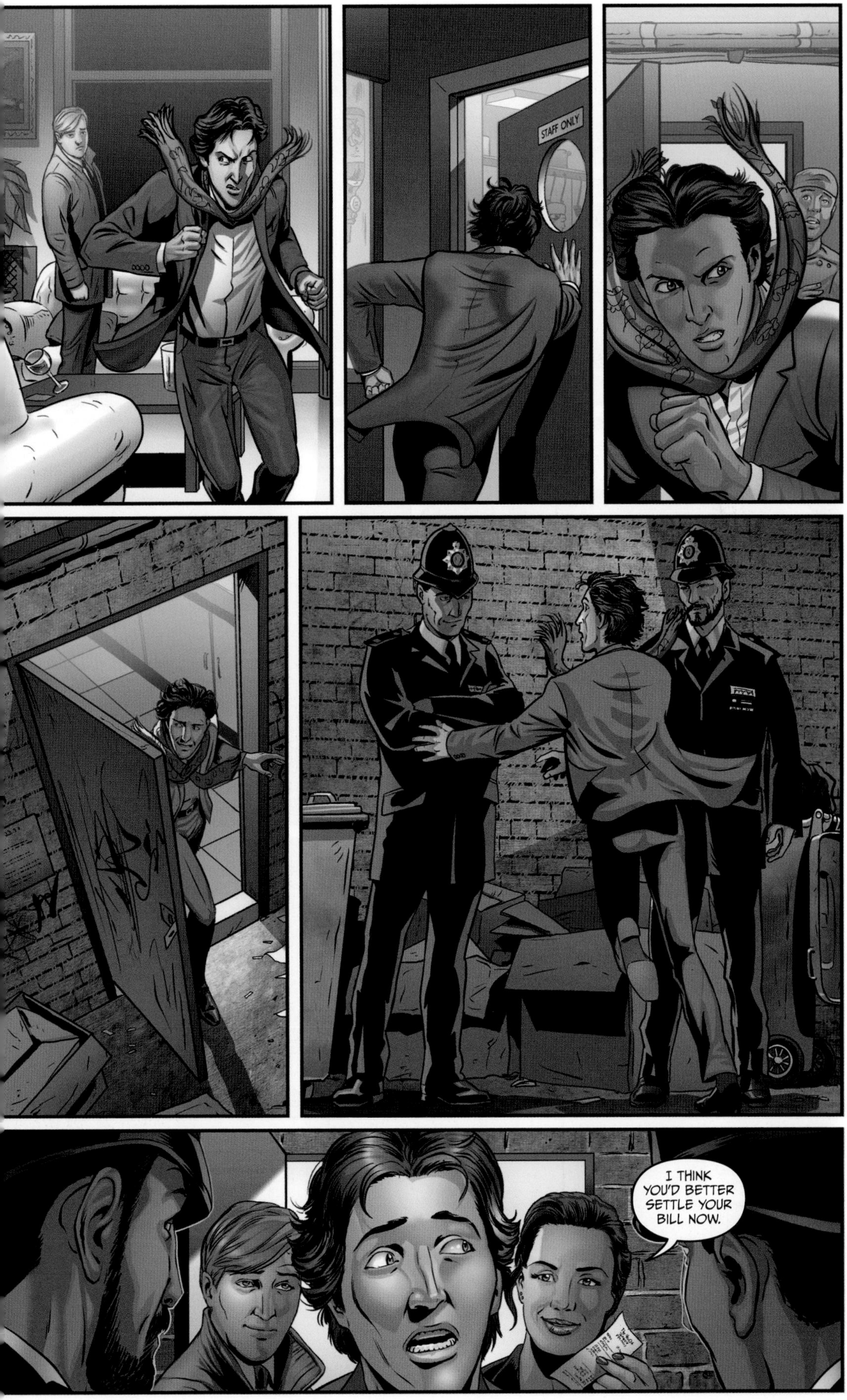
STAFF ONLY
I THINK YOU'D BETTER SETTLE YOUR BILL NOW.

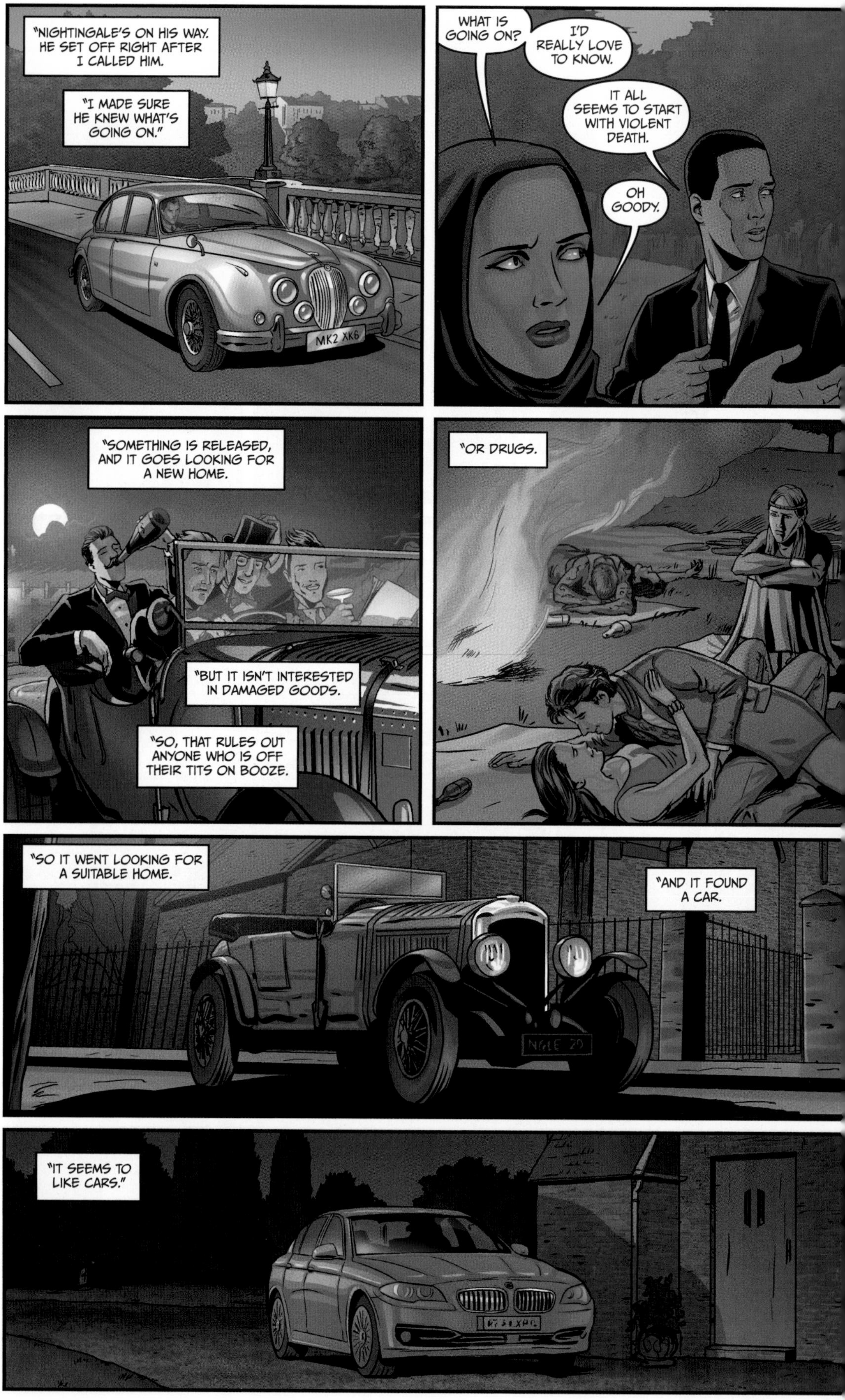
"NIGHTINGALE'S ON HIS WAY. HE SET OFF RIGHT AFTER I CALLED HIM.
"I MADE SURE HE KNEW WHAT'S GOING ON."
MK2 XK6
WHAT IS GOING ON?
I'D REALLY LOVE TO KNOW.
IT ALL SEEMS TO START WITH VIOLENT DEATH.
OH GOODY.
"SOMETHING IS RELEASED, AND IT GOES LOOKING FOR A NEW HOME.
"BUT IT ISN'T INTERESTED IN DAMAGED GOODS.
"SO, THAT RULES OUT ANYONE WHO IS OFF THEIR TITS ON BOOZE.
"OR DRUGS.
"SO IT WENT LOOKING FOR A SUITABLE HOME.
"AND IT FOUND A CAR.
"IT SEEMS TO LIKE CARS."

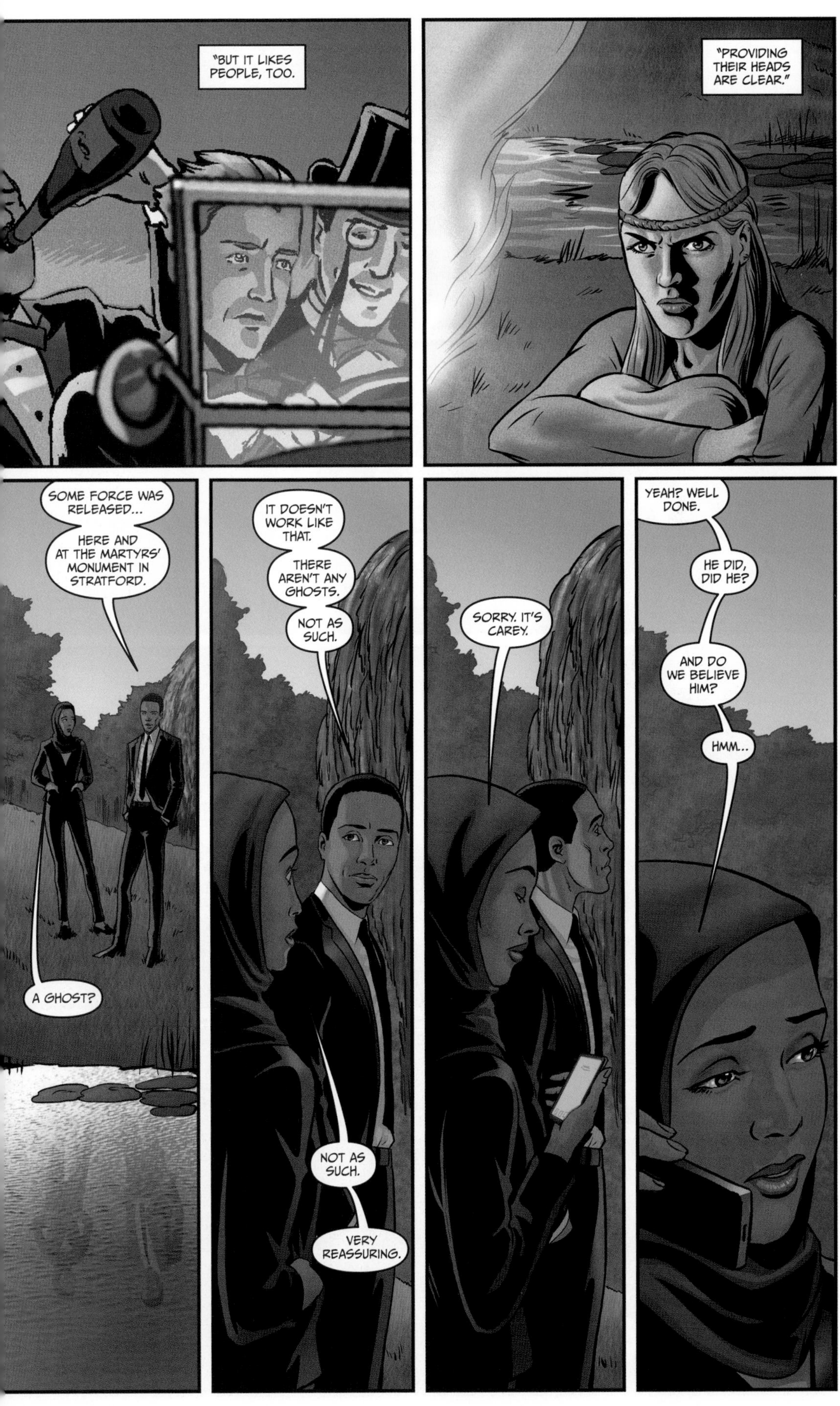
"BUT IT LIKES PEOPLE, TOO.
"PROVIDING THEIR HEADS ARE CLEAR."
SOME FORCE WAS RELEASED...
HERE AND AT THE MARTYRS' MONUMENT IN STRATFORD.
A GHOST?
IT DOESN'T WORK LIKE THAT.
THERE AREN'T ANY GHOSTS.
NOT AS SUCH.
NOT AS SUCH.
VERY REASSURING.
SORRY. IT'S CAREY.
YEAH? WELL DONE.
HE DID, DID HE?
AND DO WE BELIEVE HIM?
HMM...

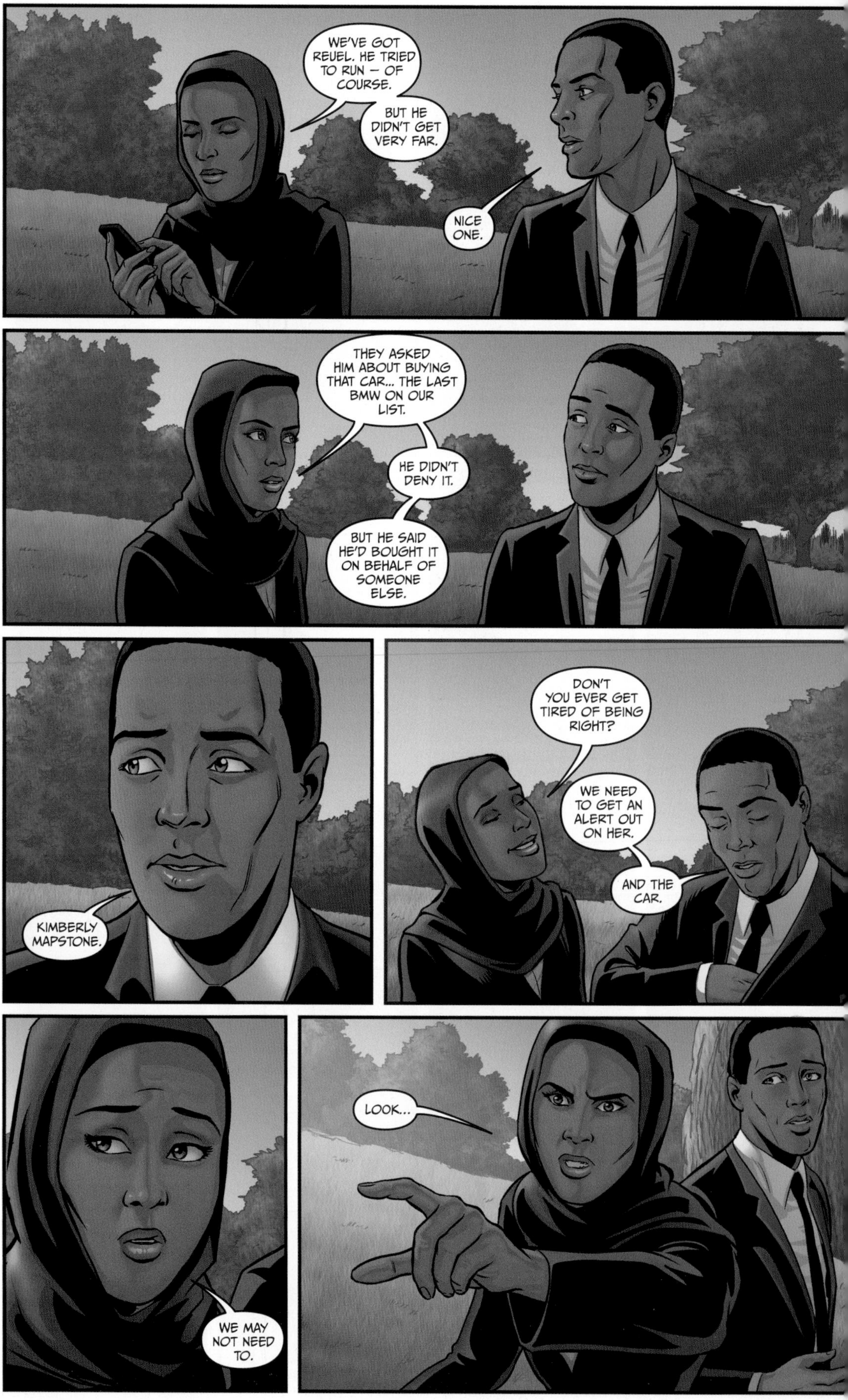
WE'VE GOT REUEL. HE TRIED TO RUN — OF COURSE.
BUT HE DIDN'T GET VERY FAR.
NICE ONE.
THEY ASKED HIM ABOUT BUYING THAT CAR... THE LAST BMW ON OUR LIST.
HE DIDN'T DENY IT.
BUT HE SAID HE'D BOUGHT IT ON BEHALF OF SOMEONE ELSE.
KIMBERLY MAPSTONE.
DON'T YOU EVER GET TIRED OF BEING RIGHT?
WE NEED TO GET AN ALERT OUT ON HER.
AND THE CAR.
WE MAY NOT NEED TO.
LOOK...

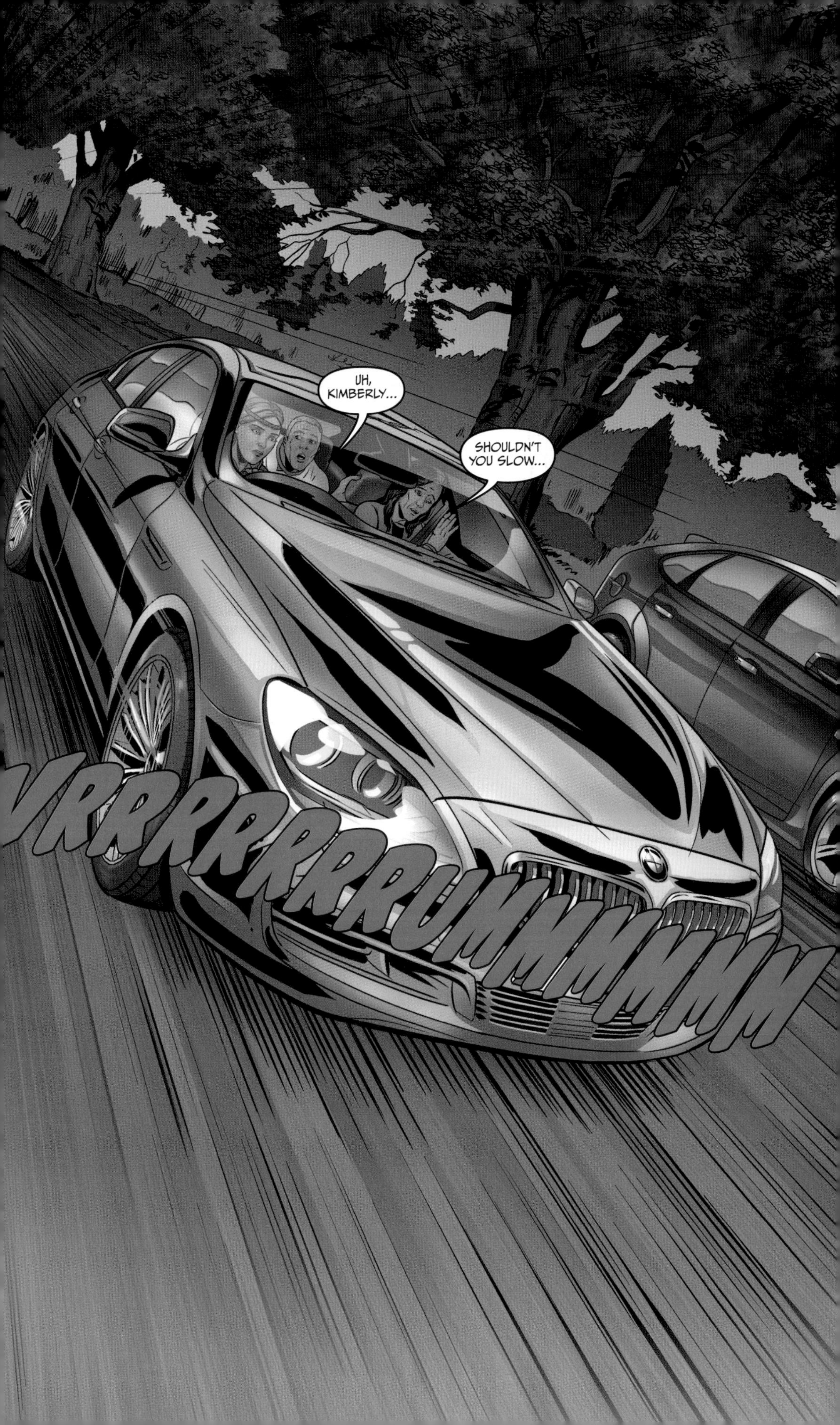
UH, KIMBERLY...
SHOULDN'T YOU SLOW...
VRRRRRRRRRUMMMMMMMN

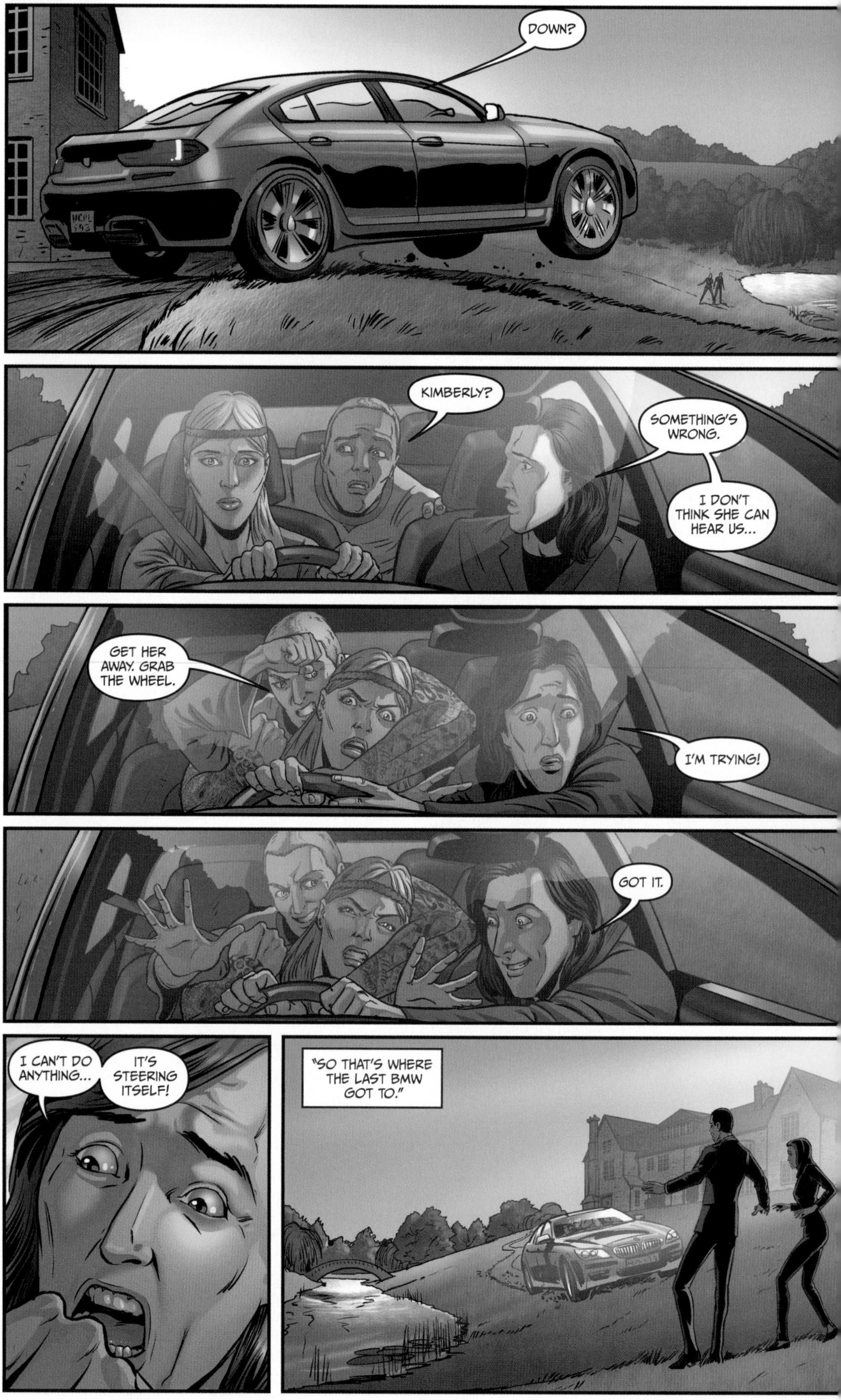
DOWN?
KIMBERLY?
SOMETHING'S WRONG.
I DON'T THINK SHE CAN HEAR US...
GET HER AWAY. GRAB THE WHEEL.
I'M TRYING!
GOT IT.
I CAN'T DO ANYTHING...
IT'S STEERING ITSELF!
"SO THAT'S WHERE THE LAST BMW GOT TO."

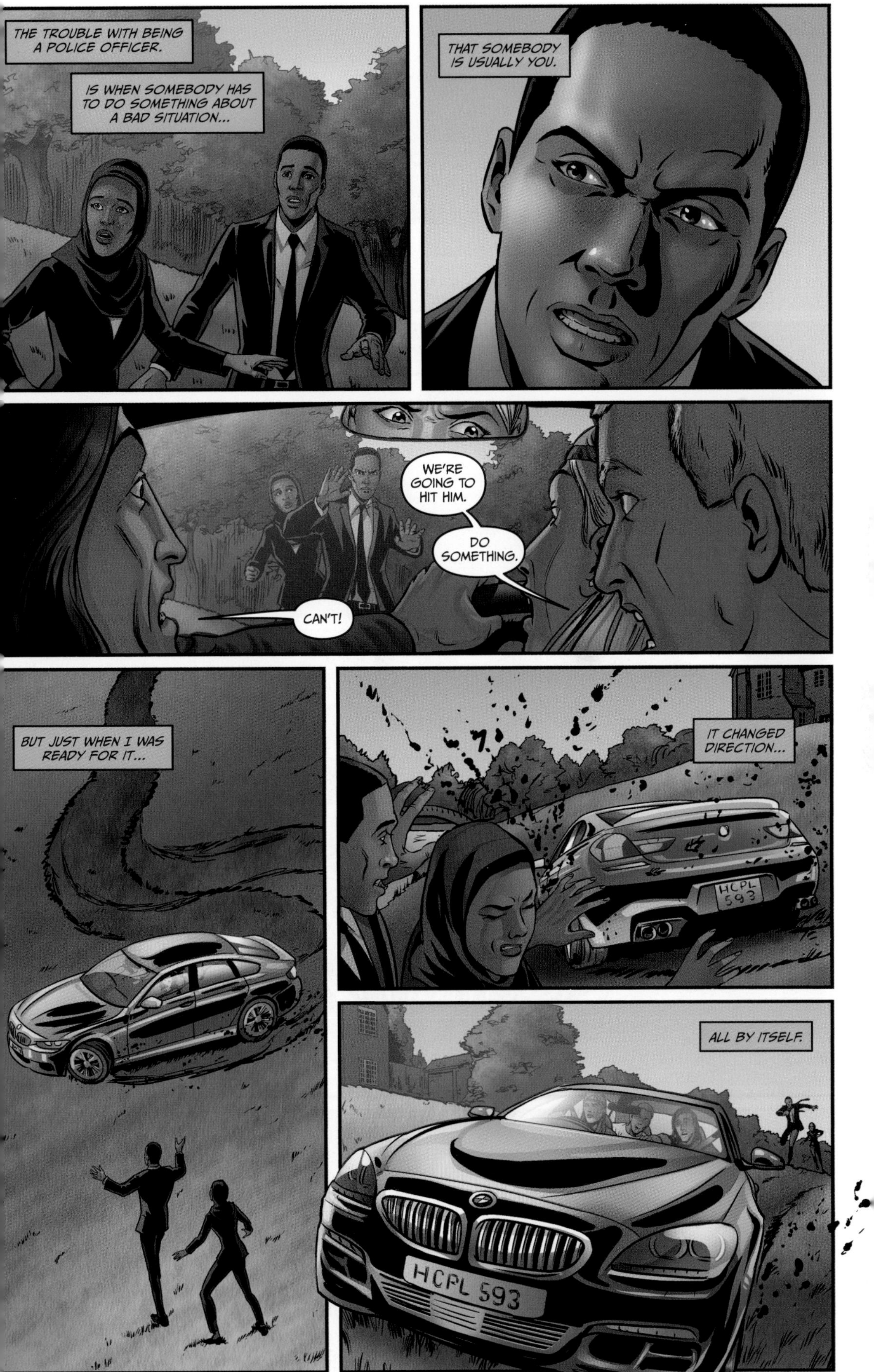
THE TROUBLE WITH BEING A POLICE OFFICER.
IS WHEN SOMEBODY HAS TO DO SOMETHING ABOUT A BAD SITUATION...
THAT SOMEBODY IS USUALLY YOU.
WE'RE GOING TO HIT HIM.
DO SOMETHING.
CAN'T!
BUT JUST WHEN I WAS READY FOR IT...
IT CHANGED DIRECTION...
HCPL 593
ALL BY ITSELF.
HCPL 593

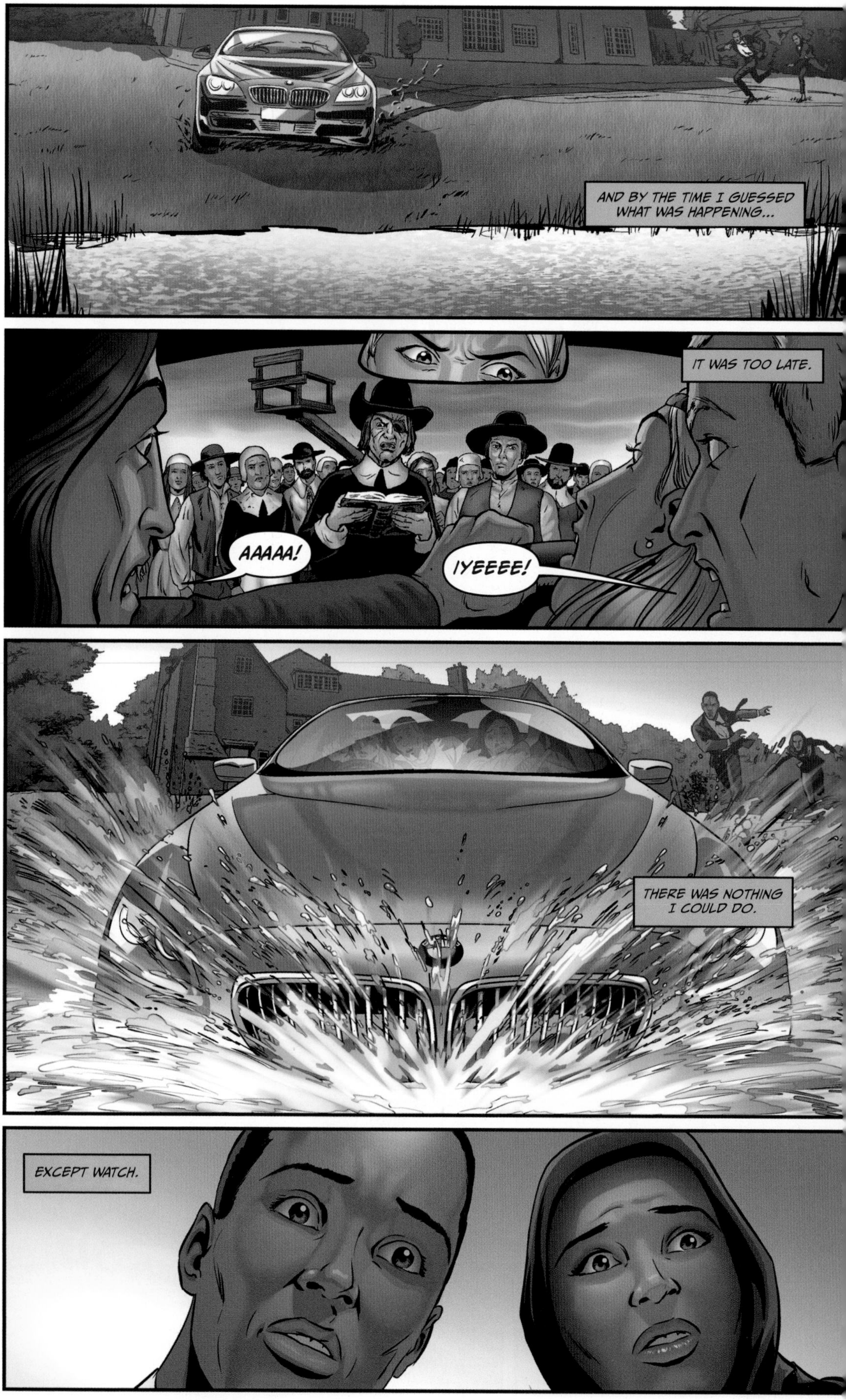
AND BY THE TIME I GUESSED WHAT WAS HAPPENING...
IT WAS TOO LATE.
AAAAA!
IYEEEE!
THERE WAS NOTHING I COULD DO.
EXCEPT WATCH.

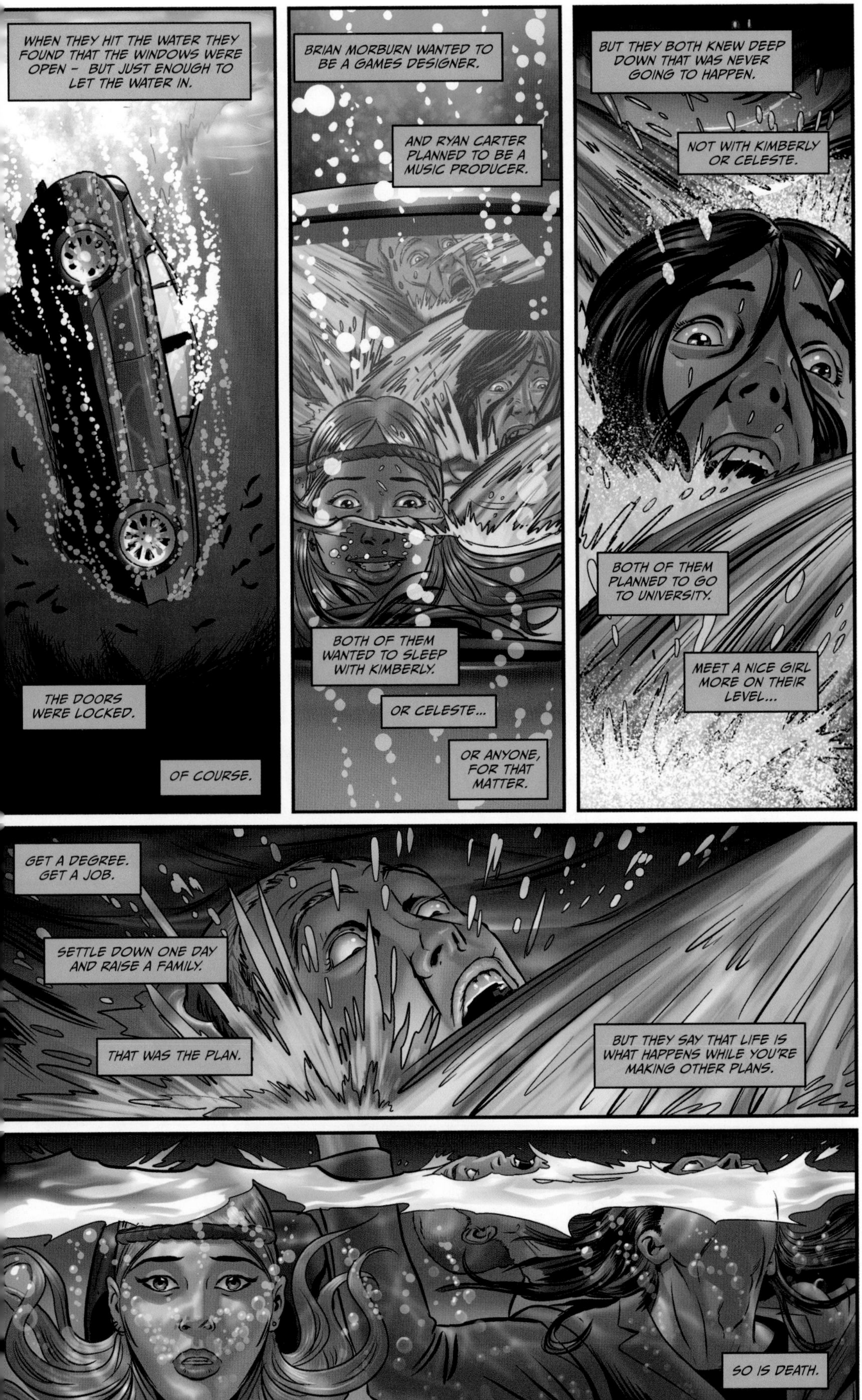
WHEN THEY HIT THE WATER THEY FOUND THAT THE WINDOWS WERE OPEN - BUT JUST ENOUGH TO LET THE WATER IN.
THE DOORS WERE LOCKED.
OF COURSE.
BRIAN MORBURN WANTED TO BE A GAMES DESIGNER.
AND RYAN CARTER PLANNED TO BE A MUSIC PRODUCER.
BOTH OF THEM WANTED TO SLEEP WITH KIMBERLY.
OR CELESTE...
OR ANYONE, FOR THAT MATTER.
BUT THEY BOTH KNEW DEEP DOWN THAT WAS NEVER GOING TO HAPPEN.
NOT WITH KIMBERLY OR CELESTE.
BOTH OF THEM PLANNED TO GO TO UNIVERSITY.
MEET A NICE GIRL MORE ON THEIR LEVEL...
GET A DEGREE. GET A JOB.
SETTLE DOWN ONE DAY AND RAISE A FAMILY.
THAT WAS THE PLAN.
BUT THEY SAY THAT LIFE IS WHAT HAPPENS WHILE YOU'RE MAKING OTHER PLANS.
SO IS DEATH.

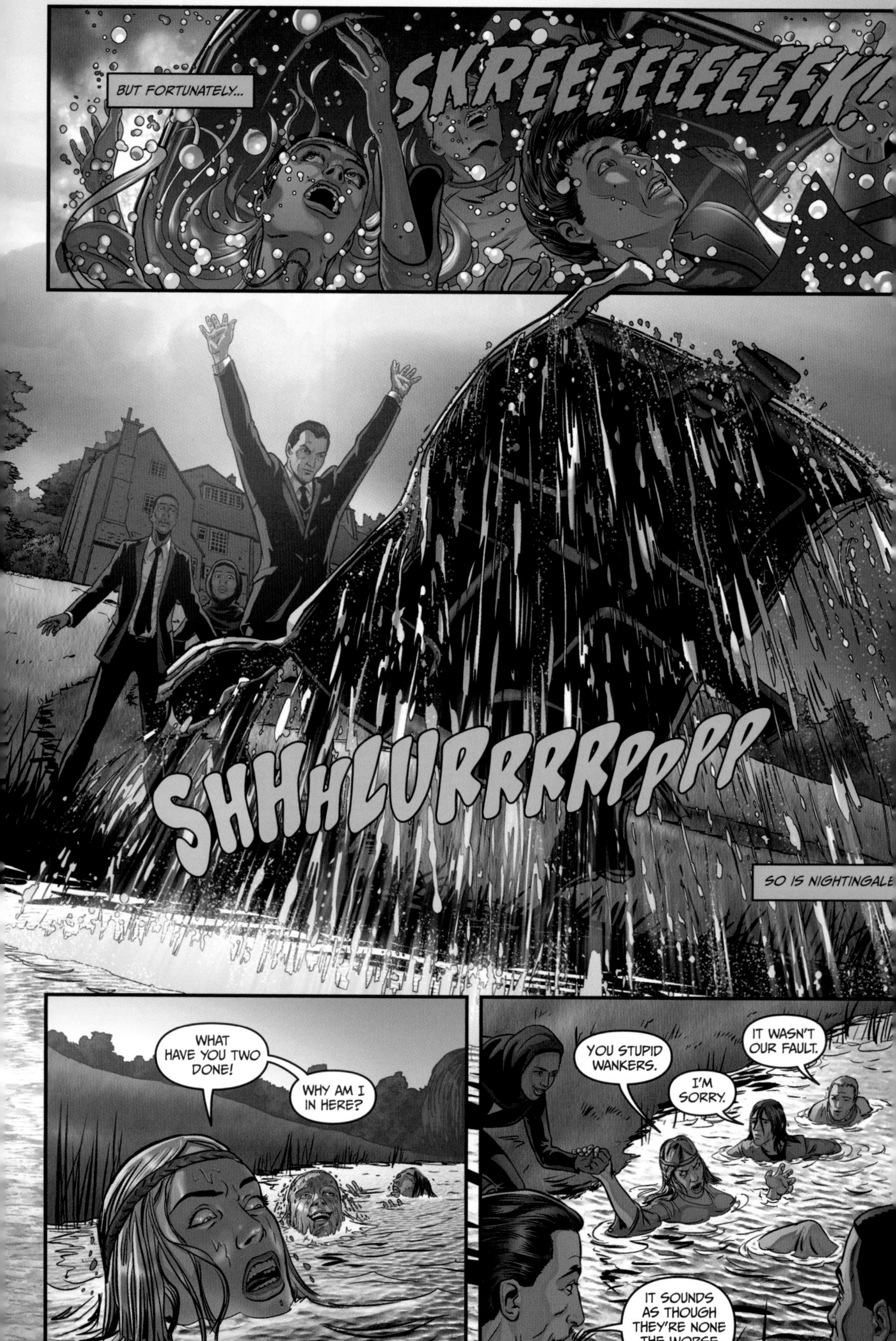
BUT FORTUNATELY...
SKREEEEEEEEEEK!
SHHHLURRRRPPPP
SO IS NIGHTINGALE
WHAT HAVE YOU TWO DONE!
WHY AM I IN HERE?
YOU STUPID WANKERS.
IT WASN'T OUR FAULT.
I'M SORRY.
IT SOUNDS AS THOUGH THEY'RE NONE THE WORSE FOR WEAR.

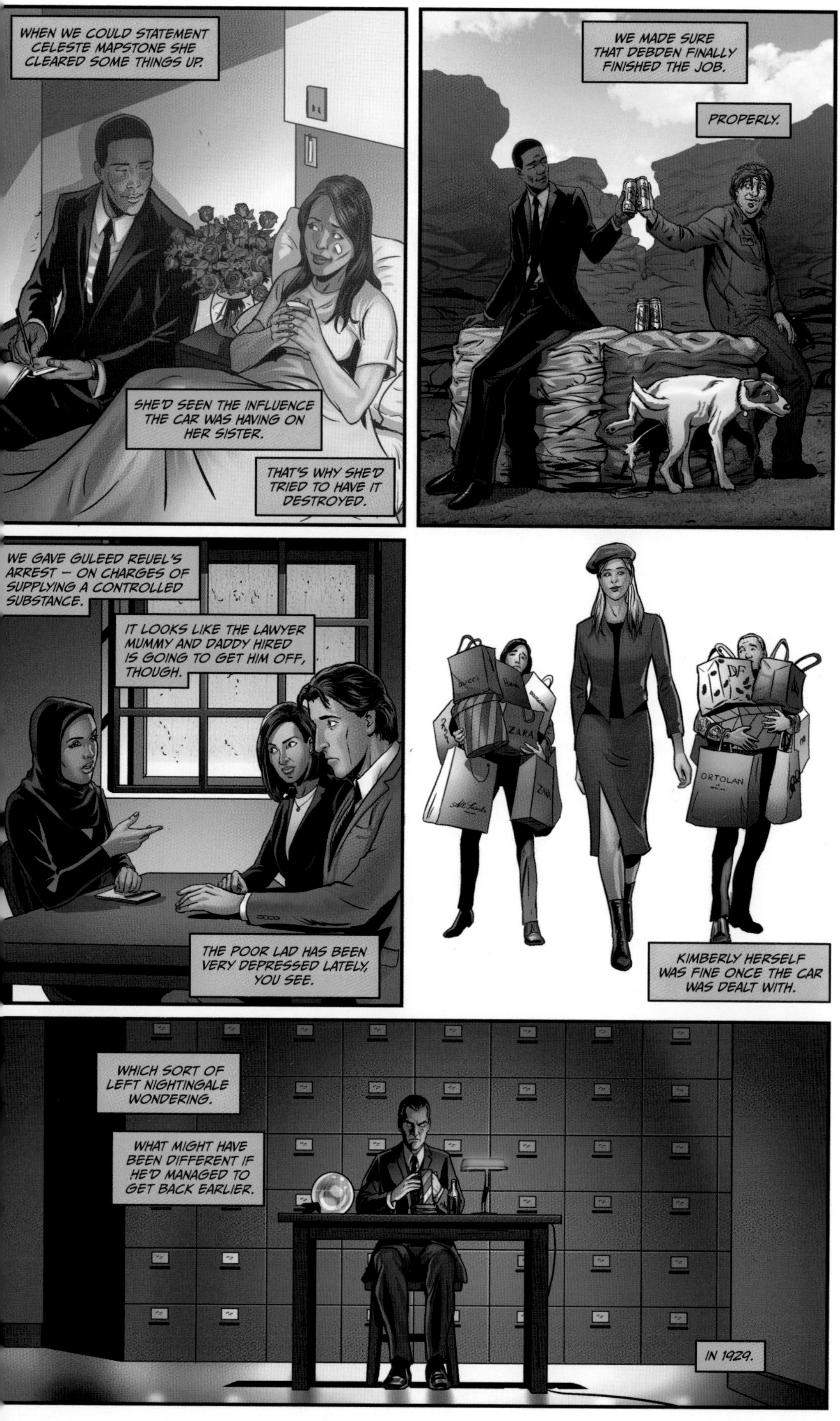
WHEN WE COULD STATEMENT CELESTE MAPSTONE SHE CLEARED SOME THINGS UP.
SHE'D SEEN THE INFLUENCE THE CAR WAS HAVING ON HER SISTER.
THAT'S WHY SHE'D TRIED TO HAVE IT DESTROYED.
WE MADE SURE THAT DEBDEN FINALLY FINISHED THE JOB.
PROPERLY.
WE GAVE GULEED REUEL'S ARREST — ON CHARGES OF SUPPLYING A CONTROLLED SUBSTANCE.
IT LOOKS LIKE THE LAWYER MUMMY AND DADDY HIRED IS GOING TO GET HIM OFF, THOUGH.
THE POOR LAD HAS BEEN VERY DEPRESSED LATELY, YOU SEE.
GUCCI
ZARA
ORTOLAN
KIMBERLY HERSELF WAS FINE ONCE THE CAR WAS DEALT WITH.
WHICH SORT OF LEFT NIGHTINGALE WONDERING.
WHAT MIGHT HAVE BEEN DIFFERENT IF HE'D MANAGED TO GET BACK EARLIER.
IN 1929.

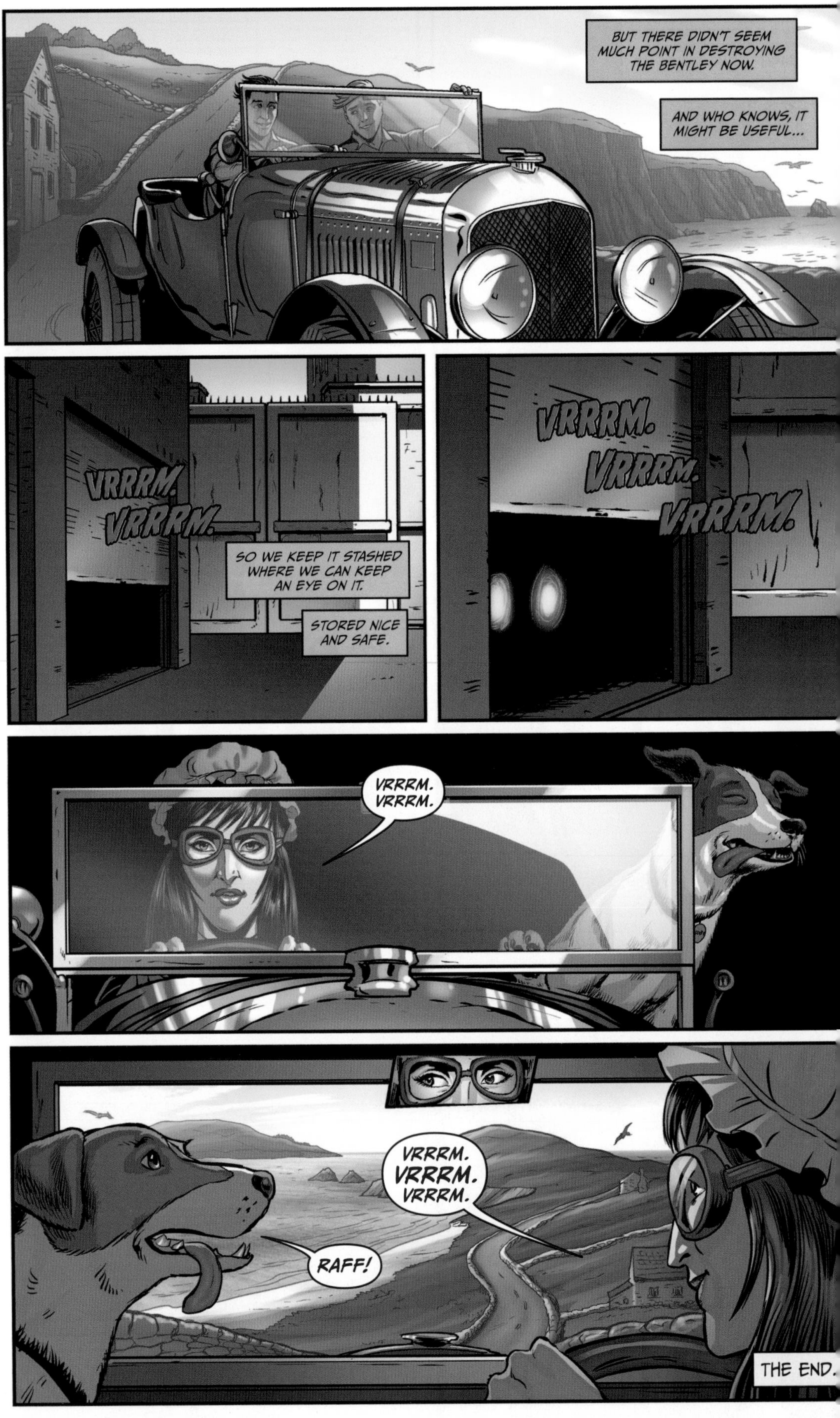
BUT THERE DIDN'T SEEM MUCH POINT IN DESTROYING THE BENTLEY NOW.
AND WHO KNOWS, IT MIGHT BE USEFUL...
VRRRM. VRRRM.
SO WE KEEP IT STASHED WHERE WE CAN KEEP AN EYE ON IT.
STORED NICE AND SAFE.
VRRRM. VRRRM. VRRRM.
VRRRM. VRRRM.
VRRRM. VRRRM. VRRRM.
RAFF!
THE END.

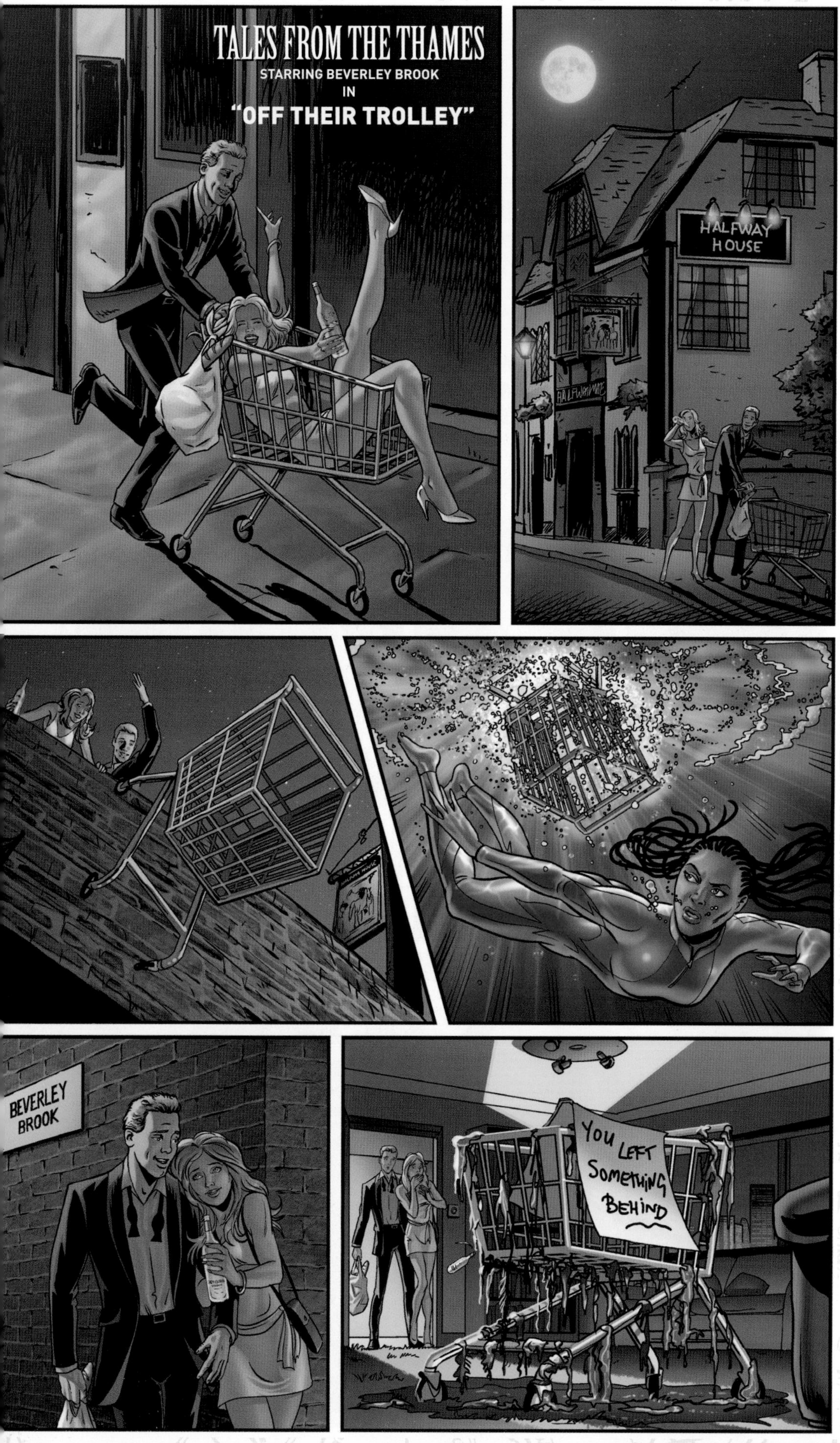
TALES FROM THE THAMES
STARRING BEVERLEY BROOK
IN
"OFF THEIR TROLLEY"
HALFWAY HOUSE
BEVERLEY BROOK
YOU LEFT SOMETHING BEHIND

TALES FROM THE FOLLY
STARRING MOLLY
IN
"RED MIST"

EEEK...
MOAN...
WHINE...

EEEEEEE...

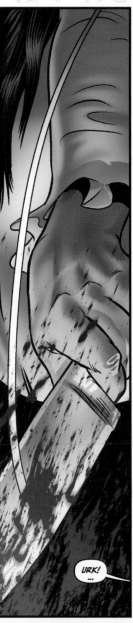

URK!
...

TOBY
SAYS IF YOU
EVER GO BACK TO
COOKING MEAT, HE'D
APPRECIATE A
SAUSAGE.

EEEEEK.
URK.
WHINE.

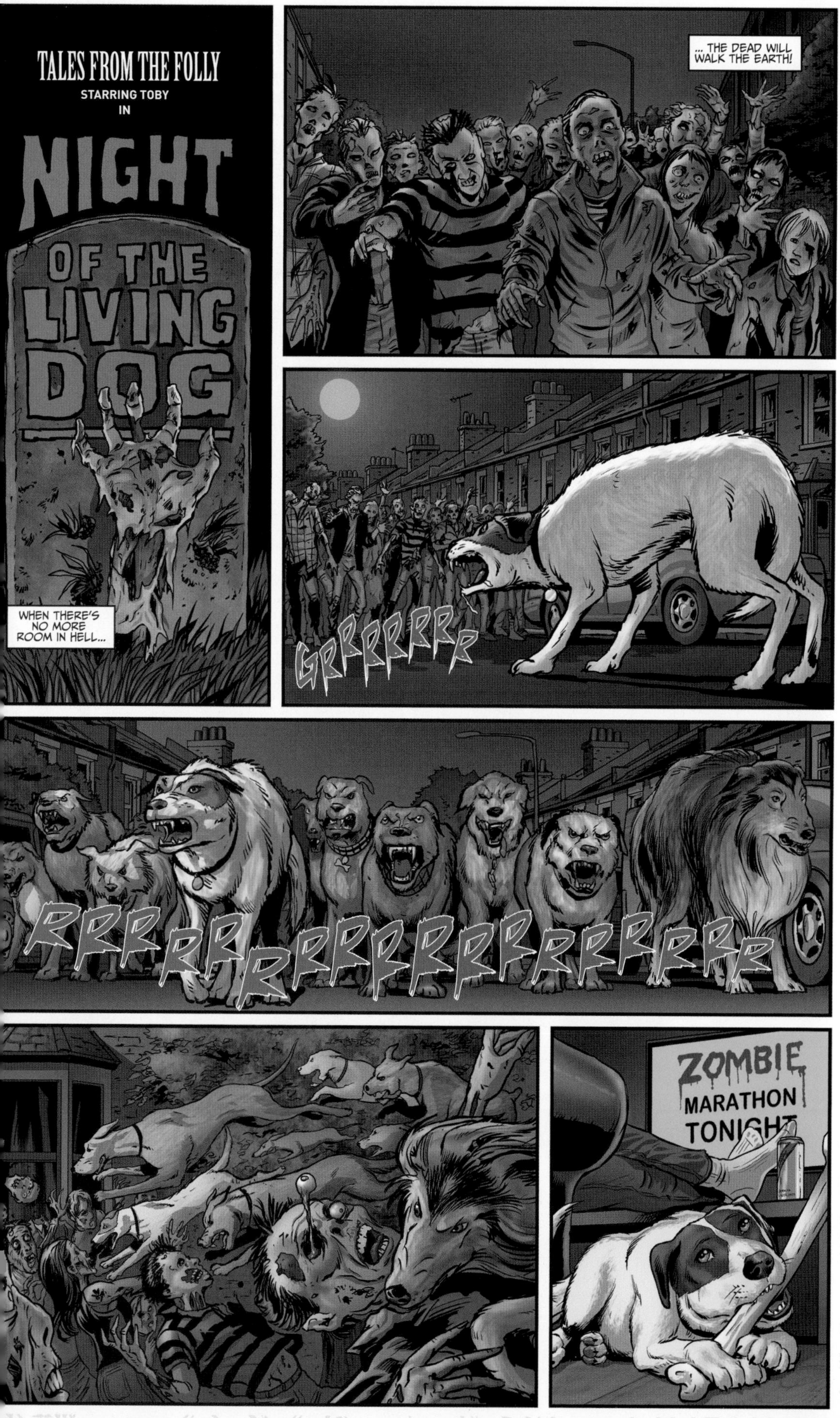
TALES FROM THE FOLLY
STARRING TOBY
IN
NIGHT OF THE LIVING DOG
WHEN THERE'S NO MORE ROOM IN HELL...
... THE DEAD WILL WALK THE EARTH!
GRRRRRRR
RRRRRRRRRRRRRRRRRRR
ZOMBIE
MARATHON
TONIGHT

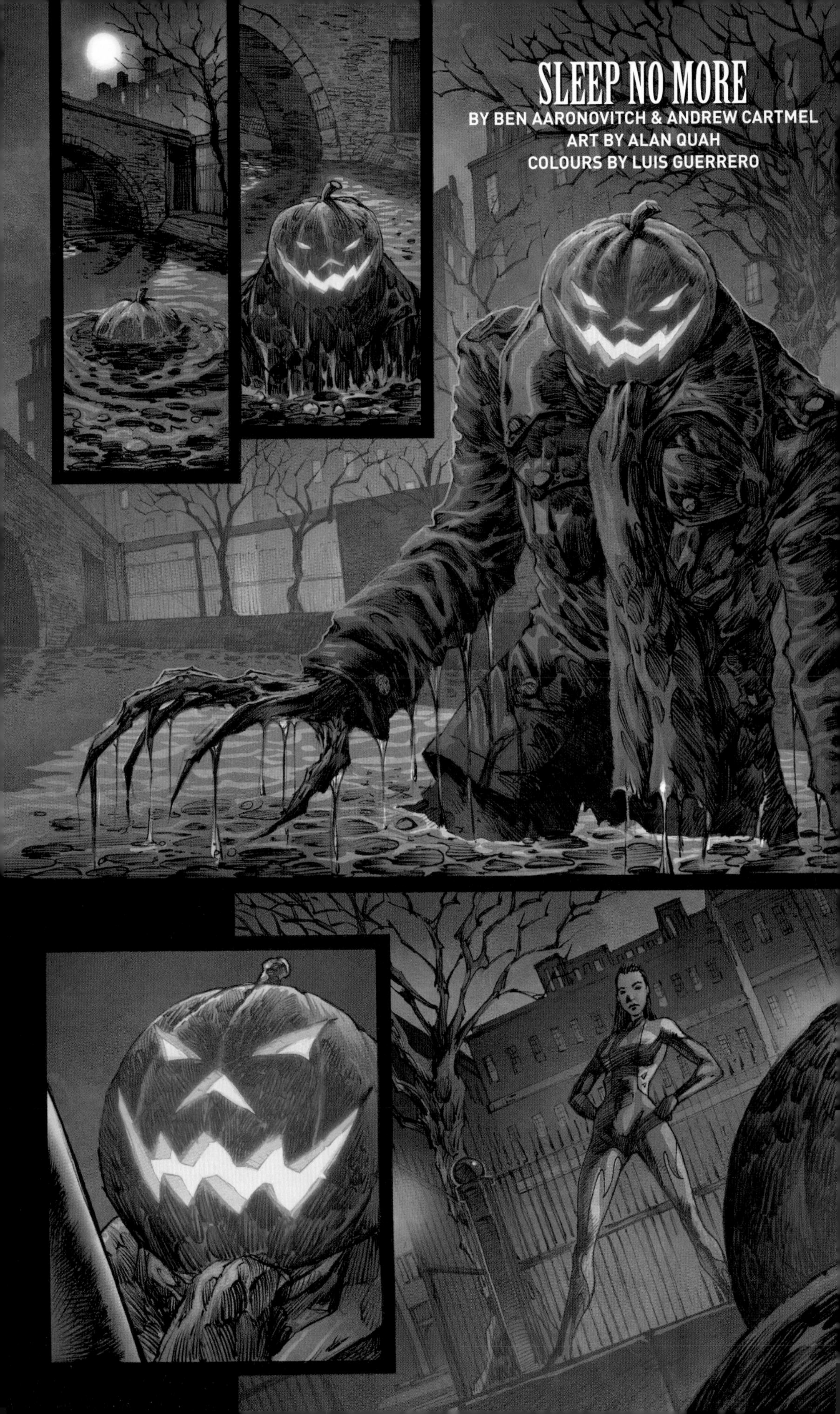
SLEEP NO MORE
BY BEN AARONOVITCH & ANDREW CARTMEL
ART BY ALAN QUAH
COLOURS BY LUIS GUERRERO

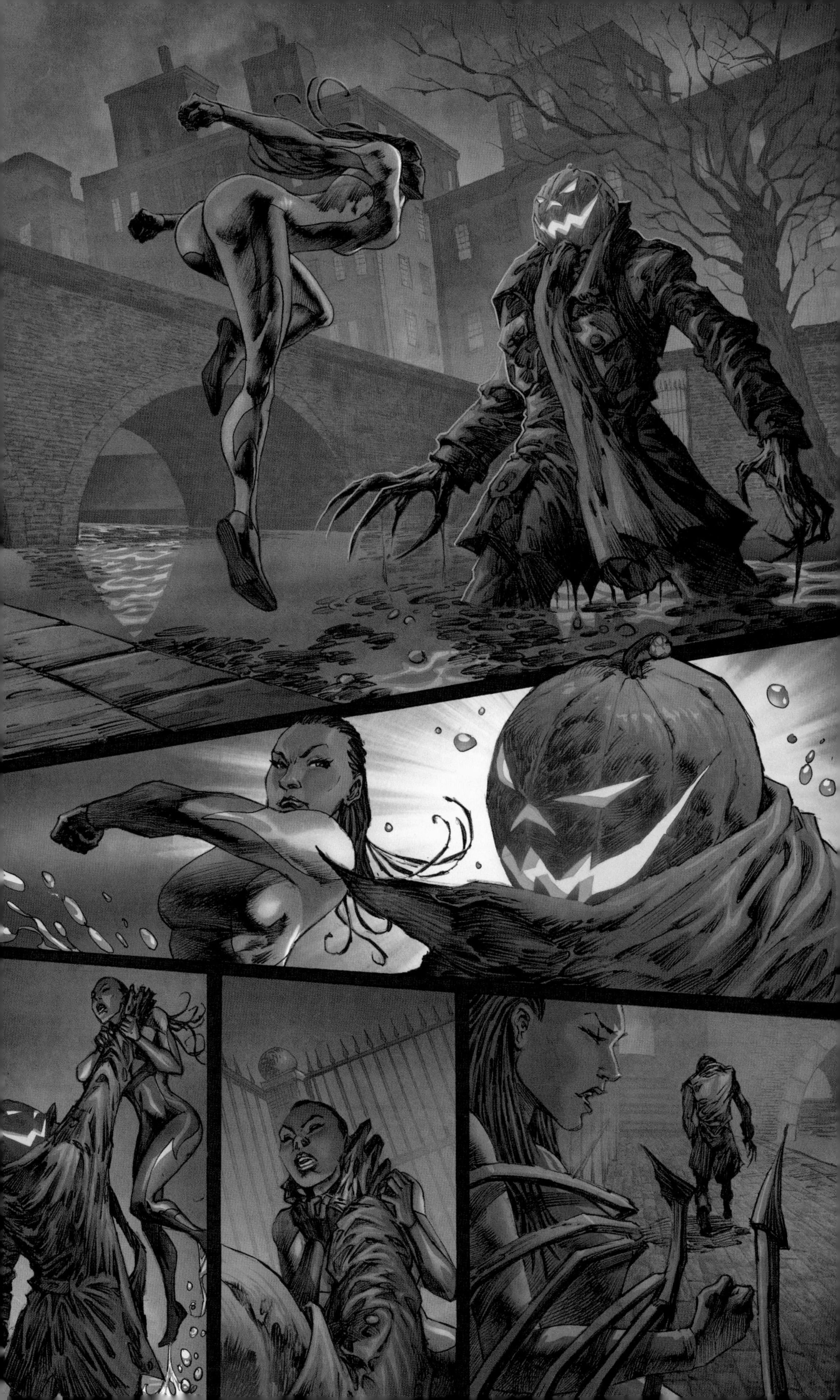

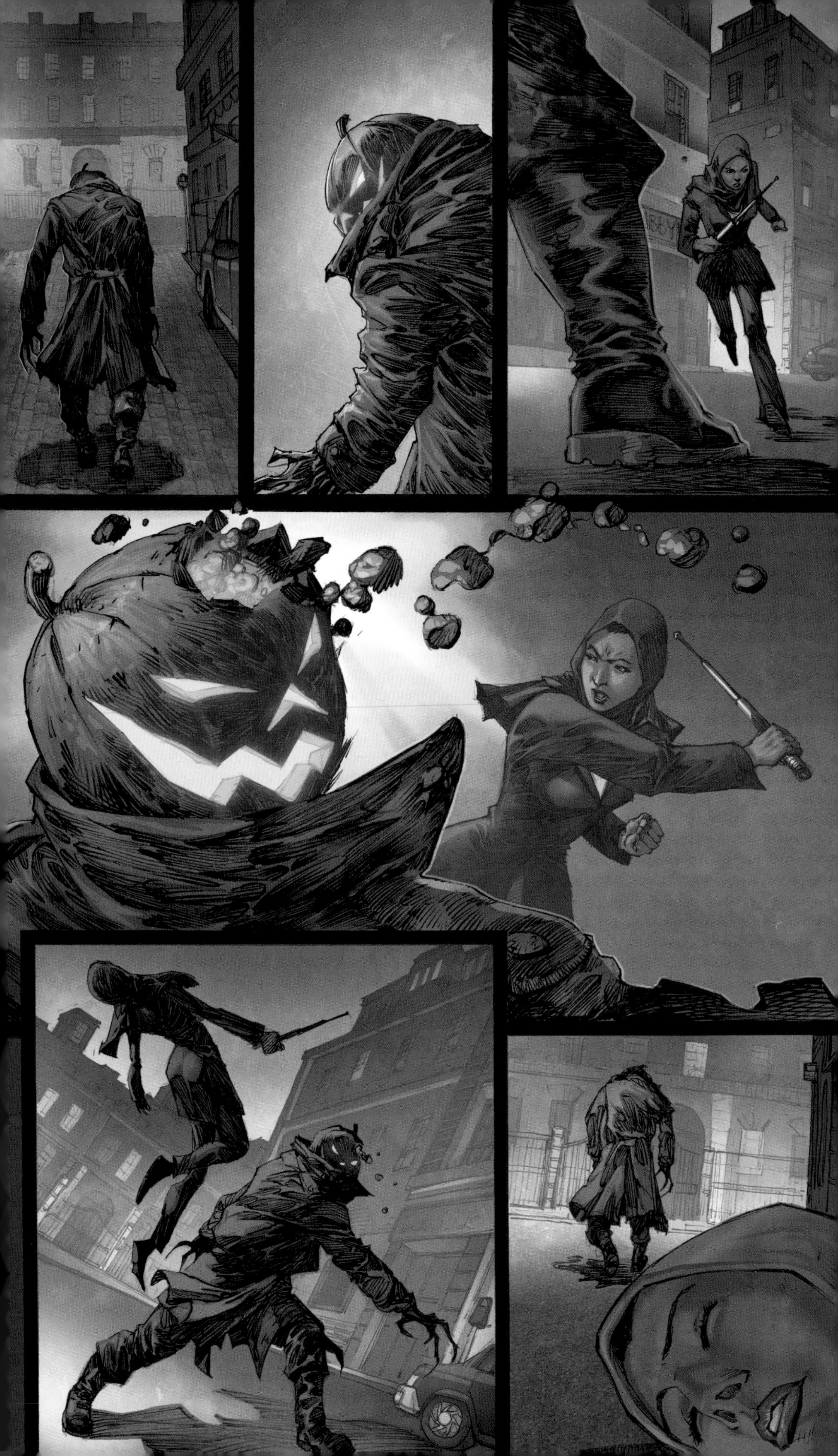

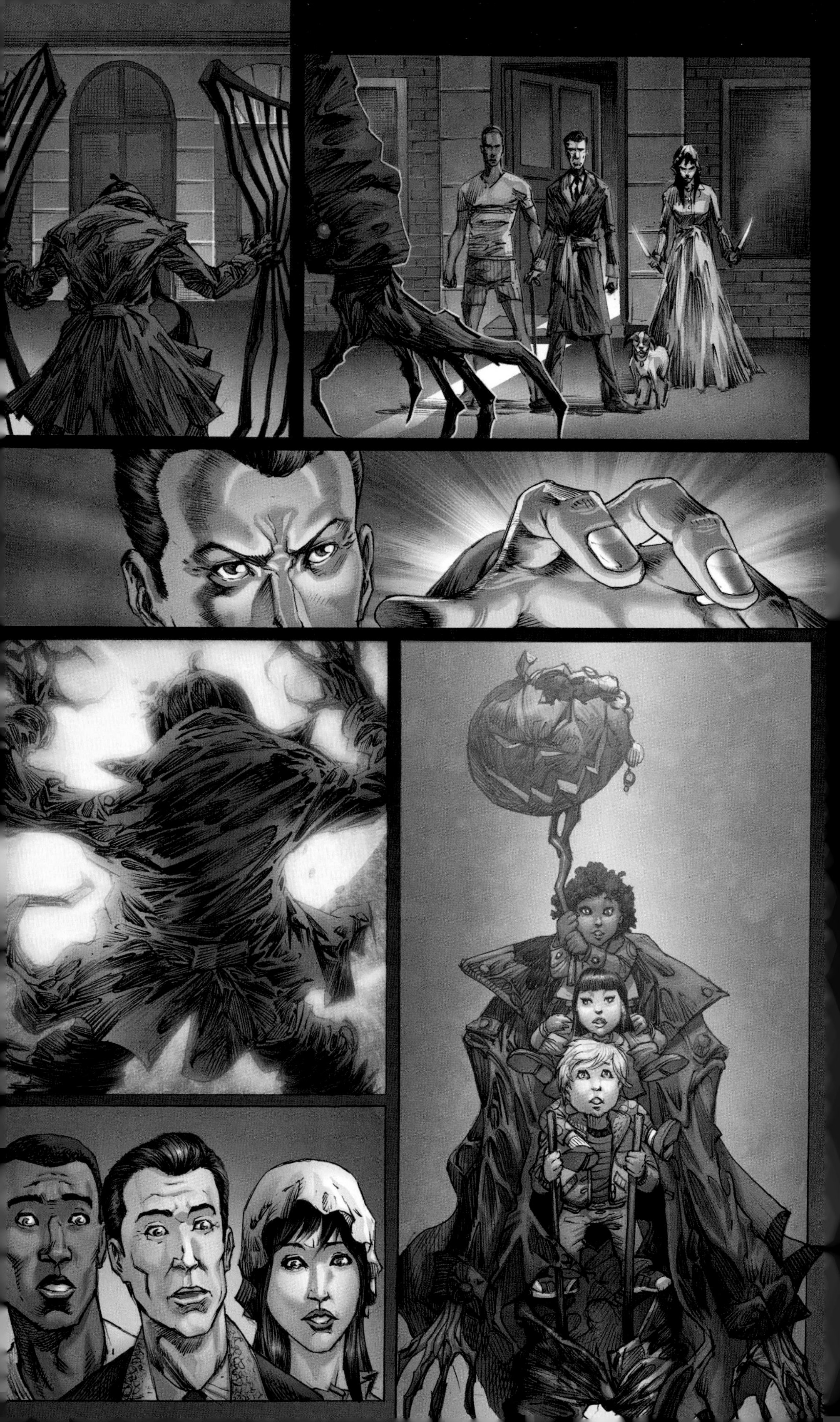

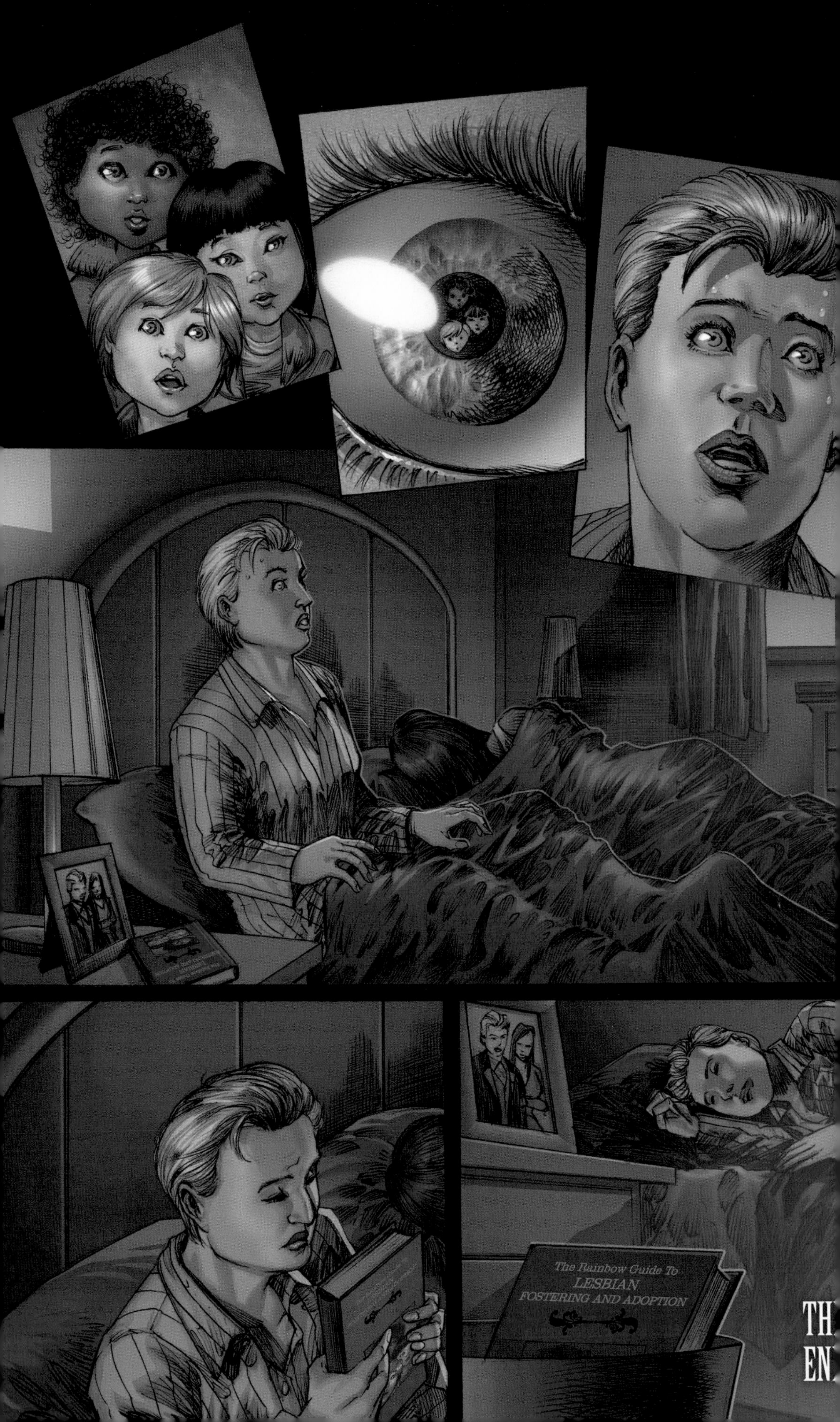
The Rainbow Guide To
LESBIAN
FOSTERING AND ADOPTION
TH
EN

COVERS GALLERY

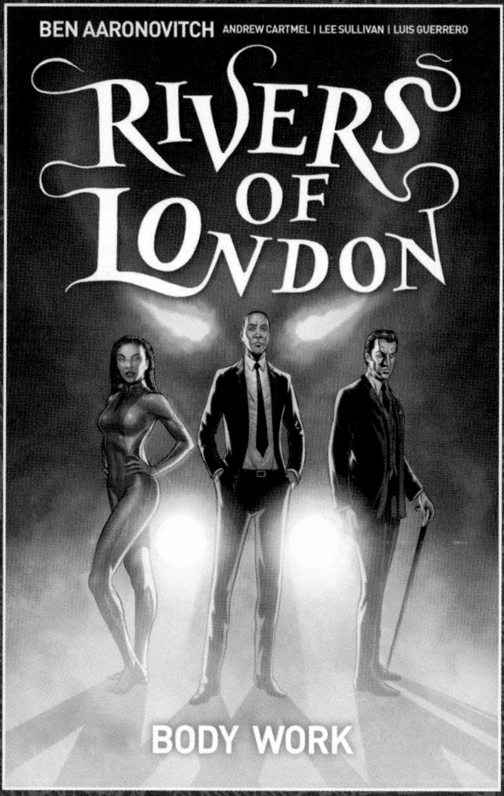
BEN AARONOVITCH
ANDREW CARTMEL | LEE SULLIVAN | LUIS GUERRERO
RIVERS OF LONDON
BODY WORK

ISSUE 1 - Cover A LEE SULLIVAN & LUIS GUERERRO

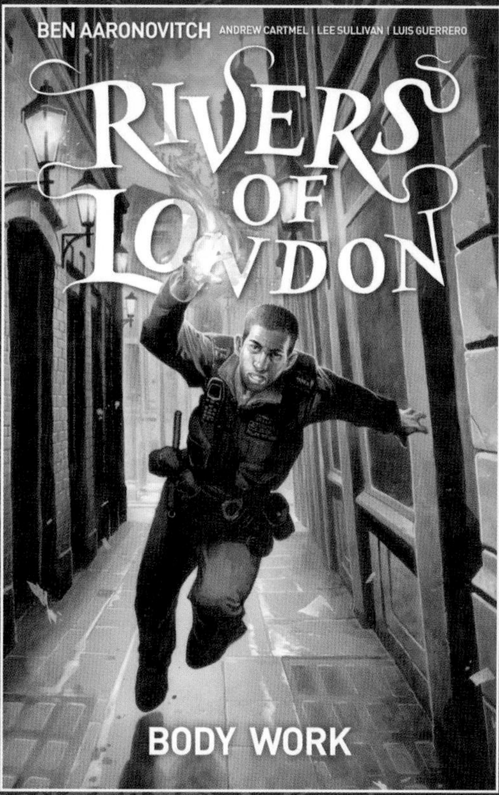
BEN AARONOVITCH
ANDREW CARTMEL | LEE SULLIVAN | LUIS GUERRERO
RIVERS OF LONDON
BODY WORK

ISSUE 1 - Cover B WAYNE REYNOLDS

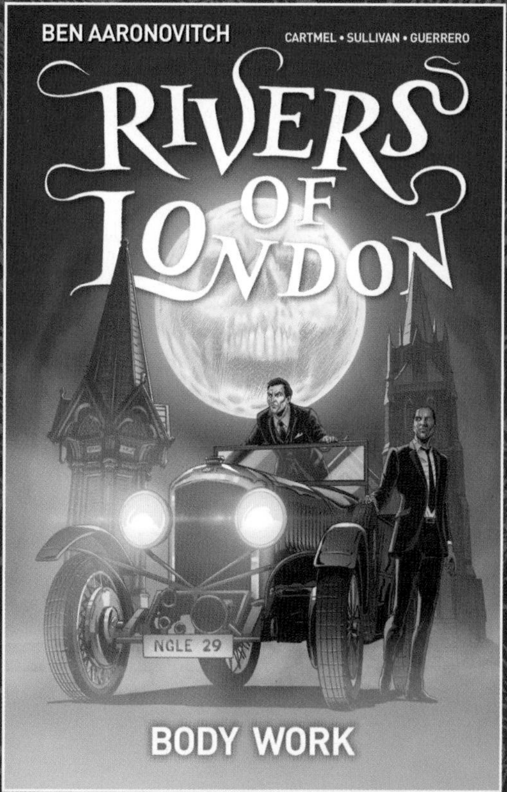
BEN AARONOVITCH
CARTMEL • SULLIVAN • GUERRERO
RIVERS OF LONDON
NGLE 29
BODY WORK

ISSUE 2 - Cover A LEE SULLIVAN & LUIS GUERERRO

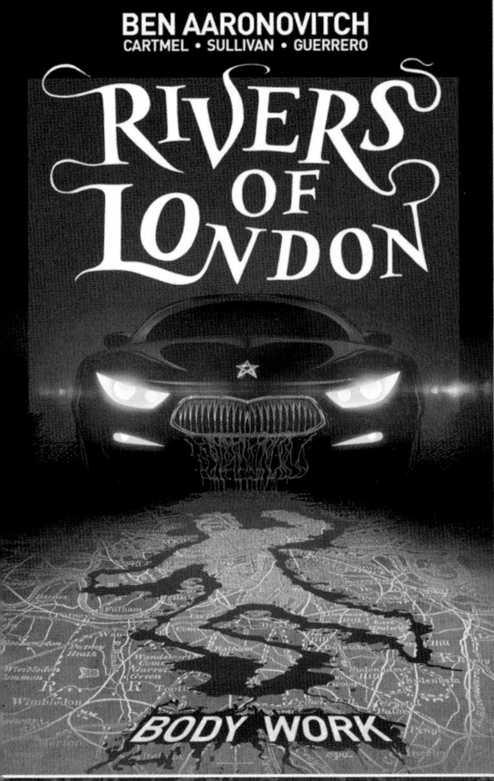
BEN AARONOVITCH
CARTMEL • SULLIVAN • GUERRERO
RIVERS OF LONDON
BODY WORK

ISSUE 3 - Cover A LEE SULLIVAN & LUIS GUERERRO

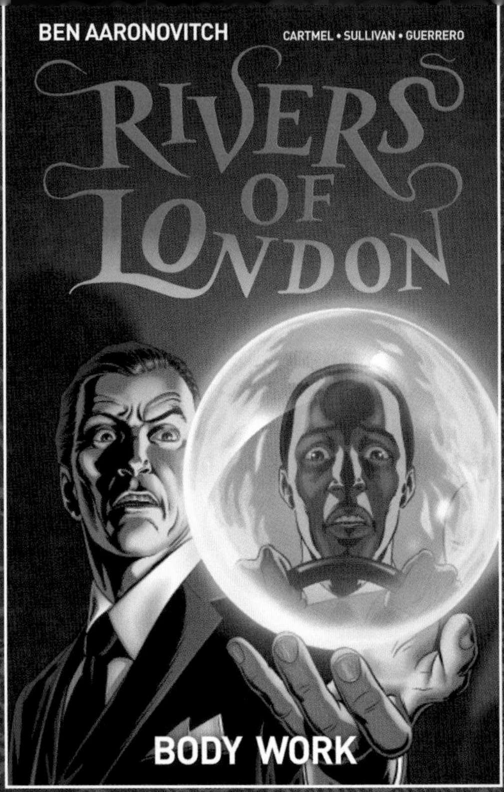
BEN AARONOVITCH
CARTMEL • SULLIVAN • GUERRERO
RIVERS OF LONDON
BODY WORK

ISSUE 4 - Cover A LEE SULLIVAN & LUIS GUERERRO

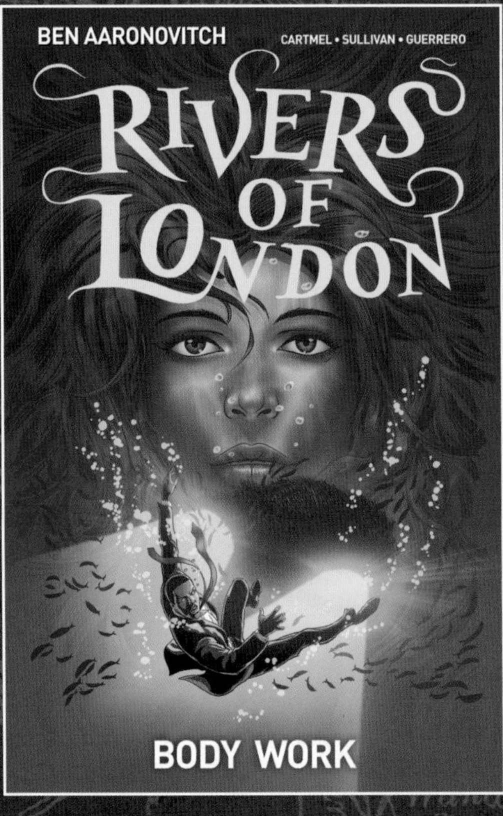
BEN AARONOVITCH
CARTMEL • SULLIVAN • GUERRERO
RIVERS OF LONDON
BODY WORK

ISSUE 5 - Cover A LEE SULLIVAN & LUIS GUERERRO

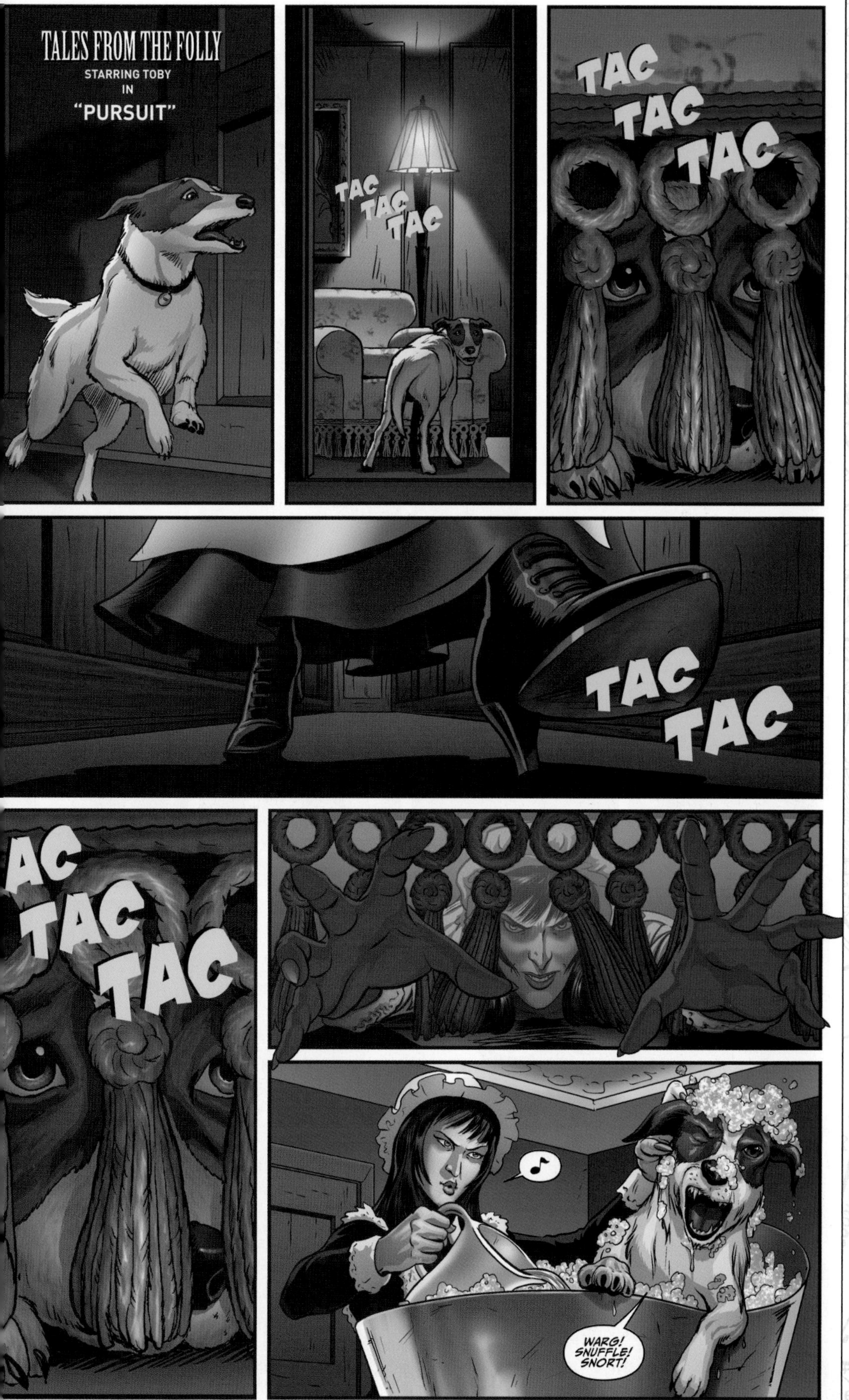
TALES FROM THE FOLLY
STARRING TOBY
IN
"PURSUIT"
TAC
TAC
TAC
TAC
TAC
TAC
TAC
TAC
AC
TAC
TAC
♪
WARG! SNUFFLE! SNORT!

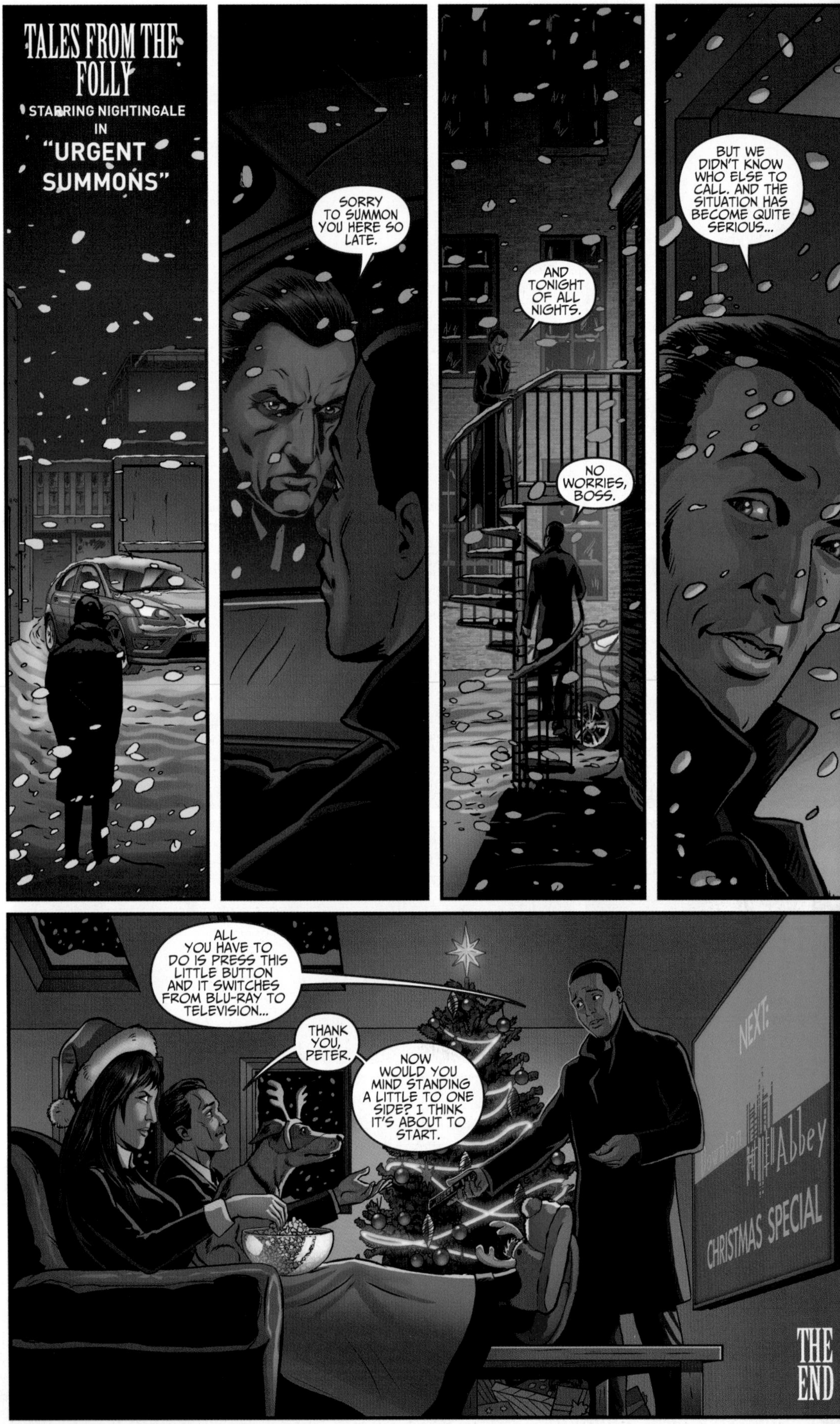
TALES FROM THE FOLLY
STARRING NIGHTINGALE
IN
"URGENT SUMMONS"
SORRY TO SUMMON YOU HERE SO LATE.
AND TONIGHT OF ALL NIGHTS.
NO WORRIES, BOSS.
BUT WE DIDN'T KNOW WHO ELSE TO CALL. AND THE SITUATION HAS BECOME QUITE SERIOUS...
ALL YOU HAVE TO DO IS PRESS THIS LITTLE BUTTON AND IT SWITCHES FROM BLU-RAY TO TELEVISION...
THANK YOU, PETER.
NOW WOULD YOU MIND STANDING A LITTLE TO ONE SIDE? I THINK IT'S ABOUT TO START.
NEXT:
Downton Abbey
CHRISTMAS SPECIAL
THE END

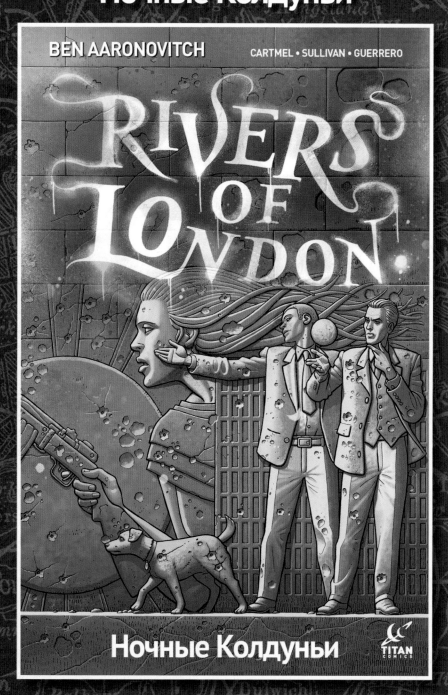

CREATOR BIOGRAPHIES

ANDREW CARTMEL

began a long and varied career in TV and publishing when he was hired as script editor on *Doctor Who* in 1986. He had a major (and very positive) impact on the final years of the original run of the TV show, after which he worked as script editor on *Casualty*. He is also writing the *Vinyl Detective* series of crime novels for Titan Books; the first, *Written on Dead Wax*, is on sale in May

In his spare time, he likes to do stand-up comedy.

LEE SULLIVAN

began his comics career at Marvel UK, drawing *Transformers*, *Thundercats* and *Robocop* – but it is with *Doctor Who* that he is most closely associated. He remains a huge fan of the show, and has continued to draw the Doctor for a variety of publishers.

He played saxophone in a Roxy Music tribute band for a decade. He has dotted various Roxy Music-related gags through this series!

LUIS GUERRER

Unlike the grizzled vetera above, Luis is a relat newcomer to comics. native of Mexico, his earli published work was Big Dog Ink's 2012 seri *Ursa Minor*. Since then, has been a regular fixt at Titan Comics, color interiors and covers fo number of series includ *Doctor Who, The Troop,* a *Man Plus,* as well as *Riv of London*.

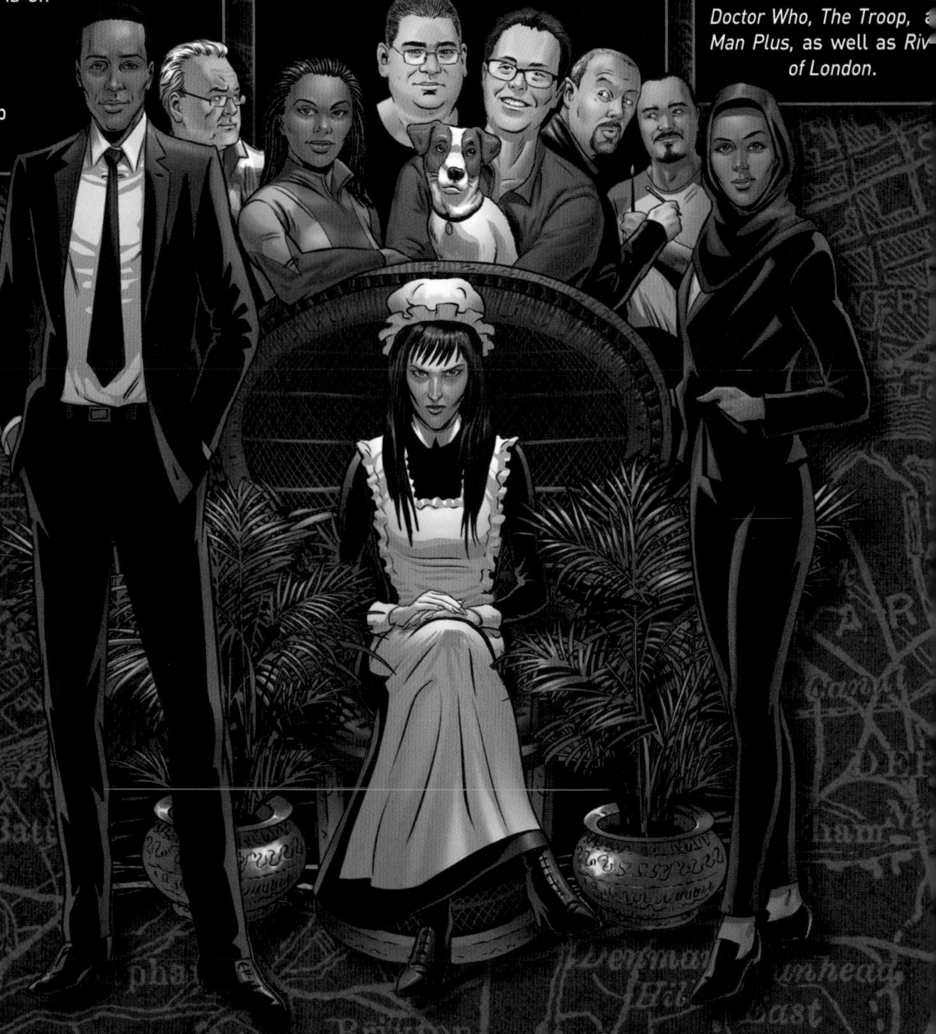

BEN AARONOVITCH

Ben is perhaps best known for his series of Peter Grant novels, which began with *Rivers of London*, released in 2011. Mixing police procedural with urban fantasy and London history, these novels have now sold over a million copies worldwide; the latest, *The Hanging Tree*, is released in 2016.

Ben is also known for his TV writing, especially on *Doctor Who*, where he wrote fan-favorites *Remembran of the Daleks* and *Battlefield*. He also wrote an episode of long-running BBC hospital drama, *Casualty*, and contributed to cult British sci-fi show, *Jupiter Moon*.

Ben was born, raised and lives in London, and says he will leave the city when they prise it out of his cold, dead fingers.